SUE KREITZMAN'S
LOW
FAT
LIFEPLAN

SUE KREITZMAN, described by *The Times* as 'the queen of low-fat cookery writing', wholeheartedly believes in good food with maximum flavour and minimum fat.

Sue lectures and demonstrates all around the country, and regularly appears on radio and television. She contributes to many national magazines and newspapers, including *BBC Good Food*, *Woman's Own*, *Woman's Realm*, *Living* and the *Mail on Sunday*.

Sue Kreitzman's Low-Fat Lifeplan is her twenty-third book. Her other books include *Sue Kreitzman's Low-Fat Desserts*, *Sue Kreitzman's Complete Low-Fat Cookbook*, *Sue Kreitzman's Low-Fat Vegetarian Cookbook*, *The Low-Fat Cookbook*, *The Quick After-Work Low-Fat Cookbook*, *Lavish Low-Fat Cooking*, *Slim Cuisine Italian Style* and *Slim Cuisine Quick and Easy*.

SUE KREITZMAN'S

LOW FAT LIFEPLAN

Your Essential Guide to a Low-Fat Lifestyle

PIATKUS

© 1999 Sue Kreitzman

First published in 1999 by
Judy Piatkus (Publishers) Ltd
5 Windmill Street, London W1P 1HF
E-mail: info@piatkus.co.uk

**For the latest news and information on all our titles
visit our new website at www.piatkus.co.uk**

The moral rights of the author have been asserted

A catalogue record for this book is available from the British Library

ISBN 0-7499-1963-9

Designed by Paul Saunders
Nutritional analysis by Jasmine Challis BSc SRD
Photographer Jean Cazals
Food stylist Janice Murfitt

Typeset by Wyvern 21 Ltd.
Printed and bound in Great Britain by
Butler & Tanner Ltd, Frome and London

Contents

ACKNOWLEDGEMENTS

For Steve and Shawm, for making everything worthwhile

Thank you to Sandie Mitchel-King for everything (I would fly into a thousand disorganised pieces without you), to Shawm and Steve for family togetherness and fun, to the McGuiness, Fairman and Doer families, Bobby, and all the rest of my neighbours who make life in Hitchin Square so pleasant and sociable, to all of the Hitchin Square children for their exuberance and enthusiasm, and to Marlena Spieler and Alan McLaughlan for their foodie friendship.

Thank you to David Grossman for always making me feel as if my work is worthwhile, to Judy Piatkus, Rachel Winning and everyone else at Piatkus who are such a pleasure to work with, to Roland at Farfalle at Bow Wharf who has brought a touch of culinary class to Bow, and to Paul Gill at Borders, a supportive friend who loves the smell of spicy beans and mushrooms wafting through his bookshop.

Thanks too to Brenda Huebler for being so dependable, to Kate Ashley, my bosom buddy, to Janet Tod for amazing colour and good natured artistic advice, to Mandy Morton for our far-reaching radio conversations, and to Lorraine Kelly and the Lorraine Live team for enthusiasm and unflappability, even in the face of a flaming kitchen set.

Finally, thanks to all my Roman Road friends for making day-to-day life such a rich and colourful tapestry.

PREFACE

This book is a bit different from my previous ones. I'm getting more lenient in my old age. The problem with writing a low-fat lifestyle manual is trying to deal with the multiplicity of problems out there. Some people want to lose weight (in some cases, a substantial amount of weight) in an intelligent, high-nutrition way, others have specific problems that demand a switch to a very low-fat lifestyle (gall-bladder problems, heart disease, arterial problems and so on). For those people who must deal with obesity or disease (and the two are very much related), all the rules of very low-fat eating are contained in this book.

But all those people who have no specific problem, yet wish to embrace a lower-fat, healthier lifestyle in order to prevent future problems, or who just want to shed a few pounds, but are not actually obese, need a low-fat regime as well, although not quite as drastic. That's where the leniency comes into play. In such cases, a little bit of fat here and there won't hurt. The question is what kind of fat, and where exactly is here and there? I'm going to try to sort this out for you, so that – whatever your problem and need – you can strike the right balance. But as a recovered fat person who has struggled to maintain a significant weight loss for many years, I must issue a warning. Adding a bit of olive oil here, a sliver of butter there, a handful of nuts, an avocado or two or three, may pose a problem. Reformed fat addicts are easily readdicted, low-fat foodies can quickly become reintroduced to the seductions of old-fashioned fat-based cuisine,

and this – especially for the middle-aged, the less active and any fat-prone person – spells instant weight gain, with all of its attendant problems. So know your needs, choose wisely, and don't be easily seduced by the fat sirens. All the recipes in this collection are marked with a series of symbols, to guide you to the very low-fat and higher-fat recipes. Pick and choose to suit your needs. Some recipes are followed by lower-fat or higher-fat suggestions.

THE LOW-FAT PALATE

If you are about to embark on a low-fat lifestyle, and fear that it means an end to gastronomic enjoyment, please stop worrying. Cutting back on the grease releases flavour in a remarkable way. When you cook by my methods, you experience fresh, vibrant, clean-flavoured and textured food that is wonderfully exciting and gratifying. Diet (that is the food we eat day in, day out) should be about health, optimum nutrition, and – above all – sensual enjoyment. My kind of low-fat cooking and eating provides all these pleasures, and will open up to you a new gastronomic way of life that is deeply satisfying. Even my new techniques that use small amounts of fats and oils here and there keep the tastes relatively clear, clean and non-cloying. You will find that your palate adjusts to the lower fat levels; soon greasy, oily, creamy and buttery food becomes unpleasant, and you crave fresh, clean tastes and textures. It is a culinary life that is worth pursuing.

Introduction

These days there is something old-fashioned – almost *passé* – about dishes that depend on rivers of oil, butter and cream, and mounds of rich cheeses. Current nutritional wisdom teaches us that an excess of fats (and of oils, which are simply liquid fats) is a risk factor for a variety of diseases. And fat, at 9 Calories per gram (more than twice that of carbohydrate and protein) – Calories the body metabolizes directly to fat stores – makes us fat in an extremely quick and easy manner. As a result, more and more people are turning to a lower-fat lifestyle in order to lose weight, to get off the dieting yo-yo, to alleviate specific medical problems, or to follow, simply and wisely, a healthier way of life so that they do not develop dietary fat-related diseases and obesity later in life.

It's easier than ever now to live the low-fat way, but there are still pitfalls. Supermarkets overflow with food – high-fat, low-fat and everything in between. Products labelled 'lite' or 'reduced fat' can be misleading. They are not always as low-fat and healthy as they seem. There is a minefield of choices to deal with in the supermarket: what type or level of fat to opt for, how much fat, which type of fats are 'good' and which 'bad', what about cholesterol, and how about olive oil – it can't possibly be fattening, can it? I'm going to try to guide you through these perplexing questions, and I'm also going to try to guide you through the really difficult hurdles – restaurant eating, snacking, socializing – and suggest strategies to avoid the junk food that still, despite the ever-growing choice of healthy foods, surrounds us every day. First, a brief discussion of fats:

About Fat

1 *All* fats – whether they are the saturated animal fats including poultry fat, lard, drippings, suet, butter fats; polyunsaturated or monounsaturated oils (including olive oil); margarines (many are highly saturated, although some are richer in mono- and polyunsaturates); the fats or oils in nuts, seeds, avocados, coconuts – provide 9 Calories per gram (approximately 120 Calories per tablespoon): Calories that are metabolized into body fat in an extremely quick and efficient fashion.

2 So-called low-fat spreads *do* contain less fat than butter or margarine because they have been diluted with something (water or air or buttermilk, for instance), but they still contain substantial amounts of health-threatening and Calorie-dense fat.

3 I'm sure that you have heard plenty about saturated and unsaturated fats (both mono and poly). *All* edible fats are mixtures of saturated and unsaturated compounds. Animal fats, including dairy fats (butter, cream and wholemilk products), lard, poultry drippings, suet and so on, contain a high percentage of saturated fatty acids. The word 'saturated' refers to the actual chemical make-up of the fat molecules. Interestingly enough, three of the vegetable oils (palm oil, palm kernel oil and coconut oil) are even higher in saturates than butter. So if a product is labelled 'made with vegetable shortening only', or 'contains vegetable fat', it does not necessarily mean that the product is therefore high in unsaturates. Other vegetable oils are higher in monounsaturates and polyunsaturates, although they will also contain *some* saturates. Again, the terms monounsaturates and polyunsaturates refer to the chemical bonding within the fat molecules. Since a fat with a higher proportion of unsaturation is often a liquid at room temperature, some solid margarines and solid vegetable shortening are manufactured by putting highly unsaturated vegetable oil through a hydrogenation process to firm it up, so that it will be 'spreadable'. This hydrogenation process actually causes the oil to become saturated. (Some so-called trans-fatty acids are formed and these hydrogenated fats are believed to cause even more health problems than naturally saturated fats.)

In evaluating this information, just remember that all fat is equally *fattening*, whatever the make-up of its chemical bonds. And an impressive history of solid scientific research reveals a connection between highly saturated fats and disease. But an excess of unsaturated fats has also been implicated in disease (several kinds of cancer, for instance), and an excess of *any* kind of fat is fattening. So merely replacing all the highly saturated fats you eat with an equal amount of unsaturates makes little sense, either for weight control or for health. This would just replace one high-fat regime with another.

4 The human body needs a certain amount of dietary fat to function. But there is plenty of what you need in a bountiful diet of fish, lean meat and poultry, vegetables and grains. And the wide variety of vegetables, whole grains, poultry, fish, fruit and lean meat (and skimmed milk powder) available will give you a full complement of fat-soluble vitamins as well.

5 What about cholesterol? Cholesterol is a fatty substance that is manufactured in the body, and is important to the body's functioning. It is the excess cholesterol levels in the blood that are of concern. On the scientific level, there have been clashing viewpoints. Does dietary cholesterol affect levels of blood cholesterol? Does it contribute to heart disease? And what about 'good' cholesterol and 'bad' cholesterol? Does olive oil (and other highly monounsaturated oils) *really* raise levels of 'good' cholesterol – as has been touted with great enthusiasm lately? The truth is that there are no easy answers. The whole cholesterol story, on both a medical and scientific level, has been fraught with debate and conflicting theories. On a practical level, there is no need to be too concerned. If you seriously reduce the added fats and high-fat foods in your diet, you will do much towards reducing your total blood cholesterol levels and restoring the proper balance between so-called 'good' (HDL) and 'bad' (LDL) cholesterol. It is now pretty generally believed that it is the *total fat intake* that may have the effect of raising blood cholesterol levels, not just frequent consumption of high-cholesterol foodstuffs. So it is probably not a wise choice to lavish lashings of olive oil or canola oil or other highly monounsaturated oils over your food to benefit your cholesterol levels. Olive oil and the others are pure fat. Eliminate excess fat from your life, and you will be doing the best thing possible to reduce and rebalance your blood cholesterol levels.

6 Do eat fish, both fatty and lean, several times a week. According to recent research, fish fat may well be beneficial to the heart, and fish is rich in fat-soluble vitamins as well. Squid and shellfish – although not particularly fatty – contain a high proportion of Omega-3 fatty acids (those compounds in fish fat that are believed to be beneficial to the heart). Although some shellfish have high cholesterol levels their low-fat, high-Omega-3 profile means that it might be wise to make both shellfish and other fish a regular part of your diet. Keep this in mind: even the fattiest fish is relatively low in Calories, and a small amount of fish fat (like the fat in whole grains) might be just the kind of healthy fat your body needs.

HOW MUCH FAT?

Medical necessity

If you must cut back for medical reasons, then you know that axeing the fat might mean the difference between life and death, or between extreme pain and comfort. In this case, dietary fat reduction is more than an interesting lifestyle choice – it is grim necessity. If this applies to you, don't worry: it is easier than you think (once you figure out how to make the proper choices), and the food (I can't emphasize this enough) will *not* bore you to distraction. Low-fat food *never* has to be boring and insipid. My methods of cooking produce lower-fat food with fresh, deep, well-rounded flavour, and plenty of colour and pizzazz. It is the kind of food that makes traditional high-fat cooking seem greasy, over-rich and cloying. You will be embarking on a deeply satisfying lifetime culinary adventure, and may find yourself eating better than you ever have in your life.

Weight control

If you need to lose weight, or have lost a considerable amount of weight and want to maintain control, then you, too, must drastically reduce the fat. In matters of obesity, there is no cure, there is only control. And a very low-fat lifestyle is an excellent way to gain control, without the all too familiar hunger, frustration and depression that haunts the constantly food-deprived. Embrace a *no-added-fat* lifestyle, and your life will dramatically change for the better.

So for medical problems, obesity, weight control in general, and weight maintenance, eliminate *all* added fats from your dietary lifestyle. Maintainers, depending on their measure of control at any particular time – this can change with stress levels, hormone activity

Banish these foods

- Butter
- All oils (with the exception of the oil-spray, page 28)
- Ghee
- Solid shortenings
- Margarine
- 'Low-fat' spreads
- Vegetable shortenings
- Dripping
- Lard
- Suet
- Poultry fat
- Poultry skin
- Bacon fat
- Fatty meats (see page 163 for a discussion of lean cuts of meat)
- Mayonnaise, vinaigrettes and other salad dressings
- Full-fat and part-skim dairy products (see page 22 for a discussion of very low-fat dairy products)

- Eat whole eggs only occasionally (check with your doctor; see page 6 for a discussion of eggs in the diet)
- Avocados – In Mexico, they call avocados 'poor man's butter', and spread the unctuous pale green flesh on bread. One avocado (about 275g/10oz) contains 320 Calories, about 280 of which are fat Calories. The oils in avocado are highly unsaturated, as opposed to the highly saturated butter fats, but if you must resist fat, then you must forgo this luscious green-fleshed fruit.
- Nuts – Virtually all nuts are extremely high in fat: for instance 25g (1oz) almonds (about 24) contains 170 Calories, 140 of which are fat Calories, and 25g (1oz) peanuts (only 3 tablespoons of the wretched things) contains 160 Calories, 130 of them fat Calories. Coconuts, brazils and macadamias are high in saturates; all other nuts, except chestnuts, are high in unsaturates.

  Chestnuts are the *only* low-fat nut. Bless them, they contain less than 1 gram of fat per 25g (1oz). All other nuts, alas, derive most of their Calories from fat. Seeds, like nuts, are rich in unsaturated fats. A tablespoon of sunflower seeds, for instance, contains 7 grams of fat.

and sun spots (well, perhaps not the last, but if you struggle with a love of food and a tendency towards obesity, you know what I mean) – can add the *occasional* dab of medium-fat cheese.

THE HIDDEN FATS

Eliminate as well all prepared foods, from frozen foods to baked goods to snacks and convenience food, and everything in between, that contain added fat. Read the labels: see page 7 for a thorough discussion of nutritional labelling.

A note about bread

You want a loaf of bread that contains no added fat. So when you buy, read the ingredients on the label first, and make sure no (or very little) oil or fat of any kind is listed.

Some packaged foods contain integral fat, even though no fat has been added in the preparation. Whole grains, for instance, contain fat, so even though no added fat may have been used in the baking of the bread, the nutritional analysis on the label will include a few grams of fat. Don't worry – that's as it should be. The naturally occurring fat in the wholegrain is beneficial, and helps provide your body with the essential fatty acids that it needs. As long as there is no fat listed in the ingredients, all is well. The same rule of label-reading applies for cereals, crackers or any other wholegrain products.

A PRUDENT LIFESTYLE

Cutting back on fat, without cutting it out

If you have no fat-related health problems, and are happy with your weight, yet have seen the light and want to cut back on fat without cutting it out entirely, there are all sorts of clever ways of going about it. Remember to keep your fat intake to 30 per cent or less of your daily intake (actually if you aim for 25 per cent, you'll probably hit 30 per cent) and choose your fat sources carefully.

A word of caution, however. If you are a fat person trying desperately to lose weight, or a controlled fat person, who has lost weight and is struggling to maintain control and stay in remission, using even these small amounts of fat and oil can put you on a slippery slope. Having butter in the fridge, tasting it again (even in minute quantities), can be a complete disaster for fat addicts. A little scraping on the toast can't really hurt, can it? A bit of oil on the salad, just a tiny mound of mayo or aïoli next to the steamed veg – and soon you are back where you started. The weight is back, all your lovely palate freshening is gone, you are back in the blunting, cloying, high-fat world you worked so hard to leave behind. I speak from bitter experience. So know yourself and your problems, and choose wisely.

Just a dab

1 Use oil (and the occasional sliver of butter) as a seasoning, rather than a sauté medium. Basically, you'll be using my tried and true no-fat techniques (see page 27–32) with just a dab of the naughty stuff to keep that touch of fat flavour that you crave. You may find, after using this technique for a while, that you don't really need that little dab at all – then welcome to the fresh clean taste of the no-added-fat kitchen. But, until that time, try this: use the basic stock sauté method on page 27. In other words, put your onions and garlic in a frying-pan, along with any flavouring (spices, if you are making a

chilli or a curry, sun-dried tomatoes, and chillies, or whatever is appropriate to the recipe). Then add a teaspoon of oil or butter. (A teaspoon of oil contains 45 Calories and 5 grams of fat, and a teaspoon of butter contain 37 Calories and 4 grams of fat.) Pour in approximately 300ml (½ pint) of stock (chicken or vegetable), cover and simmer briskly for 5–7 minutes, then uncover and simmer gently for a few more minutes until the liquid is about gone and the onions are frying gently in that dab of fat. This is a very useful technique and gives you just that taste of fat that you may feel you must have. Although butter is a saturated animal fat, here it is a seasoning, not a main ingredient, and so is used in only minute amounts. It makes no sense to use margarine this way, because this is about flavour and technique, and no one in their right mind would use marge as a flavouring (and I'm certainly not convinced that marge is a bargain, healthwise). A teaspoon of olive oil works well for just the same reason.

2 Buy several very small spray bottles (you can get little plastic ones from large chemists) and use them for very fragrant oils: truffle oil, walnut oil, hazelnut oil, and so on. Use my low-fat techniques but flavour food, as appropriate, with just a hint (one or two spritzes) of the aromatic oil. Also, try filling a small spray bottle with your favourite vinaigrette dressing, and using it to *lightly* spray your salad leaves.

3 Eggs – Although the yolks are high in cholesterol, and contain 5.2 grams of fat per large egg, they are also rich in nutrients. It is now believed that the occasional whole egg won't hurt (check with your doctor, first, if you have a medical problem). It is recommended not to exceed 4–5 a week. The whites, of course, are high in protein and are fat- and cholesterol-free, and extraordinarily useful in the kitchen.

4 Go to the source – if you have no fat-related medical problems, and are not obese, or in fat remission, then you can have the occasional avocado, or handful of nuts. Although these are high in fat, the fat is natural, highly unsaturated (except for Brazils, macadamias and coconuts, which are high in saturates and really – alas – to be avoided) and comes with a nice complement of fibre, vitamins and minerals. (See page 4 for the fat levels in avocados and nuts.) The problem with nuts is their extreme moreishness; it really is hard to establish control once you start nibbling the damn things. And just remember, a mere ounce of almonds contains 170 Calories, 140 of which are fat Calories, so moderation is of the essence. It is best to keep them in the freezer (because of the high oil content, they tend to go rancid rather quickly) and use in small quantities in recipes here and there. See Creamy Pesto (pages 52–3) or Cranberry-Apple Sauce (page 206) for examples.

Now that Thai cooking has become so popular, coconut milk and coconut cream are easily available in most supermarkets – a superb ingredient for all sorts of Thai dishes. Because of the high saturated fat content of coconut, these ingredients are not a particularly healthy choice. If you want to add a hint of coconut to a Thai-style dish, or to a pot of rice, buy a solid block of creamed coconut (it comes in 200g blocks). Once opened, store in the freezer. Grate, frozen, and add in very small amounts towards the end of cooking.

LABEL READING

No matter what your reason for taking on a low-fat lifestyle, if you want to make wise choices in the supermarket you must read the labels, tedious though this may be. There are three things to look for on the label when choosing packaged foods (these rules pertain to *manufactured* food, and not to fish, poultry, meat or dairy products).

1 How much fat? If a food is labelled low-fat it must – by law – contain less than 5g of fat per 100g (3½oz) (or per serving, if a serving is greater than 100g). So this a good rule of thumb: for healthy low-fat eating, choose packaged foods that contain 4 grams or less (preferably less) of fat per 100g or per serving.

2 What kind of fat? It's best to choose packaged foods with no added fat at all. If there is fat listed in the nutritional percentage, it should be the naturally occurring fat in the whole grains (if the product is bread or cereal) or in the fish flesh (as in tuna or salmon in brine) and so on. If there *is* added fat, yet the percentage is within the guidelines, check it out on the ingredient listings. If the fat is hydrogenated (or partially hydrogenated), or palm, coconut or palm kernel oil, think hard before making that particular choice.

3 If there is no percentage of fat listed (there is less and less chance of this happening these days, but just in case) and some fat is listed in the ingredient listing, note where it is on the list. Ingredients are listed in descending order of amount – the first ingredient is the one there is the most of, and so on down the line. Just

remember *not* to depend on terms such as 'reduced fat', 'healthy eating', 'healthy choice', or even 'cholesterol-free'. A cholesterol-free food may be loaded with much too much vegetable fat, a 'reduced fat' product may be lower in fat than the high-fat original but still woefully high in fat, and 'healthy choice' or 'healthy eating' might mean lower salt and lower sugar, rather than low-fat. So read the fine print, and make your own decision.

TO SUM UP

If you must cut out fat for medical reasons, or to lose weight, or to maintain a large weight loss, then it is wise to cut out all added fats and all hidden fats found in manufactured products, as well as excess egg yolks, and full fat and part skim dairy products. Avoid as well high-fat meats, and poultry fat and skin. Keep your daily fat intake to 25 per cent or less of total Calories.

If you have no weight or health problem, yet want to live a healthier, lower-fat lifestyle, then eliminate all hydrogenated fats and tropical oils (palm, coconut and palm kernel oils). Since these are contained in many manufactured foods, it is important (although tedious) to read the labels as you food-shop. Keep saturated fats to a bare minimum and don't overload yourself with eggs and full-fat dairy products. Four to five eggs a week will strike a good balance. Use skimmed milk dairy products with the occasional small addition of quality medium-fat cheeses to keep things interesting. Choose mono- and polyunsaturated oils, and use them (and the occasional sliver of butter for flavour) as a seasoning, in conjunction with basic low-fat cooking techniques (pages 5–6).

Cooking for the Family

If you are responsible for cooking for your family, it doesn't pay to cook one way (high-fat, creamy, buttery-oily-greasy, health-threatening) for them, and another way (low-fat, disease-fighting, healthy, fresh, clean and vibrant) for yourself. It doesn't seem fair at all, does it? And of course, planning multi-meals is exhausting, expensive and makes a ridiculous amount of extra work for the cook. And it certainly doesn't pay to have stashes of 'goodies' (sweets, biscuits, doughnuts, crisps and so on) hidden away for them, but not for you. It's hard enough resisting the subversive siren song of such destructive snacks when you are out and about – how much more difficult it is to avoid them in your own home. It is very destructive to your well-being and healthy eating regime to play such games: 'real' food for them, and 'diet' food for you. As far as I am concerned, the so-called 'diet' food is the real thing. Even if some members of your family or your house-mates are the kind who can seemingly eat any-thing without putting on weight, and have no apparent health problems, do they really need an excess of butter and cream, high-fat meats, sugary, fatty sweets? Do they really have to have deep-fried chips regularly? Why should it be proper for you to cherish your own heart and arteries and general physical well-being, but not theirs? My kind of cooking is about celebrating food and health for everyone for a lifetime; juggling menus should simply not be necessary.

Do remember, though, that children need plenty of Calories to develop properly, and it won't hurt them to have a bit of fat as well. But I firmly believe that they don't need tons of junk – biscuits, sweets, pastries, deep-fried everything, fast-food hamburgers and so on. These things only predestine them for later suffering, muddy their taste perceptions, and encourage them to develop a lifetime of bad habits. They will be exposed to enough of this in the outside world. It's no surprise that childhood obesity is on the increase. What they should be able to depend on in your kitchen is the special, delicious, comfort-ing and health-giving mother (or father) food that sets them up for life. Childhood culinary nostalgia is the most powerful, sustaining and evocative there is – make your family food the best it can be.

SNACKS

Keep plenty of healthy and compelling snacks on hand, to keep everyone's mind off sweets, crisps, and other rubbish.

Fresh fruit

There has never been such a global profusion of fresh fruit as can be found in modern supermar-kets. Unfortunately, it has never been so tasteless, flabby, underripe and unsatisfying. By the time supermarket fruit arrives in our kitchens, the orchard is a dim and distant memory, and the fruit has been picked unripe from that orchard to minimize damage during shipping. To be sure that fruit you ultimately eat is luscious and juicy, it pays to know a few things about it – which ones will ripen after picking, how to ripen them, how to choose them wisely in the supermarket – so that the fruit really is the aromatic marvel it should be (or as close to an aromatic marvel as today's supermarket fruit can be). Of course, the best way to eat perfect fruit is to eat it in season, and grow your own, or obtain it from a local grower. But in these supermarket-dominated days, such luxury is not always possible, so here are some clues and tips to help:

• These fruits will never ripen after picking; *what you buy is what you get*: soft berries, cherries, citrus fruit, grapes, litchis, pineapple and watermelons.

• **These will ripen in colour, texture and juiciness after picking, but will get no sweeter:** apricots, blueberries, figs, melons (other than watermelon), peaches, nectarines, plums, passion fruit.

• **These will get sweeter after picking:** pears, apples, kiwi, mangoes, papayas (and, of course, the dependable and gorgeous banana will ripen in flavour, colour, texture and tenderness after picking).

• **To ripen underripe bananas, cantaloupes and mangoes (and tomatoes as well), gas them:** tomatoes, bananas and apples give off ethylene gas as they ripen. To ripen underripe bananas, mangoes, cantaloupes or tomatoes, place them in a paper bag with a couple of apples or ripe bananas. Close loosely, so that some air can get in, and leave on the worktop for a day or so (or more, depending on how underripe the fruit is). If you allow yourself an avocado now and then (see page 4), ripen it in the same way.

How to tell if fruit is ripe

Galia and cantaloupe melons, and pineapples, will be swooningly fragrant when ripe. A pineapple will 'give' a bit when you squeeze it. A melon will give a bit as well, when you press the blossom end. If you rap hard-shelled melons with your knuckles, they will sound hollow when ripe. (I'm told that when rapped they emit a perfect concert A, but you'll need perfect pitch to test this out.)

Fragrance, and bit of a 'give', are excellent tests for peaches, plums, pears and kiwis too. Ripe fruit also feels heavy for its size. Lift citrus fruit in your hand – if it feels weighty it is probably fully mature. With cherries and grapes do the obvious: taste one.

Bananas, of course, are easy – they are tender and bright yellow, with a few brown specks, when ripe. Some people like them thoroughly soft and blotchy, when they become gorgeously, decadently sweet. (My assistant loves them this way. She cherishes and cossets them until they are soft, sweet, and perfect, and then I often filch them to make Poppy Seed and Sherry Banana Loaf (pages 190–1). I think I owe her an entire plantation of bananas by now!) Bananas are very low in fat indeed, they ripen nicely at home and – in a paper bag – help ripen other fruit, and are indispensable in many pudding recipes. Who needs empty Calorie sweets, and greasy chips, with such bounty in your fruit bowl?

Canned fruit

It's fashionable to sneer at canned fruit, but I think that is a great mistake. Although canned fruit can never measure up to the real orchard-picked, seasonal, local, impossibly fragrant, juicy, luscious thing (calm down, Sue!), few things can, including supermarket fruit. Supermarket fruit has had quite an odyssey from farm to table, and plenty has been lost on the way: flavour, texture, even nutritional value. This is not to say that such fruit is worthless – just that it is not quite so bursting-with-virtue as the term 'fresh fruit' might lead us to believe. Canned fruit has been processed very close (in time and place) to its growing point. Inevitably, texture and some nutrients are lost, but plenty of goodness still remains. Why not keep a selection of canned fruit in the fridge? Icy cold, sweet and refreshing, it is excellent for snacking. I particularly like canned litchis, pineapple and pears. No one can pretend that eating canned fruit is like eating fresh, but it is a very good food in itself, especially for low-fat snack purposes.

Dried fruit

Dried fruits are power packs of nutrition and taste, concentrated in sweetness and fibre. The sugar is concentrated as well, so the fruit can pile on the sugar Calories at great speed, but the nutrient concentration is so high that the Calories are far from empty. Because of this, and because of their compelling taste, dried fruits are marvellous low-fat snacks for children. Nowadays, in addition to the usual apricots, figs, prunes, raisins and so on (they may be familiar, but they are never boring), there are exciting new dried fruits easily available as well: cranberries, blueberries, sour and sweet cherries, mangoes.… At one time all of these were only available by mail order, or in lofty and pricey speciality delis, but now – as with the ubiquitous sun-dried tomato – more and more supermarkets carry them.

Frozen Fruit

There is not a huge variety out there, but what I've seen is good: raspberries, summer fruits, strawberries, blueberries (fabulous!) and cranberries. Keep plenty in the freezer, not so much for eating as they are, but for turning into instant ice creams or sorbets in your food processor – no defrosting necessary. The ice creams and sorbets here (made in less than 5 minutes, see pages 199–201) are great for both kids and adults, and do much to assuage the craving of those who have a sweet tooth *and* an ice cream addiction. They are cheaper than the designer ice creams, *much* lower in fat and Calories, bursting with nutrition, delicious, and vividly colourful – what more can you ask?

Raw vegetables

As you can see, I believe that the best snacks contribute to the day's nutrition – it is not just a matter of blindly satisfying that recurring need to crunch and munch between meals. Raw vegetable crudités do both: they supply a most satisfying 'crunch' factor, and add plenty of low-fat, low-Calorie, very high-nutrient goodness to the day. I am passionate about vegetables and think that they should always be the centre of culinary attraction, even when snacking. The problem with vegetable crudités is that they take time and attention – all that peeling, trimming and cutting into nice, bite-sized pieces. For optimum texture and nutrition they should be prepared as close to the time of consumption as possible. It *is* possible to make a batch in the morning and keep them in a bowl of very cold water in the fridge; they stay wonderfully crisp and fresh-tasting, although they do lose some nutrients. But, presumably, you are taking in such an exquisite array of nutrients every day that the leaching out of a few stray vitamins from your crudités won't really matter.

Ready-prepared crudités of various sorts are available in the greengrocery section of most supermarkets, but they sometimes taste rather

Raw snack vegetables

- **Carrots** – The best of all raw veg: blazingly orange, heavenly crunchy, sweet and full of good nourishment.

- **Beetroot** – If you can find small raw beet-roots (they are easier than ever to find these days), peel them and cut them into bite-sized chunks. I think you'll be surprised and pleased by their sweet and earthy crunch. Pair them with carrot sticks and Grilled Red Pepper Spread (page 56) for a stunning technicolor snack.

- **Cabbage** – White and red. Cut small cabbages into chunks so that you can see their fascinating and unique inner whorls and swirls.

- **Celery** – A dieter's cliché, surely, but still … raw celery is delicious especially when it's young, seasonal and local. Celery sticks and Blue Cheese Dip (page 54) – what bliss!

- **Baby corn cobs** – Adorable little mini sweet-corn-on-the-cob, eaten cob and all. They add a lovely yellow to your colourful crudité array, and are great with dips.

- **Cherry tomatoes** – Plan ahead with toma-toes. The small variety usually have bags of real tomato flavour, but you must think ahead. Buy them before you plan to use them, and let them sit, loosely covered or uncovered, on the counter for a few days – even a week – so that the flavour can develop. Or ripen them in a bag with a banana (see page 9).

- **Cucumber** – Best peeled (if the skin is bitter), cut in half lengthwise and then seeded (scrape out the seeds with a teaspoon, leaving two 'boat' shapes). Then cut into sticks.

- **Courgettes** – Small ones are tender and sweet eaten raw. No need to peel – the skins are tender as can be.

- **Fennel** – It looks like bulbous celery and has a haunting anise freshness. One of my favourites, raw *or* cooked, fennel adds a unique dimension to a crudité selection.

- **Peppers** – I wouldn't enjoy cooking half so much without red peppers (yellow and orange ones too) – their colour, sweetness, texture and amazing versatility and brilliant nutritional profile make them invaluable in the kitchen of anyone who craves excitement and colour in their low-fat cooking. To achieve maximum satisfaction from peppers (perfect texture, no bitterness, no intestinal ructions), peel them first: cut the peppers into their natural sections and peel with an ordinary vegetable peeler. This results in a raw, crisp pepper – just right for salads, and for stir-frying or sautéing.

- **Radishes (and mooli)** – Crisp, scarlet, peppery little radishes, in season, served with just a little salt, some crusty bread and perhaps some herbed, drained yogurt (pages 29–30), are as good a snack, light lunch or first course as you are likely to have anywhere. A mooli is simply a large radish: cut it into sticks and add to the crudités.

- **Sugar-snap peas** – Sweet, green, and more of a crunch when raw than mangetout.

- **Turnips** – Buy tiny white ones in season, peel and cut into sticks. They are sweet and peppery; lovely for crudités.

tired and flabby. Ready-cut carrots in particular seem to have lost quite a lot in the preparation, and sometimes they develop an off-putting 'bloom' from – I assume – whatever preservative is used on them. Far better to keep a big bag of carrots in the fridge, and peel and munch as needed. The chart on page 11 contains a complete list of the best raw veg for snacking.

Dips

Have bowls of gorgeous dips in the fridge for crudité dabbling. Most of the dips on pages 52–8 keep very well. In lieu of vegetable dipping, you could spread them on melba toast, motzah crackers or any other no-fat cracker (read the labels!). Keep plenty of Quark and fromage frais (page 22) and drained yogurt (page 29) in the fridge as well, for instant snacking. A little marmalade, jam, conserve or French no-added-sugar fruit conserve swirled into fromage frais is a splendid, quick pick-me-up. Or try my all-time favourite quick snack: melba toast spread with Quark and a tiny bit of Sambal Oelek (a hot chilli condiment – and it *is* hot!). Slice a few cherry tomatoes, or so-called vine tomatoes that you have carefully ripened (see page 9), and arrange the slices on top. Eat at once. I find this snack completely irresistible. If you can't take the heat, spread on mild chutney instead of Sambal Oelek.

'Junk-food' type snacks

There are lots of low-fat snacks that mimic the junk-food experience. They are not as nutrition-packed as fruit and veg, but they satisfy that inevitable urge for mindless crunching. Of course dieticians would tell us that the best option is to conquer and ignore these urges, but I'm the first to admit that this is much easier said than done.

Find solace in the low-fat junk-food listed opposite.

Store-bought baked goods

The problem with many of the very low-fat baked goods that are becoming available is that many are – to my taste – far too sweet, often oddly textured and not at all delicious. At the time of writing, I'm very impressed with Marks & Spencer's very low-fat cookies, made with rolled oats and heavenly chewy. They come with dried apricots, stem ginger or sultanas and contain 0.9 grams of fat per large cookie. They're endearingly like old-fashioned oatmeal cookies. And Entenmann's very low-fat New York Danish Style pastries (available in most supermarkets) are not too bad. It can be problematic having these things in the house, however; exercising control is not always easy. One or two cookies, or a slice of the low-fat pastry, is no problem, but it's so easy to eat another, and another, until you've polished off the whole package – after all, it's very low-fat, isn't it? If obesity (and establishing control) are your problems, these, although low-fat, could be your downfall. But for the rest of you, these products might be a real pleasure.

Low-carbohydrate snacks

Some people find that too many high-carbohydrate snacks (including fruit and veg) can act as a trigger for over-eating. In this case keep low-fat high-protein snacks on hand: thinly sliced lean deli meats (turkey, chicken, lean fat-trimmed ham), canned tuna and salmon in brine, the occasional hard-boiled egg (don't exceed 4–5 eggs a week in total), Quark, very low-fat fromage frais and yogurt.

Low-fat snacks

- **Popcorn** – Wonderful stuff. Buy plain popcorn kernels (not microwave popcorn, which contains fat) and store in the freezer. The final popped product will be much fluffier than that made from unfrozen kernels. Invest in a hot-air corn-popper, so you can pop the corn with no fat or oil (see the mail order guide, page 213). It is a great luxury to have the real fresh, hot, fluffy-crunchy thing on tap whenever you want it, and it can easily take the place of more destructive snacking. Popcorn improves any film that you choose to watch at home. Cinema popcorn is not a great low-fat bargain – it has too much oil (very likely hydrogenated). Sneak in your own; no one should be forced to watch a popcorn-less movie.

- **Crisps** – So called lower-fat crisps are still far too fatty for a proper low-fat régime – read the labels next time you shop. But you can make your own, quite easily, from potatoes, pitta bread, or corn tortillas (see pages 67–8). Tortilla crisps and pitta crisps will keep for weeks in an airtight tin; potato crisps should

be eaten on the day they are made. Eat these crisps on their own, or with some of the dips on pages 52–8.

- **Cereal** – Crunchy, bite-sized no-added-fat cereal makes wonderful crisp-type snacks. I'm devoted to bite-sized Shredded Wheat: on their own, with dips, covered in dark chocolate (page 181), or even as soup croûtons. Have a good trawl through the cereal aisle next time you go supermarket shopping, read labels so that you can avoid added fat, and take a few home for snack purposes. I've heard rumours that some people actually eat these products all mushed up with milk and sugar, but to my mind their strength is in their crisp-textured nibble factor.

- **Rice cakes** – More and more types of rice cakes, large and small, are appearing these days – some, imported from America, are flavoured with strawberry, almond and blueberry and come in savoury versions as well. They are virtually fat-free and very good indeed. Look for other American fat-free imports in up-market groceries: pretzels, tortilla chips and flavoured crisp flatbreads.

The Outside World

Once you get into the rhythm of low-fat food planning, shopping and cooking, keeping a low-fat kitchen becomes easy, enjoyable and gratifying. Alas, trying to deal with fat levels in the outside world (i.e. restaurants, travel, dinner parties, and so on), where you have no direct control, is another story entirely. This is a battle I seem to be constantly fighting, both on a personal and a professional level, and I fear that there are no easy solutions. I'm going to try to give you some strategies to use out there in the fat jungle. Those who suffer from fat-related disease and obesity must work very hard indeed at implementing these strategies. Those who simply want to live a healthier lifestyle can afford the occasional inevitable slip.

Lunch ... let's begin with lunch, since I think that this is the easiest outside meal to control. (I must emphasize here that the important thing is to *enjoy* the meal – don't turn it into some kind of grim fat-and-Calorie-accounting session. Learn the choices, try to make the right ones, and then relax.) Lunch at home, of course, is easy – it's the outside world that's hard. I'll try to give you some suggestions, but ultimately you'll have to use your intelligence, and try to ignore the lure of all the fat sirens out there.

If you eat your lunch in conventional restaurants, see suggestions below, in the restaurant section. If you bring your own, you're essentially beating the system: you can control exactly what you eat, and your choice runs from the obvious sandwiches and fruit to more creative choices. For packed sandwiches, see the sandwich chapter.

If you have a microwave at work, then you can bring soup (see pages 70–5), which I think makes the best lunch possible, especially paired with really good bread. (Or bring soup in a Thermos.) Don't wrap your good bread in plastic; nothing turns bread flabby and ruins its crust like a plastic bag does. Instead, wrap it in a small paper bag, or in kitchen paper. Dips with crunchy dippers and/or vegetable crudités are great for packed lunches as well. If the dip is dairy-based, keep the lunch cold in a cold bag with a small, frozen gel cold-block, or keep your lunch in the fridge, if one is available at work.

I'm all for splashing out on a Godzilla or a Little Mermaid lunchbox, or something else really silly, although you may want to choose something a bit more staid. But if you have this feeling that you are restricting yourself – no Mars bars, no crisps, no doughnuts – in short, none of that mindless fun stuff that everyone else is eating, you might as well have some childish fun in other ways. Far better to tote around a silly lunchbox (why not throw in a small action figure, nestled next to your healthy lunch, for luck – Xena, or Superman, or Luke Skywalker, for instance) than to load up your arteries and fat cells with rubbish. But I digress. Salads (again, keep them cold) are great for lunch as well – not lettuce-based ones which get horribly wilted, but grain salads and bean salads that just get better as they sit. Obviously, if beans give you problems, forget them as a lunch option – farting at work is never the done thing. And if you are a dentist, an ensemble actor, or have frequent board meetings, you might consider leaving out the garlic. In the recipe section of this book I have indicated the recipes that are suitable for packed lunches.

If you grab lunch out, it is best to stay away from American-style fast-food restaurants; the fat levels are extraordinarily high. The exception is those places that offer corn-on-the-cob and baked beans. Both, with unbuttered bread, make a fine lunch (no butter on the corn). Sandwich places that make sarnies to order are perfect; specify no mayonnaise, no butter/marge, no olive oil, no cream cheese. Although highish in fat (see the fish chapter, page 135), smoked salmon – with lemon and pepper if you like them – is a great choice because of the beneficial Omega-3s in the salmon; what could be better than a bagel (there is no added fat whatsoever in a bagel) filled with the lovely smoked fish? But if you have gall-bladder problems, or any other medical condition that requires the lowest possible fat intake, choose a different filling (sorry). There are plenty of good ones – sliced chicken or turkey (smoked or not), lean ham (all great with mustard), plain tuna (no mayo) or prawns and any combination of tomatoes, cucumbers, salad, sprouts, as long as they contain no oily dressing. In fancy sandwich shops and in supermarkets where the sandwiches are pre-made, low-fat choices are often offered along with the buttered and mayoed selection, but do be careful: their idea of low-fat does not necessarily match ours. Read the label first. Reduced-fat mayonnaise contains plenty of fat, as does medium-fat cream cheese. Always check the ingredient list, and the fat grams per sandwich, so that you can make an intelligent choice.

If you decide on a salad instead of a sandwich, make sure that the dressing is separate so that you can studiously ignore it. A baked potato makes a splendid lunch with lemon and pepper, or baked beans, or very low-fat cottage cheese.

I've been told that soup is the new sandwich, and soup bars do seem to be on the increase. Soup can be a wonderful lunch option – filling, delicious, warming and comforting – but you must ask about the fat levels. Obviously, creamy soups are bad choices, but do ask about the others – hidden fat is everywhere. Some of the non-cream Covent Garden Soups are very low-fat indeed, and their quality is high, although I do find that I have to employ my arsenal (see below) to zip them up a bit.

THE ARSENAL

Here's a great trick to add pizazz to a low-fat lunch: keep a flavour arsenal with you at all times so that your lunch will be in no danger of austerity.

1 Buy a small hip flask and keep it filled with balsamic vinegar (page 24). A few dashes improve so many things: salad, of course, but also tuna or prawn-cucumber sandwiches, or baked potatoes.

2 I never leave the house without a bottle of hot sauce tucked into my handbag. I'm devoted to Mexican Chipotle Chilli Sauce (smoked jalepeño sauce – I buy it at Si Señor in St Anne's Court in Soho), but Tabasco is great too, as are many of the Caribbean and Chinese chilli sauces. If you love a soupçon of edible fire, find one that pleases you and dash it into soups, baked beans, over salads and baked potatoes, any bland place at all.

3 If you have a tiny battery-operated pepper grinder, and fill it with mixed peppercorns (page 25), you will be able to add a bit of fragrant zip to your lunch with the flick of a switch.

These three secret weapons enable you to lunch with panache, even though you are carefully avoiding all those things everyone else seems to be eating. They've got the fat, but you've got the flair – it seems a fair trade, especially when you add in all the advantages your healthy lifestyle provides.

COFFEE BARS

Cappuccino, latte, double decaff, espresso – serious coffee is everywhere. Many coffee bars now offer skimmed milk, so it is possible to have a no-fat cappuccino or latte. Once you have refined or retrained your palate to the low-fat life, you'll find it impossible to go back to full-fat milk in your coffee.

RESTAURANT EATING

This is a minefield. All traditional cookery, whether classic, rustic, ethnic, sweet, savoury or basic 'caff', is fat-based. And nowhere is it more fat-based than in restaurants. Whether the controlling personality behind the stove is a renegade young genius, a dignified elder culinary statesman, a catering school grad, an old ethnic hand, or a plain old hashslinger, he or she will fling the fats and oils around with frightening abandon. And once you enter one of these temples of grease, powerful emotive forces, olfactory assaults, and all the excitement and sense of occasion that swirl around such places undo your resolve in an instant. Perhaps I'm overstating the case; restaurant food can be exquisite, delicious, fun and rewarding. But – no doubt about it whatsoever – it is heavily fat-based. If you are medically restricted, and really must keep the added fat to as close to nil as possible, restaurant dining can be a wretched,

embarrassing and frustrating experience. Your best bet is to avoid establishments run by great chefs. It just doesn't do to tell such a chef how to cook his food, to insist that he leave out the butter and oil (really impossible in many cases), to attempt to – in effect – totally emasculate his genius. I certainly wouldn't want anyone to waltz in and tell me to change my ways.

Nathan Pritikin, the late American guru of austere, extremely low-fat, low-salt, low-protein diets, went so far as to provide (in one of his books) cards to be photocopied and carried on one's person at all times. The cards stated: 'No oil, no salt, no sugar. Especially no MSG. Assorted steamed vegetables, please. Thank you.' He reproduced this card in six different languages, including Hebrew and Chinese. Please stay calm – I am not about to impose such austerity on you. And why enter a temple of gastronomy, only to eat a plate of steamed vegetables? If you have serious medical problems it's best to just steer clear of these joints.

Try, instead, to eat in more modest and informal establishments, where it is possible to reason with the proprietor and waiting staff. If you become a regular in such a place, they will come to know your needs, and you may not have to plead your case from scratch each time. In dire straits (when you really *must* avoid all added fats), steamed vegetables, poached fish or chicken breast, undressed salads, and fruit or sorbet will have to be your foods of choice. With the right ingredients, in the right hands (and with some fresh herbs, lemon and lime juice and balsamic vinegar), these simple foods can be intoxicatingly delicious, and much more attractive, in their way, than heavily fat-marbled meats, cream and butter-glutted sauces, oil-laden salads and killer desserts. Just be sure to explain yourself clearly when ordering: no oil, no butter, no cream, no margarine, no fat *of any sort*. Many people still believe that olive oils, or other unsaturated oils, pose no problem, so it really needs to be spelled out.

For those who do not suffer intense pain or exacerbation of medical problems as a result of eating small amounts of fat, the restaurant situation is a bit easier. I'm going to give you a general idea of what sort of things to order in various types of restaurants, but do use your head and think things out for yourself; techniques, recipes and menus differ from place to place and I can only give you general guidelines.

Italian

Olive oil is almost a religion these days, and you won't get out of an Italian restaurant without an almighty battle to avoid an excess of the stuff. Remember, whether it's extra virgin, or thoroughly experienced, it's 120 Calories per tablespoon, and pure fat. Ciabatta bread, in the bread basket in many Italian restaurants, contains a modest amount of olive oil, so to avoid an excess of oil you'll have to regulate your bread consumption. Melon and Parma ham make a great starter, but you must discreetly trim the fat from the ham. Your best bets are tomato-based pasta sauces and grilled or roasted vegetables (with the exception of aubergine, which soaks up oil like a sponge), and salad with balsamic vinegar in place of oil and vinegar dressing. Fish, lean, well-trimmed meat, poultry without the skin, are all good, but specify that any sauce be omitted, or served on the side, so that you can have a tiny taste. Mussels are marvellous too, as long as they are in a wine or tomato broth – no cream. Minestrone-type soups and thick tomato soups (non-creamy) are good, but be sure to specify with *everything* that you order in an Italian restaurant:

'No added oil please!' You must look the waiter straight in the eye, and enunciate well – no one really believes that you don't want to totally anoint yourself with the oil of the blessed olive at every possible opportunity, and the fashion right now is to lavish it, as an oily garnish, over everything. You will not be able to avoid oil altogether in an Italian restaurant – the tomato sauce, the soups, just about everything will have used some in the preparation, but *you* can avoid the gratuitous extra oily benison.

Pizza

You can actually have a splendid and healthy meal in a good pizza restaurant. Simply ask for a pizza with plenty of vegetables (no fatty meats) and specify 'No oil, no cheese.' You'll be amazed at how good it is. If you are cutting back on fat, but not cutting it out, then ask for half, or one quarter of the usual amount of cheese.

Mexican

In a Mexican place, it's the Margaritas that get you – a couple of these babies, and you'll eat anything, so be careful. (I speak from experience; I once ate a plateful of fried grasshoppers in a restaurant in Puebla – what's more, I actually enjoyed the crunchy little things.) Real Mexican food is complex, regional, highly developed and full of lard. As far as I know, there is no real Mexican food in the UK; it is all a cobbled-up combination of Tex-Mex, New Mexican Mex, and fast food, with all sorts of odd fusion (or confusion) touches thrown in: I've seen a London 'Mexican' menu with dishes that included teriyaki sauce, Brie cheese, and Linda McCartney 'meat' and 'poultry' vegetarian products on the menu – Montezuma would faint with shock.

Fajitas – strips of lean meat, skinless chicken breast or vegetables, with tortillas and garnishes – might do if you ask them to use a bare minimum of oil, and *not* to sizzle the dish with extra oil when they serve it. Without these caveats, it will be an oily disaster. Avoid the guacamole (avocado purée) and soured cream garnishes, and choose corn (maize) tortillas, which are made with no added fat. In Mexico wheat tortillas are made with lard; here they are made with hydrogenated vegetable oil. Neither fat is a good choice, although one wheat tortilla only contains 3 grams of fat. One won't hurt, but concentrate on the delicious maize ones. Ask for whole beans (they'll have marvellous black beans if you're lucky) instead of mashed refried beans which tend to contain more fat, and eat them with plenty of salsa – a real Mexican salsa contains no fat. Instead of fried tortilla chips, ask for soft, warm maize tortillas, and tear off pieces to dip into the bowl of salsa. Soft shell tacos are better than fried ones, obviously, but try to avoid all the cheese ladled over everything. It is best to order a stack of soft, warm corn tortillas, a big bowl of salsa, a mess of black beans, some plain rice and salad and a few lime wedges. Then fill the tortillas, squeeze on the lime juice, wrap and eat with gusto.

Indian

Indian food is loaded with ghee (clarified butter) or vegetable ghee (hydrogenated vegetable fat) or tropical oils. In fact there is very little in an Indian restaurant that falls into the low-fat range. I have a standard low-fat meal that I eat at my local Indian, and by now they know me and my little foibles and serve it to me happily; in the early days, the waiter would be distressed that the meal was too 'dry' and didn't contain enough

vegetables. Now, as is well known, no one adores vegetables more than I do, but not when they are swimming in an oily sauce. So I enjoy my clean, fresh-tasting meal, while all around me people spoon up buckets of ghee. Enter an Indian restaurant without fear, and try this: order chicken tikka or tandoori chicken and ask that it not be sizzled in oil upon serving. (At my local, they sizzle it on the hot platter for me *without* extra oil.) Order plain rice (pilau rice is loaded with oil), plain nan bread (*without* a brushing of ghee), raita with cucumbers or onion (raita is made of yogurt, but it may *not* be the very low-fat kind, so beware if a bit of fat causes you pain; the same point applies to the yogurt-based sauce served with the chicken tikka), and assorted chutneys and relishes. It makes a simple meal but a very satisfying one, and you'll leave feeling well fed, yet fresh and unbloated.

Japanese

Sushi is everywhere, even in supermarkets. And aren't sushi bars fun, whether they're the kind with conveyor-belts, or the kind where you sit at a counter and watch the sushi-maker at work? Japanese cuisine is a low-fat one; eat sushi, sashimi, chicken teriyaki, soups, vegetable dishes, rice and noodle dishes and sauces without problems. Watch out for tempura (fried morsels) and fat-marbled beef, but the vast majority of the food will be quite low in fat indeed. Japanese noodle bars, springing up everywhere these days, are healthy and low-fat as well, and have plenty of delicious low-fat choices.

Chinese

For a basically lowish-fat cuisine, Chinese restaurants can be amazing fat traps. Again, it's best to make yourself known at your local and ask that your food be stir-fried in the barest minimum of oil. I often ask that vegetables (particularly various Chinese leaves and Chinese greens) be braised in stock, then served with a dash of oyster sauce on plain rice, with a little dish of chilli sauce (not chilli oil) and rice vinegar with ginger on the side to drizzle on. Soups (hot and sour, won ton), are low in fat but not *no-fat*, and char siu (barbecued pork) with plain rice is a good choice – the meat is usually lean – any bits of surrounding fat can be trimmed away. Anything steamed is wonderful, but even pan-fried dumplings can be good – usually they are grid-dled, and come out of the kitchen crisp but not greasy. Should they be a bit greasy, blot them with paper napkins.

Dim sum (my favourite restaurant celebration experience) can be perfect for the low-fat diner – ignore the fried food and concentrate on all the steamed goodies, and the wonderful bowls of chicken broth with noodles, greens and lean pork. For dessert, ask for wedges of fresh orange, or litchis – a perfectly refreshing pud. In some dim sum restaurants, they even offer luridly coloured wobbly jelly – what could be more cele-bratory, fun, low-fat and refreshing than that?

Turkish

Turkish barbecue restaurants can be miracles of low-fat gastronomy. Have a kebab of grilled skinless chicken with a mound of gorgeous, herby salad, and some grilled vegetables. Ask that no oil be poured on. Squeeze fresh lemon over every-thing. Or try Turkish pizza and ask that *no oil* be added (it's made with a small crisp crust, lean minced lamb, wonderful spices, and *no* cheese (hurrah!)).

Thai

If you avoid the deep-fried items, nuts and anything made with coconut, you can have a marvellous feast in a Thai restaurant. Tom yum (hot and sour) soups are low-fat wonders, Thai salad dressings are usually made from lemon and lime juice and fish sauce (fabulous), and the steamed fish dishes tend to be exquisite. Usually even the dessert list will feature many fruit and rice dishes.

A few more thoughts on restaurant dining

I'm not listing French, Greek or Spanish (tapas) restaurants, because it's just too difficult to achieve a low-fat meal in such places, and you end up feeling like a fool when you start in on your 'no butter, no oil, no cream' theme. If you have to eat in such a place for social or business reasons, it doesn't hurt to discreetly call ahead to see what they can do for you. Be nice about it. Don't *demand* – simply explain that you have a medical problem and ask them for suggestions. Most restaurants will cater to vegetarians, and will understand allergy problems; it's not unrea-sonable to expect them to understand your prob-lem as well. (Just be sure that they understand that olive oil is *not* OK; I have heard too many chefs exclaim with great conviction that olive oil is a low-fat choice.)

I once attended a conference in a posh hotel in Lugano as a guest speaker, and knew that the food would be extremely rich. I called ahead and explained that I would like – if possible – food prepared with no added fat and oil, or as little as was humanly possible. At first, they were shocked and affronted ('But Madam, we'll have to serve you raw vegetables at every meal!'), but once they had had a little think, they agreed to try. As a result, during the week of the conference, while the others were served huge portions of fatty meats, creamy, buttery sauces, olive oil every- where, I was served equally huge portions of the freshest, brightest, most vivid, herb-strewn, light (without ever being 'lite' if you know what I mean) and delicate food you can imagine. In fact, many of the other attendees sent back their meals and demanded to have what I was having. So it really does pay to make your needs known.

DINNER PARTIES

If you are giving a dinner party yourself, there is no problem at all – see the chapter on celebrations, page 203. Don't make a big deal about the fact that the meal is very low-fat indeed (unless one of your guests will be very pleased to hear it); nothing about the meal will seem odd, stingy or unsatisfying. If you are to be a guest at someone's dinner party, and you have a medical problem with fat, then you must say something to your host or hostess at the time of invitation: no one wants to be responsible for a guest's physical discomfort as a result of the food at his or her table. There is no need to feel like a prude, a fanatic or a spoiled child; there should be no shame in caring for your health. If you have no specific problem, but just want to keep your life at an intelligently low-fat level, other people's dinner parties may be the time to compromise; it really doesn't pay to start dictating to your host, unless there's a very good reason to do so. On the other hand, when inviting guests to your own dinner party, it is quite right to ask if there are any foods the guest can't eat. After all, there are plenty of people who are allergic, diabetic, vege- tarian, religious or what have you. If a host asks you this question there is nothing wrong with saying that you can't eat an excess of fats or oils.

The Low-fat Kitchen

SHOPPING

Low-fat cooking should never be about austerity and punishment, but should be about celebration; of health, food, life and the glory of being a sensual food-loving being. Start by organizing your kitchen. First, get rid of the fat. Turn to the 'Banish these foods' list on page 4. You'll need a little oil (preferably extra virgin olive oil) for your oil-water spray (page 28), but that's about all, so ruthlessly clear your kitchen of all the rest. You're starting a marvellous new way of cooking, so there is absolutely nothing to be nervous about. Once the kitchen has been stripped for action, and you have whipped yourself into a frenzy of excitement and anticipation, hit the supermarket. Conventional wisdom dictates doing your food shopping when you are not hungry, so that you don't lose your head. But I suggest browsing the shelves when you *are* a bit hungry, and all fired up about your new regime: ignore the old destructive fat traps (the acres of sweets, the crisps, the fatty baked goods, the truly frightening array of fats, oils and greases) and concentrate on the brave new world of fruit, veg, bread, dried fruit, fabulous condiments, herbs and spices, pickled veg, canned beans, packaged grains and pasta, lean meats and poultry and sliced deli meats (forget salami, think smoked turkey). Revel in all the delicious low-fat meal possibilities that leap to mind. For your first, serious low-fat sortie, try to visit the supermarket at an off-time, when you can browse the shelves in a leisurely way, read labels, ponder on the choices, enjoy the spectacle of all this food – fresh, frozen, canned, pickled, dried – under one vast roof, and think about the glorious things that you will be eating very, very soon.

Supermarkets are enormous, contemporary museums of food (and cleaning supplies – also endlessly fascinating and indicative of the turn of the century mindset – but that's another story entirely), and it pays to take time every once in a while to really look at the spectacle and to think hard about all these choices. You can run through the place in record time, blindly filling your basket with rubbish that will make you fat, clog your arteries and might even make you ill over the long term, or you can take a few cultural steps back, take control, and take the time to choose those things that encourage health, clear, unmuddied flavours, and intense culinary enjoyment. Food is such an important part of life in every way – physical, emotional, sensual, familial, social – and taking the time to make it the best it can be is endlessly rewarding. Focus in on the things you *can* have, and how delicious they will be, and how much fun to cook with.

STOCK UP YOUR KITCHEN

You won't be buying butter/marge/oil (other than small amounts of oil for your oil-water sprays (page 28), full-fat dairy products, and many other staples you used to depend on. Stock up on these instead:

• **Stock** – Chicken and vegetable: very important

for basic sautés (see sauté technique, page 27). Buy small tubs of fresh stock found in chill cabinets in the supermarket, store in the freezer, and thaw in the microwave or under the hot water tap when needed. It's concentrated, so you can dilute it with water up to 2–3 times its volume. Keep some tubs of fish stock in the freezer as well, for fish cookery. And try to find the excellent Marigold Swiss Vegetable Bouillon powder (I like the low-salt vegan version) to use for sautéing when you have none of the tubs. There's a useful new bouillon concentrate available called Touch of Taste (chicken, fish and vegetable); add a small amount to water and use as you would any other stock. I try to avoid stock cubes; they contain more fat than is prudent, and the fat is often hydrogenated vegetable fat, or a highly saturated tropical oil. And they have a rather pervasive, salty, chemical taste that I find gets in the way.

Dairy products

- Skimmed milk

- Skimmed milk powder (it's vitamin-fortified, and adds extra nutrition and richness to skimmed milk)

- Very low-fat fromage frais

- Very low-fat yogurt

- Quark – Smooth and creamy no-fat curd cheese

- Medium-fat Italian style mozzarella cheese (sometimes called 'Mozzarella light') – 10 per cent fat

- Boursin Léger – A lower-fat version of the French herbed cheese spread

- Medium-fat creamy goat's cheese, in little pots (14 per cent fat)

- Parmesan cheese – Medium-fat, with a wonderful strong flavour; a little goes a long way. Buy real Parmigiano Reggiano, and grate it as you use it (or you could grate the whole thing and keep it in the freezer in a covered plastic tub). This, although medium-fat, is far from a low-fat food – the idea is to use it as a powerful seasoning. Save the rind and use it as a seasoning in soups and stews. It gives great taste, but leaves little fat in its wake. Remove before eating the soup

- Ricotta cheese – A lovely, sweet (dairy-sweetness, not sugared), very slightly grainy yet creamy cheese. It comes in little pots, and is a great stand-in – at 15 per cent fat – for mascarpone, crème fraîche and whipped cream (80 per cent fat)

- Very low-fat soft cheese (6 per cent fat) – Essentially a very low-fat cream cheese, just right for very low-fat cheesecakes (pages 196–9)

- Sweetened condensed skimmed milk – This sweet, thick and sticky stuff comes in cans and adds an amazing richness to all sorts of low-fat puddings

- Longlife skimmed milk in boxes – It has a cooked taste rendering it inappropriate for drinking, but it's great for cooking

- Eggs – Highly nutritious, and although the yolks do contain fat and cholesterol, it is now believed that 4–5 eggs a week won't hurt. The whites contain no fat or cholesterol, and are endlessly useful in all sorts of recipes

Freezer staples

A well-stocked freezer makes life so much easier. I like to cook large batches of things like tomato sauce, bolognese sauce, stews and soups, and keep usable portions in the freezer for busy days. And of course, keep a good supply of stock (see above) in the freezer as well. And fill the freezer with these:

• **Frozen fruits** – Summer fruits, raspberries, blueberries, cranberries, plus fruit that you've cubed and frozen yourself (see page 199)

• **Frozen vegetables** – Corn and peas freeze very well. Others lose texture, but this doesn't matter if they are to be used in puréed soups. Frozen vegetables are usually frozen very quickly indeed after harvesting, so may – in a way – be 'fresher' than supermarket green-grocery department produce that travels the world to reach our local supermarkets

• **Microwave rice** (in individual sachets) – My word, what a convenient food this is!

Dried goods

• Assorted dried fruits: apricots, cherries, blueberries, cranberries, figs, raisins, sultanas

• Lentils, dried beans

• Dried mushrooms

• Shake O'cini (dried mushroom powder in a shaker can) – Adds va-va-voom to mushroom cookery

• Sun-dried tomatoes – Snip them into pieces with scissors, and use as part of a flavour infusion (see page 27). (Be sure to buy them dry-packed, not packed in oil.) They add a compelling, smoky, caramelized dimension to savoury dishes. Italian brands are salty, so be careful about adding additional salt. There is no need to reconstitute them first – they rehydrate as they cook

Tomato products

• Canned tomatoes: whole and chopped

• Passata: in boxes or jars

• Tomato paste (purée) in tubes (you will be using only a small amount at a time)

• Canned Italian tomatoes

• Mexican-style salsa. Buy one that contains no modified starch, so that the taste will be fresh. Pace brand is good. There are some good bottled American brands available as well.

Canned (and bottled) goods

• Corn

• Lentils

• Borlotti beans

• Cannellini beans

• Pinto beans

• Red kidney beans

• Flageolets

• Chickpeas

• Roasted peppers in natural juice or brine

• Tuna in brine

• Salmon in brine

• Black olives in brine, or vacuum pack

• Capers

- A selection of canned fruit: pears, peaches, pineapple, mangoes, litchis

Wines and spirits

Use wines in your basic sautés to give wonderfully deep flavour. (The alcohol evaporates in the cooking.) Use rum and liqueurs to give your desserts a boozy dimension.

- Dry white vermouth (my favourite cooking wine)

- Dry red and dry white wine

- Medium dry sherry and cream sherry

- Port

- Dark rum

- Liqueurs: Cointreau, Crème de Pêche, etc.

Flavourings and seasonings

- Assorted mustards – Invaluable in vinaigrettes, cooked sauces, dips and spreads. Become a mustard connoisseur. Try to keep Dijon mustard and a milder dark mustard on hand at all times, along with grainy mustards and flavoured mustards, as long as they contain no fat

- Grated horseradish – Now available in jars. Make your own creamed horseradish by stirring it into fromage frais

- Sambal Oelek – A fiery red Indonesian chilli paste

- Chinese-style chilli sauce – Milder than Sambal Oelek, but packs a good punch

- Chinese black bean sauce – A small amount gives a rich, salty edge to all kinds of dishes

- Hoisin sauce – 'Chinese barbecue sauce' is how this thick, complex sweet/musty sauce is often described. It is very good as a component of a stir-fry sauce, or smeared on to a steamed Chinese pancake which is then used to wrap grilled meat and vegetables

- Tabasco and Worcestershire sauces – I list these together because I invariably use them together, and consider them almost as essential as salt and pepper. Keep them right next to the cooker, to dash into soups and sauces – they are a wonderful short-cut to building deep flavour. (NB: Because Worcestershire sauce contains anchovies, it is not suitable for vegetarians.)

- Teriyaki sauce – Another essential to keep next to the cooker, for dashing into things when you want to enhance flavour. It is, essentially, a flavoured soy sauce. Low-fat mushroom cookery wouldn't be the same without it

- Thai fish sauce – Now available in most major supermarkets. It seems rather smelly, but don't panic – small amounts (a teaspoon or less) give excellent results in all sorts of Thai-inspired dishes. A bottle will last for quite a while

- Ketchup – A tablespoon or so of this old standby is great in dipping sauces, spreads and dressings. It is a bright, dependable and homely presence on anyone's store-cupboard shelf

- Balsamic vinegar – Great stuff, even the supermarket bottles – not quite the real thing, but delicious, none the less. It does wonders for low-fat salad dressings (see pages 58–60). Keep cider vinegar, white wine vinegar, and sherry vinegar as well

- Mango chutney – I particularly like hot mango chutney, and use it in dressings, sauces and marinades. Buy the best you can find. Also look for other interesting chutneys and pickles to zip things up

- Citrus fruits: lemons, limes and oranges

- Onions (particularly red ones)

- Garlic

- Chillies (seed and rib them before using unless you are seriously dedicated to edible fire)

Sugars and sweeteners

All of the following are valuable seasonings that are useful in both sweet and savoury cookery:

- Honey – Use in dessert cookery, and also in marinades, sauces, dressings – all the usual places you want to build complex and pleasing flavour in a hurry. It blends beautifully with mustard to coat chicken and pork

- Molasses and treacle

- Marmalades, jams, preserves and conserves, including French no-added-sugar conserves

- Assorted sugars – Caster, icing, soft brown, granulated brown, muscovado

Dried herbs and spices

Buy spices in small jars or cartons and store them *near* the cooker for convenience, not on shelves *over* the cooker or they will turn stale very quickly. Some useful spices are:

- Dried oregano

- Dried tarragon (most herbs are better fresh, but both oregano and tarragon dry well)

- Ground cayenne

- Crushed dried chilli flakes

- Mild chilli powder

- Ground coriander

- Ground cumin

- Fennel seeds

- Ground ginger

- Whole nutmegs (keep a little grater handy)

- Hungarian paprika

- Smoked paprika (look in speciality food halls and Italian or Spanish delis)

- Ground white pepper

- Salt and pepper (keep sea salt, whole mixed peppercorns and whole black peppercorns in grinders next to the cooker)

- Sesame and poppy seeds

- Piri piri seasoning

Flavour extracts for desserts

See mail order guide, page 213 – buy only pure natural extracts.

- Vanilla

- Chocolate

- Almond

Carbohydrate Basics

- Potatoes

- Quick-cooking polenta

- Ready-cooked polenta (shrink-wrapped blocks) – cube it and add to soups and stews

- Couscous

- Bulghur

- Assorted rices

- Wild rice

- Assorted dried pasta, including lasagne

- Potato gnocchi

EQUIPMENT

You'll need a few heavy-bottomed non-reactive (in other words, they will not react with acid ingredients to produce off-colours and tastes) pots and pans: one or two each of enamelled cast iron and weighty non-stick would be perfect. A large, flat-bottomed wok with a good cover will come in very handy as a saucepan and as a steamer or smoker (with a bamboo or folding metal steamer insert) as well as for the more obvious stir-frying. Useful as well are one or two good-sized (20cm/8in diameter), deepish, heavy-bottomed, non-stick frying-pans, and a ridged grill pan, to be used on the hob. Grill pans are heavy and non-stick, and will allow you to barbecue on the hob – the ridges give that appealing striped grill effect (it helps if you have a good induction fan over the cooker).

I prefer wooden cooking implements; they feel good, are the perfect weight (they almost become an extension of your hand as you use them over the years), and will not scratch your non-stick and enamel pots. Get a few spray bottles for your oil-water spray, along with a few sturdy non-stick baking trays for roasting or oven 'frying'. For oven-frying potatoes (see page 106) I like perforated baking trays (see mail order guide page 213) – they speed things up nicely. Buy a few baking dishes (Pyroflam or Pyrex) as well, for lasagne, crumbles, etc., and a few non-stick cake tins.

Handy gadgets and utensils

- Flexible palette knife

- Kitchen scissors

- Citrus zester

- Efficient can opener

- Vacu-van (for keeping opened bottles of wine fresh)

- Sharp knives (dull knives are dangerous and slow you down)

- Measuring jugs and spoons

- A reliable set of kitchen scales

- Brush (for brushing on marinades, milk washes, etc.)

- Thin skewer or cake tester

- Whisk

- Food processor

- Blender

- Microwave (invaluable for thawing, warming, even some cooking – very low-fat white sauces for instance)

- Airpopper for popcorn (see mail order guide, page 213)

Techniques and Secret Weapons

Now for the fun: get into the kitchen and start cooking. Low-fat techniques are easy and rewarding – they become second nature very quickly.

1 Basic Sautéing

How do you sauté without fats and oils (especially butter and olive oil)? Substitute stock – or even better, stock and wine – for the fat or oil. Make your own fat-free stock (chicken, vegetable or fish, depending on the recipe), or buy those excellent little pots of stock now available in the chill cabinet of many supermarkets, which can be diluted with water to three times their volume. Keep the pots in the freezer, and defrost (approximately 5 minutes in the microwave) when needed. An excellent alternative is Marigold Swiss Vegetable Bouillon powder, available in many whole-food and health-food shops. Avoid stock cubes. Their fat content is too high, and they tend to be salty and over-seasoned. To sauté, put chopped onions and garlic in the pan, pour in about 300ml (½ pint) of stock and a few fluid ounces of dry wine (red, white, vermouth or sherry, depending on the recipe), and bring to a boil. Simmer briskly, covered, for 7–10 minutes, then uncover and simmer briskly for a few minutes more, until the onions and garlic are meltingly tender, and 'frying' in their own juices. If they catch and brown a bit, deglaze the pan with a splash of stock and wine and scrape up the browned bits with a wooden spoon or spatula – this deepens the colour, and intensifies the flavour. Red onions, yellow onions, leeks and spring onions (for speed and great delicacy) can be sautéed this way. For deep taste make a flavour infusion of the basic sauté by adding flavour ingredients – chopped dry-packed sun-dried tomatoes (for ease, chop them with kitchen scissors), slivered black olives (use vacuum-packed or brine-packed black olives – *not* oil-packed – and always on the stone. Pre-stoned olives tend to be flabby, and canned olives are invariably tasteless). Two or three olives add glorious olive oil flavour for a fraction of the Calories and fat grams of olive oil – 4 olives will provide 2 grams of fat and 19 Calories, a tablespoon of olive oil contains 14 grams of fat and 120 Calories. To your flavour infusion you can also add spices, chopped chillies or dried red chilli flakes, or a dash or two of Tabasco, as well as a dash of Worcestershire sauce, or – for mushroom cookery (see below) – a dash of teriyaki or soy sauce. And various extra vegetables can be added to the basic sauté: chopped carrots, peeled, chopped peppers, chopped fennel, and so on.

2 Stir-frying

Heat a small amount of stock (or stock and wine) in a wok, toss in the vegetables and flavour components (ginger, garlic, chillies, soy sauce, etc.), and stir and cook until crisp-tender. If you wish, spritz the wok with oil-water spray (see below) before adding stock. Fresh lemon and lime juice make good additions to stock for either sautéing or stir-frying vegetables such as sliced fennel, diced or sliced courgettes, asparagus tips or broccoli. Stir-fry and cook until the vegetables are done as you like them and coated in a syrupy glaze.

3 Oil-water Spray

Occasionally a few drops of oil can be just what you need, despite your low-fat regime: a baking dish needs a light greasing, a frying-pan needs oiling, roasted vegetables need lubricating, and so on. For a low-fat lifestyle, frying – even shallow pan-frying – is out. But you can grill-fry or oven-fry very successfully if you make yourself an oil-water spray. Fill a clean, new plant mister or small plastic scent spray seven-eighths with water and one-eighth with good oil. To use, just shake and spray. This gives you a light even misting of oil and water (in the heat of cooking the water evaporates, leaving a hint of oil), just enough to do the job. Keep a spray bottle for olive oil, one for sunflower oil, and one for sesame oil (for seasoning Oriental dishes). With oil-water spray and a sturdy non-stick baking sheet, you can oven-fry chicken and potatoes and potato pancakes (see below) and you can grill-fry fish and cutlets with great success.

4 Oven-frying

Instead of a deep fryer, depend on a good non-stick baking sheet. With the shake and spritz oil-water spray and the baking sheet, you need never again drown potatoes in boiling oil. Home-made oven chips are a gastronomic experience to cherish. Or try Mediterranean-style roasted vegetables: spray aubergine, courgettes, garlic and tomatoes with the oil spray and roast in a hot oven. Or try a British version with chunks of root vegetables, or cauliflower florets. Oven-roasted vegetables take on a swooningly well-rounded, caramelized flavour that is deeply satisfying. Lightly oil-sprayed vegetables, Bean Cakes (page 80) or polenta rounds can be grilled to great effect as well.

5 Wok-smoking

I've borrowed a brilliant Chinese low-fat technique for wok-smoking, and applied it to all sorts of interesting recipes, not necessarily Chinese. This method of Chinese smoking is used as a seasoning, not an actual cooking method. It adds an amazing, subtle smokiness to low-fat food. Usually the food is cooked first, then smoked. I reverse the process when smoking poultry: smoke first, then cook on a ridged grill pan. For some vegetables, I cook first, then smoke. Here's how to do it:

Choose a flat-bottomed wok, with a cover, and line the wok with heavy-duty foil, leaving a generous overhang. Make-up the smoking mixture: 3 rounded tablespoons Lapsang Souchong tea (or the contents of 6 Lapsang Souchong teabags), 3 rounded tablespoons raw white rice, 3 rounded tablespoons brown sugar. Mix together and scatter into the bottom of the wok. Choose a folding metal steamer basket or a Chinese bamboo steamer and set in the wok. Arrange the food to be smoked in the basket (i.e. raw skinned duck breasts or boneless, skinless chicken thighs). The duck or chicken can be seasoned first with a spice rub or a bit of soy or teriyaki sauce. Cover the wok, then fold up the foil overhang and seal all around so that the kitchen does not fill with smoke. Turn the hob to high, then begin the timing – usually on high for 5 minutes, medium for 5, low for 5, then 5 minutes sitting time in the closed wok. Timing depends on the weight of your wok, the strength of your hob, and the ingredients, so you will eventually learn what works best for your equipment. On some occasions, seasoning ingredients can be added to the smoking mixture: thyme sprigs and bayleaf for instance, or cinnamon sticks and star anise.

6 Bread

Eat your bread *without* the usual butter or margarine. Good bread is delicious on its own. Or use yeast extract, mashed fruit, a bit of jam, marmalade or honey, or no-fat fromage frais or Quark flavoured with herbs, spices and garlic, or with honey or marmalade.

7 Dairy products

Substitute skimmed-milk dairy products for the full-fat versions. You will be surprised at how quickly your palate adjusts to the change, in fact after a (short) while, whole-milk products will seem unpalatably fatty and cloying. Try non-fat fromage frais – thick, creamy and wonderful on its own, or in all sorts of interesting recipes. Quark – a non-fat smooth curd cheese – is endlessly useful as well, as is no-fat yogurt, especially when drained to make luscious, tangy Greek-style yogurt. Buttermilk, cultured from skimmed milk, and thick as pouring cream, has many uses as well, as does skimmed milk, especially when combined with skimmed-milk powder, for added nutrition and richness

(skimmed-milk powder is fortified with fat-soluble vitamins).

There are no skimmed-milk hard cheeses but there are outstanding medium-fat ones. *If you can tolerate a small amount of fat in your low-fat lifestyle*, choose a few that you like and use them sparingly. Italian Parmesan is one of the best. It has a gorgeous, deep taste, so a little goes a long way. Cube it, then put it into the blender and blend it to a powder, or grate it on the small holes on a box grater. Store it in the fridge or freezer. Gruyère and Fontina cheeses are also medium-fat and fabulously flavourful – a little bit goes a long way. And half-fat Italian mozzarella (in the liquid-filled pouches – it's sometimes called 'mozzarella light') melts like a dream.

8 Cream

In place of crème fraîche, soured cream, double cream or mascarpone cheese (at least 80 per cent fat), use ricotta (15 per cent fat). (But those who must avoid fat entirely should avoid ricotta.) It is beautifully creamy, and has an exquisite sweetness. Whip it in a food processor with a spoonful of good marmalade, jam or preserves or a bit of icing sugar for a creamy topping that surpasses whipped cream.

9 Using Low-fat Yogurt

Very low-fat yogurt separates when heated – if you try using it in a sauce, you invariably end up with a curdled mess. I've seen recipes that suggest that stabilizing the yogurt with cornflour or egg white, but I find the finished sauce unsatisfactory with these methods. One way of reducing the yogurt's tendency to curdle is to drain it: line a sieve with a dampened double layer of muslin, blue J-cloth or jelly-bag, and place over a deep bowl. Pour the yogurt into the sieve, fold the cloth over the top and refrigerate overnight. (If you are draining yogurt for use in a raita or a dip, refrigerate for 2–3 hours only.) The next day, drain the liquid from the bowl (it can be used as part of the liquid in bread-baking), then rinse and dry the bowl and scrape in the drained yogurt. Refrigerate until needed.

Another trick is to stir Dijon mustard into yogurt (and sometimes – for colour and smoky flavour – a puréed grilled pepper as well). The Dijon stabilizes the yogurt so that you can stir it into a sauce at the end of a recipe and simmer it *gently* until smooth and thickened. Also, yogurt/mustard makes a wonderful coating for pork cutlets, fish, aubergine and courgette slices; they can then be grill-fried. Dredge in the yogurt/mustard (mixed with puréed grilled pepper if you wish), coat with crumbs (or crumbs and Parmesan cheese) and grill until golden. The yogurt protects the meat, fish, fowl or veg and keeps it moist, the mustard keeps it from curdling and adds delicious taste. For a sauce, blend the yogurt, mustard, pepper in the blender. Blending thins it down to a good consistency for finishing sauces. For coating, just whisk it lightly together with a fork, so that it stays nice and thick.

10 Salad dressing

Give up conventional salad dressings – with their high oil content, they rack up the fat Calories. Dress your salad instead with lemon or lime juice, no-fat fromage frais or buttermilk whisked with balsamic vinegar and a dab of Dijon mustard, or just plain balsamic or sherry wine vinegar. Or see pages 58–60 for some very sexy no-fat dressings.

VEGETABLE TECHNIQUES

1 Mushroom stock and sauté

An entire pound of mushrooms contains 120 very low-fat Calories – a single tablespoon of fat used in the sauté adds another 120 (fat-packed) Calories – and of course a pound of mushrooms takes much more than a tablespoon of butter or oil. For a deeply flavourful mushroom sauté, substitute the low-fat mushroom trinity for the fat: dry wine (sherry is great with mushrooms, but red wine is good as well), stock and a splash of teriyaki sauce. These bring out the mushroom flavour like nothing else, and result in a splendid sauté that tastes rich, deep and anything but low-fat. To make things even more intense, soak some dry mushrooms in a generous amount of very hot water, then strain to eliminate the grit. Save the strained liquid to use in place of other stocks in the basic mushroom sauté (add the soaked mushroom pieces as well). I keep containers of this mushroom stock in the freezer to use in all sorts of ways, from rice and other grain pilafs, to bread-baking. To add even more wildness, shake in some Shake O'cini (page 23).

2 Aubergine

This glorious, glossy purple bulbous vegetable makes low-fat cooking richer, easier, and much more interesting.

Roasted purée: Pierce a whole, unpeeled aubergine in several places and bake in a 180°C/350°F/Gas Mark 4 oven for about 40 minutes, until it is soft and collapsed. It loses its glossy beauty, but strip off the skin, chop the tender flesh, and use the resulting rough purée as an addition to very lean mince. It makes the leanest of mince, usually dry, juiceless and unrewarding, become juicy and succulent, and it stretches the meat so a small amount goes a long way. Most importantly it does these things discreetly and deliciously – there is no added taste or off-putting texture. The overall impression is lighter, but not at all insubstantial.

Flavour infusion: A peeled aubergine, cubed and simmered with stock, wine and flavour ingredients (sun-dried tomatoes, garlic, onions, spices, slivered olives), becomes meltingly tender, and the cubes soak up the flavours like little sponges. Roughly purée the mixture in a food processor, and use it – as with roasted aubergine – with extra lean mince (it's marvellous in a bolognese sauce; a small amount of very low-fat meat becomes lavish and luxurious) or try it in stuffings and vegetable casseroles.

3 Garlic: roasted and braised

Roasted or braised garlic purée adds marvellous texture and depth of flavour to soups, stews and sauces. It is mild and rich, unlike the harsh rudeness of raw garlic. An entire bulb of roasted or braised garlic is actually milder than a single clove, crushed in a garlic press, and browned in oil.

To roast garlic, remove its papery covering but don't peel the cloves and don't separate them. Make sure that you choose large, firm, non-blemished, non-sprouting bulbs for this technique. Slice off the point end, so that a cross-section of the garlic flesh within the clove is revealed. Spray with oil-water spray. Wrap in foil (a well-sealed but roomy packet – one bulb per packet), shiny side in, and roast in a 190°C/375°F/Gas Mark 5 oven until the garlic turns

into a meltingly tender purée. This takes about an hour. Squeeze the purée from the cloves, and use in sauces, stews and dips; or just spread it on good crusty bread, and eat with great pleasure.

To pan-braise the cloves, peel as many garlic cloves as you like, but don't crush them. Spread them in a heavy-bottomed pan, cover with stock, and simmer gently, covered, until tender, about 10–15 minutes. Add a bit more stock as needed. Mash the cloves, or rub through a sieve.

A note on crushing raw garlic: I believe that garlic presses reduce the glorious bulb to an evil-smelling mush. Instead, buy a sturdy wooden carpenter's mallet from a DIY shop. Separate the garlic cloves and hit them lightly with the mallet. Remove the skins, then use the mallet to beat the garlic cloves to a pulp.

4 Roasted onion

When an onion is roasted at high heat it becomes sweet and smoky, just the flavours you need for enriching low-fat soups, stews and sauces.

1. Preheat the oven to 220°C/425°F/Gas Mark 6.

2. Put the onions on a double sheet of foil, shiny side out, but do not wrap them. Roast for 1¼ hours, or until very soft and almost collapsed.

3. With a sharp knife, cut off the stem and root ends of the onions. Remove and discard the blackened skin and first layer. Serve as they are with pepper and lemon juice, or put the onions into a liquidizer and purée for use in other recipes.

5 Peppers

Glowingly attractive red and yellow peppers (green ones lack sweetness) are endlessly useful in low-fat cookery. They make food beautiful, delicious and rich-tasting without adding fat and they add valuable nutrients too – what more is there to ask? In these techniques the peppers are divested of their skins, and they are cooked, not raw, therefore they are exquisitely sweet and digestible. There are so many ways to use peppers, a complete listing would fill an entire book.

Grilled: Char (really char, until burnt, and blackened) peppers under the grill, on a barbecue or directly on the gas hob. Let them sit for a few minutes in a covered bowl, or in a closed plastic bag, and then strip off the blackened skin (don't use running water, or you will wash off the wonderful smokiness). The supple, smoky sweet peppers are perfectly gorgeous as they are, of course, but are even better puréed and used as a cooking ingredient. They add a blaze of lovely colour, a perception of richness, and a compelling flavour.

Peeled and simmered or sautéed, or infused and sieved: Cut raw red or yellow peppers in half, remove the stems, ribs and seeds, and cut them into their natural sections. With a swivel-bladed vegetable peeler, peel off the skins. The peeling is quick and easy to do, and makes an enormous difference to the finished dish; the pepper flesh cooks to melting, sweet, digestible tenderness, the skins do not. The peeled peppers can then be cut into strips and stir-fried or sautéed in stock (or stock and wine) or diced and sautéed in a basic flavour/vegetable infusion (see below). Or they can be simmered with seasonings in stock and wine, and then puréed to form a vivid, silky, clinging sauce. In some cases, the initial peeling can be skipped. If the sauce is to be puréed, and then sieved, the skins will be left behind in the

sieve – no need to peel first. It's fun to make a red pepper sauce *and* a yellow one, and then coat a plate with both – vivid puddles of red and yellow meeting in the middle. Place fish fillets, grilled meat or poultry on the sauces, and surround with sautéed pepper strips and red onion shreds, and sprinkle with shredded herbs. It's easily done, but it's a visual feast.

And *finally*, some quick essentials

1 Grill, steam, oven-poach or bake fish 'en papillote' (in a greaseproof paper or foil packet). Or see the yogurt-mustard method (page 30) for grill-frying. Use fresh herbs, lemon or lime juice, your oil-water spray, wine, mustard and so on to season fish, rather than oodles of butter and olive oil.

2 Over half the fat in poultry is in the skin, so remove it, preferably before cooking, or – so roasted chicken doesn't dry out – remove it after cooking. Then skim the pan juices of fat.

3 Trim all visible fat from meat and poultry, even the rim of fat on ham and lean bacon. Kitchen scissors do the job nicely. Try to reduce the amount of red meat you have a week, or, for stews and pasta sauces, replace half of it with chunky vegetables or roasted aubergine purée. When you do eat meat, choose lean cuts.

4 If you do make a meat stew always chill (a quick chill in the freezer, if necessary) the stew or pan juices. The fat rises to the top, and hardens, then just lifts off.

A NOTE ABOUT THE RECIPES

This book is full of simple, robust recipes for home cooking. Restaurant cooking is for restaurants. Exquisite teetering towers of elegantly drizzled and embellished morsels of expensive foodstuffs are not ultimately satisfying at home – time is short, and we want to tuck into something richly, roundly satisfying, but not precious, fiddly, or over-engineered. There is no need to hanker for chef's cuisine, when home cooking can be so good. Aim for interesting texture, big flavour, high nutrition and simple, colourful, rustic presentation, and you won't go wrong.

All quantities are given in metric measurements and in the approximate imperial equivalents. Follow one or the other.

Cooking times especially must be taken with a grain of salt. The size and shape of the oven, the thickness of the pots and pans, the number of things you are baking at one particular time, the state of the thermostat – all these variables and more will affect the total cooking time.

And finally, my great bugaboo, number of servings. Whenever possible, I give the yield in volume (900ml/1½ pints, for instance) so you can picture it, and decide how many it will feed. It changes with the shape of the meal, the appetite and habits of the diners, the time of the year, the emotional climate at the table, and God only knows what else. So take my suggestions as just that – suggestions – and apply your own logic to the question of serving size.

A NOTE ABOUT THE NUTRITIONAL ANALYSIS

All nutritional figures given are approximate and should be used as a guide. They are based on data from food tables or from manufacturers' data rather than by direct analysis. The symbol <1g indicates the recipe is estimated to contain under 1g of fat. Likewise <0.5g in the analyses means the recipe quantity stated contains less than 0.5g of fat. Neg (negligible) means 0.1 or 0.2g fat.

The Symbols

All the recipes in this book are low-fat. Some are very low-fat indeed; others – because of a little Parmesan, ricotta, eggs etc – are somewhat higher and the recipes have been given symbols to help you adapt the plan to your own lifestyle and needs. If you are seriously over-weight and want to lose weight, or have a health problem that requires a very low-fat diet, or if you want to lose some weight in a hurry, stick to the recipes with the very low-fat symbol. (Many recipes can be made lower fat by simply using Quark, fromage frais or very low-fat yogurt instead of ricotta, and by omitting the Parmesan cheese, and so on.)

Those who want to lose weight but are not seriously obese can have the *occasional* foray into higher fat territory, but people with a fat-related medical condition should be very careful indeed. The higher fat recipes are – in the context of our high-fat world – not all *that* high fat, but should be taken in moderation by slimmers, and pretty much avoided by the medically compromised. But under ordinary circumstances the occasional indulgence with these recipes can be good for the soul.

Often a higher fat recipe will seem as low fat as the others (when you look at the analysis). It's the *type* of fat that concerns me – dairy and animal fat – rather than the actual numbers. So feast on the vegetables, fruits, skimmed milk products and grains, and hold back sensibly on the medium-fat dairy products, the eggs and on the higher fat meats.

The other symbols are self-explanatory and should help make your cooking life easier. The packed lunches include sandwiches but I've also included salads, vegetable stews, soups and so on that can be taken to work in a wide-mouth Thermos or insulated bags.

Key to the symbols

♥ Very low fat

⊘ Higher fat (avoid if you are slimming, or have specific health problems)

Ⓥ Suitable for vegetarians

🍎 Suitable for packed lunches

Y Suitable for celebrations

✳ Suitable for freezing

⊘ Quick and easy

CHAPTER 1

Breakfast

Breakfast is important; it kick-starts the day, and helps avoid frenzied, destructive snacking on doughnuts and such junk later on, but my word, breakfast itself can be unbelievably unhealthy. Once upon a time, a sturdy, fat-laden breakfast seemed like a good idea. Central heating was unknown, and clothing and fabrics were not nearly as efficient as they are now at keeping out the cold. Labour-saving devices as we know them didn't exist, and people did *real* work; they had no food processors, lifts, elevators, word processors, remote control devices, power steering, and all the other miracles of modern science and technology that do our work for us these days. Add to this daily energy-expending labour the vagaries of an uncertain food supply, and you can see why stocking up on fat and stodge was once the done thing. But those days are long gone. It's still wise to feast at breakfast, but not on fat. Make it a low-fat feast.

A FEW QUICK BREAKFAST IDEAS

- A toasted bagel with Quark or fromage frais. ♥
  Add smoked salmon, if you can tolerate a bit of a (healthy) fat dimension. ❂

- Cereal (read the labels and choose a no-added-fat cereal) with skimmed milk and fruit, and a sprinkling of sugar if you like. A cereal that is fortified with vitamins and minerals is not a bad idea at all. ♥

- Porridge or other hot cereal, with honey, sugar or maple syrup if you like it. Add some cinnamon and vanilla extract to make it fabulous. ♥

- Very Quick Pizza (a great breakfast; my son grew up on this) – page 46. ❂

- Fresh fruit or fruit compote (for example see page 195) topped with no-fat fromage frais (page 29) and toast. ♥

- Sliced lean cold meats (turkey, chicken, fat-trimmed ham) with Quark. ♥
If you can tolerate a little fat add a few slices of half-fat mozzarella cheese. ⊘

The Great British Fry-up

This classic is easily de-fatted, and much improved by the defatting: the taste will be cleaner. If you are devoted to your daily morning fix of grease, it will take a while to get used to its lack, but you will learn to love it. Substitute this for the classic fry-up, and save approximately 650 Calories and 55 grams of fat (and you will revel in the taste of the food, unmasked by grease).

- Poached egg ⊘
- Oven-fried Potatoes (page 106) ♥
- Sautéed mushrooms (page 130) ♥
- Grilled tomatoes (spray with oil-water spray before grilling) ♥
- Low-fat Sausage (page 171) ⊘
- Lean back bacon (trim the rim of fat, and grill, or dry-fry in a non-stick pan) ⊘
- Baked beans (if you want them) ♥
- Toast with marmalade (no butter) ♥

Huevos Rancheros

Huevos Rancheros are the Tex-Mex equivalent of the Great British Fry-up: fried eggs on tortillas, with plenty of refried beans and salsa and perhaps a spicy sausage or two. Make a vibrant and colourful healthy version (it will turn a week-end breakfast into a fiesta) with a poached egg on a warmed maize tortilla, surrounded by Unfried Beans (page 82), and Cherry Tomato and Mango Salsa (page 62), and Orange and Red Onion Salsa (page 65). Add Spicy Oven-fried New Potatoes (page 106) and Mexican Sausage Patties (page 174).

Breakfast Eggs

Scrambled eggs, omelettes and frittatas can all be prepared with a few yolks removed, to reduce the fat and cholesterol. The colour will be a bit paler, and the flavour a bit less rich, but overall the finished dish will taste quite good. Like switching from whole milk to skimmed, once you've made the change, it's very hard to go back to a full-yolked dish.

Frittata

SERVES 2

A frittata is an open-faced omelette, very good for breakfast. Fill it with potatoes, as suggested, or with anything that catches your fancy. Cold wedges of frittata make a great starter or packed lunch.

2 whole eggs	3 tablespoons Potato Hash or whatever
2 egg whites	filling you like (see page 38)
salt and freshly ground pepper	a sprinkle of grated Parmesan cheese
to taste	1 tablespoon mixed snipped chives and
oil-water spray	chopped parsley

1 Preheat the grill. Beat together the eggs, egg whites, salt and pepper. Don't over-beat, or the egg protein thins out. Beat just enough to combine the yolks and whites properly.

2 Spray a 22cm (8½in) non-stick frying-pan with oil-water spray and heat until the droplets of water skitter about the pan. Pour in the eggs and give them a few seconds to set on the bottom. Then, with a spatula or a fish slice, push the edges of the eggs towards the centre forming soft moist curds, working your way around the perimeter, and tilting the pan as you go, so that the uncooked portion of the egg spreads underneath to the edges of the pan. Shake the pan, and loosen with the fish slice to keep the frittata moving – you don't want it to stick.

3 When the frittata is set on the bottom, but still quite moist and runny on top, spoon in the potatoes and cook for a few moments more. Sprinkle on the cheese, then flash under the grill to set the top. Strew on the herbs. Serve it right from the pan, or slide it onto a plate. Cut into wedges to serve.

CALORIE COUNT 111 Kcal　**FAT CONTENT** 7g　**PER SERVING**　

Note

To make an omelette, no need for the grill. Spoon the potatoes and herbs into the centre (step 3) when the eggs are almost set on top, and shake and cook for a few moments more. Slide the omelette on to a plate tilted against the pan; when it's half-way on to the plate, fold it over to enclose the filling.

Potato Hash

MAKES 900ml (1½ pints)

Potato hash can be used as a vegetable accompaniment as well as a frittata filling.

---

oil-water spray
750g (1½lb) boiling or new potatoes,
    unpeeled, finely diced

1 red onion, finely diced
salt and freshly ground pepper
300ml (½ pint) stock

---

1 Spray a heavy-bottomed non-stick frying-pan with oil-water spray and heat. Tip in the potatoes and onion and stir for a moment. Season and add the stock. Simmer, briskly, uncovered, stirring occasionally until the potatoes and onions are tender and sticking a bit (about 10 minutes). Pour in a splash of stock to loosen the browned bits in the pan and stir them up. Add a bit more stock during the cooking, as needed.

CALORIE COUNT 33 Kcal   **FAT CONTENT** Neg   **PER 3 TABLESPOONS**

Other fillings for an omelette or frittata

Almost anything is possible. Try these:
• Grilled vegetables, roughly chopped (courgettes, aubergines, peppers)
• Sautéed mushrooms (page 30)
• Sautéed peppers (page 32)
• Peperonata (page 149)
• Roasted fennel (page 121)
• Crumbled de-fatted chorizo (page 178)

Oven-baked French Toast

In America, where I grew up, French Toast – slices of bread soaked in a rich custard mixture, and then pan-fried in butter until puffy, custardy inside, and crisp on the outside – is a beloved and traditional breakfast dish. Typically, it is served with a big pat of butter melting on top, and rivulets of maple syrup melding into the rivulets of melting butter. Whew! It was good, but hellishly fattening. And perhaps the rich custard, *and* the butter for frying, *and* the butter for melting on top, *and* the maple syrup were just a wee bit over the top. Make a festive weekend breakfast with a more restrained version; oven-baked in a light custard, no butter, no maple syrup, but still very good indeed.

French Toast

SERVES 6

175g (6oz) day-old sliced bread, 5mm (½in) thick, each slice halved into triangle shapes

2 whole eggs

2 egg whites

2 tablespoons orange marmalade

1 teaspoon vanilla extract

500ml (16fl oz) skimmed milk mixed with 2 tablespoons skimmed milk powder

½ teaspoon ground cinnamon

2 tablespoons granulated brown sugar

1 Arrange the bread slices in overlapping rows so that they cover the bottom of a 30 × 20cm (12 × 8in) rectangular baking dish.

2 Beat the eggs and whites with the marmalade, then beat in the vanilla, milk and cinnamon. Pour over the bread; then, with a broad spatula, push the bread into the liquid so that it soaks up quite a bit. Preheat the oven to 180°C/350°F/Gas Mark 4. Put the kettle on. Push the bread down again. Scatter the brown sugar granules evenly over the surface.

3 Put the baking dish into a larger dish. Pour in hot water to come half-way up the sides. Bake for 35–45 minutes until puffed, set, and browned and crunchy on top. Serve warm.

CALORIE COUNT 173 Kcal   **FAT CONTENT** 3g   **PER SERVING**   Ⓥ

VARIATIONS

• Add a few tablespoons of raisins, dried cherries, blueberries or cranberries, or a combination.

• Use ¼ teaspoon of almond extract, and reduce the vanilla to ½ teaspoon (very good with a scattering of dried cherries added in step 2).

Clafoutis

A clafoutis is a puffy, oven-baked pancake, usually filled with cherries or other fruit (see the dessert chapter, page 194). The clafoutis principle works brilliantly with savoury ingredients, and would make a festive and special weekend breakfast or brunch. Of course, any of these recipes would be excellent as a lunch or light supper as well.

Grilled Pepper and Courgette Clafoutis

MAKES 450ml (¾ pint) **SERVES** 4–6

Ratatouille (pages 126–7) or peperonata (page 149) would fill a clafoutis beautifully, as well as this fresh and smoky mix of courgettes, grilled peppers and parsley. If you want to emphasize the smoky dimension, add ½ teaspoon of smoked paprika in step 1. You could also add a chopped chilli if you want a piquant start to the day.

Infusion
1 red onion, sliced thinly
2 garlic cloves, crushed
2–3 sun-dried tomatoes, chopped
3 black olives, slivered off their stones
150ml (¼ pint) stock
90ml (3fl oz) red wine
1 small courgette (about 125g/4oz), diced
1–2 grilled peppers, skinned and diced
1 tablespoon chopped fresh parsley

Batter
100g (3½oz) light plain flour
salt and freshly ground pepper
300ml (½ pint) skimmed milk
3 tablespoons skimmed milk powder
6 tablespoons very low-fat natural yogurt
3 egg whites
1 whole egg
oil-water spray
2 tablespoons Parmesan cheese, grated

1 Preheat the oven to 190°C/375°F/Gas Mark 5.

2 Simmer together all the infusion ingredients except the peppers and parsley until the onions and courgettes are tender and the liquid just about gone.

3 Add the pepper and the chopped parsley.

4 For the batter, put the flour into a bowl and season. Whisk together the remaining ingredients except the spray and Parmesan and pour into the flour, stirring until just mixed with no lumps. Do not overmix.

5 Oil-water-spray a 25cm (10in) non-stick flan tin. Pour in the batter. Scatter in the filling, leaving a 2.5cm (1in) border all around. Sprinkle the cheese over the top. Bake in a preheated oven for 30–40 minutes until set, lightly brown and puffed. Cool on a wire rack.

CALORIE COUNT 178 Kcal   **FAT CONTENT** 4g   **PER SERVING**

Spinach Filling for Clafoutis

MAKES 450ml (¾ pint)   **SERVES** 6

A sweet and sour Sicilian-influenced spinach mixture gives clafoutis a totally different character. The spinach mixture (and the grilled pepper-courgette mixture in the previous recipe) would make a delicious vegetable accompaniment or a wrap filling (see page 45) as well.

Infusion
1 red onion, chopped
2 garlic cloves, crushed
2 tablespoons sultanas
a pinch of cayenne pepper
¼ teaspoon ground cinnamon
¼ teaspoon ground coriander
300ml (½ pint) stock

juice and grated zest of ½ a lemon
salt and freshly ground pepper

Spinach
250g (8oz) young leaf spinach, washed
  and ready to eat, shredded
chopped fresh mint and parsley
Clafoutis Batter (page 40)

1 Combine the infusion ingredients in a pan and simmer, uncovered, until the onions are tender and almost no liquid remains.

2 Add the spinach and stir and cook until wilted (2–3 minutes), then stir in the herbs. Drain in a sieve.

3 Pour the batter into a prepared tin and proceed as in step 5 in the previous recipe, omitting the cheese.

CALORIE COUNT 170 Kcal   **FAT CONTENT** 3g   **PER SERVING**

Smoked Fish Clafoutis

SERVES 6

To me, smoked fish means breakfast, whether it's smoked salmon, a kipper, or – as here – smoked haddock. I don't like warm or hot smoked salmon, but many do. If you are one of the many, try it in place of the haddock – just omit step 3.

Filling
150g (5oz) button mushrooms, quartered
125ml (4fl oz) mushroom stock or vegetable stock
125ml (4fl oz) sherry
dash of teriyaki sauce

¼ teaspoon dried tarragon, crumbled
1 × 250g (8oz) undyed smoked haddock fillet
freshly ground pepper

Clafoutis Batter (page 40)

1 Preheat the oven to 190°C/375°F/Gas Mark 5.

2 Combine the mushrooms, stock, sherry, teriyaki sauce and tarragon in a frying-pan or wok. Simmer briskly, stirring occasionally, until the mushrooms are tender and the liquid just about gone.

3 Meanwhile, wrap the fish fillet in a piece of foil, shiny side in, so that the fish is in a roomy, well-sealed pouch. Put into the oven for 5 minutes, until just barely flaking, and not quite done. Flake the fish, discarding the skin and any bones. When the mushrooms are done, stir in the fish.

4 Oil-water-spray a 25cm (10in) non-stick flan tin. Pour in the batter. Scatter in the filling, leaving a 2.5cm (1in) border all around. Bake in a preheated oven for 30–40 minutes until set, lightly brown and puffed. Cool on a wire rack.

CALORIE COUNT 171 Kcal   **FAT CONTENT** 2g   **PER SERVING**

CHAPTER 2

Sandwiches

A sandwich can make a satisfying meal, and not just for lunch. Why not feed your hunger with a nice sloppy, overflowing sarnie? – life isn't all hot meals.

Sandwich making is just as easy for a low-fat lifestyle as for a high-fat one. Choose the bread or rolls you like – brown or white. Fortunately many breads are relatively low in fat. Those to avoid are croissants (horrendously fatty!) scones, brioche, chollah and other brioche-type loaves, and most sweet breads. Baguettes, pain de campagne, rye bread, crumpets (unbuttered, of course!), muffins (English ones, not the super-rich, fairy-cake-shaped American-style ones), pitta bread, bagels, soda bread (and many others) tend to be very low in fat indeed. Other breads will most likely fall into the low-fat range. Even the marvellous ciabatta, made with olive oil, has only a modest amount of oil. At the time of writing, Marks & Spencer's is selling an organic ciabatta that contains no added oil at all. As always, it is a good idea to read the label (if there is one). If there is any fat or oil in the ingredient listing, it should be towards the end of the list: ingredients are always listed in descending order of amount.

Low-fat sandwich fillings are very like 'ordinary' (high-fat) ones; just choose low-fat versions of sandwich-making staples. For instance, buy tuna canned in spring water or brine instead of in oil. Mix it with very low-fat fromage frais, fromage frais 'mayo' (fromage frais whisked with a dash of Dijon mustard and a dash of good vinegar), Rémoulade (page 57), or one of the vinaigrettes (see pages 58–60). It will taste just fine, and you will have saved *hundreds* of fat Calories. Choose lean ham, sliced turkey breast and sliced chicken breast instead of the higher-fat delicatessen meats.

A FEW INFORMAL SANDWICH SUGGESTIONS

1 Banana sandwich: This is a wonderful sandwich – perfect when you are on the go, and want to grab a sandwich while you are out. Buy the crispest small baguette you can find. Buy a ripe banana. Peel the banana. Split the baguette, but not all the way through. It should open like a hinged book. Insert banana into baguette. Bite into baguette. Crunchy outside – banana-y inside. Shards of crumbs on shirt front. Bite again. Mmm... Ⓥ 🍎 ♥

2 Freshly baked filled petit pain: Have you seen those wonderful no-fat ready-to-bake French rolls (Kool French Experience brand) in the chill cabinets of some supermarkets? They come 4 to a cylinder – simply pop open the cylinder, separate the pieces of dough and put them (on a non-stick tray) into a hot oven. Twelve minutes later, hot bread! To make hot filled rolls, flatten each piece of dough, spread the dough with something wonderful – Classic Tomato Sauce (page 91), Sautéed Mushrooms (page 30), Roasted Onions (page 31), a dab or two of one of the bean or vegetable stews, some sliced lean ham and a piece of half-fat mozzarella cheese, then fold over, crimp all around and bake. 🍎 ❂

3 Split a bagel like this: perforate it all around its perimeter with a fork, then pull the bagel apart on the dotted line. This method yields two bagel halves that each have a rough surface – much nicer to spread on to. A smooth-surfaced bagel is an insipid bagel – don't even consider it. Spread the bagel halves with Quark, Boursin Léger, Herbed Goat's Cheese Spread (page 54) or fromage frais (with some snipped chives if you like), and top with slices of the ripest, juiciest tomato you can find. Grind on a little black pepper. A bit of smoked salmon under the tomato certainly wouldn't hurt. 🍎

4 Spread rye bread with Roasted Beetroot Purée (page 119). Top with shredded raw baby spinach leaves and a sprinkle of balsamic vinegar. Ⓥ 🍎 ♥

5 Halve pitta bread crosswise, yielding 2 pockets. Fill the pockets with great stuff: salad, grilled vegetables, braised vegetables, bean or vegetable stews, pan-braised potatoes, and top with one of the fromage frais 'mayos', or Raita (page 55). Ⓥ 🍎 ♥

6 How about a chip buttie? Fill a bap with Oven-fried Potatoes (page 106) – smear the top half of the bap with one of the fromage frais spreads and the bottom half with Spicy Ketchup (page 57). Ⓥ ♥

7   Split a crusty small baguette, fill it with sliced ripe, juicy 'flavour' tomatoes, add some very thinly slivered red onion or sliced spring onion, a slivered black olive, some crushed raw garlic or pan-braised or roasted garlic purée (page 31), shredded fresh basil, chopped fresh parsley, and a sprinkling of balsamic vinegar or one of the vinaigrettes (pages 58–60). Wrap and weight (with a plate topped by a heavy can) for a few minutes, so that the juices permeate the bread. Ⓥ 🍎 ♥

8   Sliced cucumber on thinly sliced white or brown bread, with balsamic vinegar or one of the vinaigrettes (pages 58–60) and a sprinkling of dill. Ⓥ 🍎 ♥
     Add some flaked, drained canned salmon or some shredded smoked salmon to make a substantial and special sandwich. 🍎 ⏱

9   Sliced smoked turkey and salad (herb salad, or mixed leaves with watercress) on rye or wholemeal bread. Spread mustard on one slice, and Rémoulade (page 57) on the other. 🍎 ♥

10 Cheese on toast: if you have a microwave, you can turn a piece of full-fat Cheddar cheese into a medium-fat one. Put a 125g (4oz) piece of Cheddar on a microwave-proof plate. Microwave on high for 2–3 minutes until it melts into a bubbly, slightly-toasted-on-the-edges blob of melted cheese. Tilt the plate and drain off the rendered fat (you should be able to discard *at least* a tablespoon). Lavishly spread the melted cheese on toast. (To make things really interesting, rub the toast with the cut side of a split garlic clove first.) Ⓥ ⏱

Wraps

These are the latest sandwich sensation, although they are based on ancient peasant food from all over the world. Use Mexican tortillas or Mediterranean lavash or pitta bread with a choice of fillings, for instance:

• Slices of spice-rubbed, tea-smoked, skinless duck breasts (page 160) with grilled vegetables 🍎

• Spice-rubbed chicken breast with Orange and Red Onion Salsa (page 65) and Honey Mustard Vinaigrette (page 60) 🍎

• Grilled vegetables with a dollop of herbed fromage frais Ⓥ 🍎 ♥

• Marinated roasted sliced pork tenderloin with Mango and Fennel Salsa (page 61) 🍎

• Moroccan-inspired Sausage Patties (page 172) with Herbed Raita (page 55) and Orange and Red Onion Salsa (page 65) 🍎 ⏱

Crostini

Finally, don't forget crostini – thick grilled or toasted wedges or slices of baguette, pain de campagne or ciabatta bread, rubbed with a halved raw garlic clove and a black olive, so that the bread is saturated with garlic and olive pulp, then topped with a choice of spreads or toppings, for instance:

- Grilled vegetables and melted mozzarella Ⓥ ❂
- Herbed Goat's Cheese Spread (page 54) and Roasted Beetroot slices (page 119) Ⓥ ❂
- Creamy Pesto (pages 52–3), sliced 'flavour' tomatoes and fresh basil leaves Ⓥ ❂
- Spicy roasted beetroot purée and baby spinach leaves Ⓥ ♥

SIMPLE SPREADS

Butter and margarine are virtually pure fat, as is mayonnaise. 'Lower'-fat spreads are somewhat lower, but they are still fat, and no part of a low-fat diet. But home-made spreads can be very simply made out of Quark or very low-fat fromage frais: sweet spreads by flavouring the Quark or fromage frais with a bit of honey, jam, marmalade, maple syrup or low-Calorie sweetener; savoury spreads by flavouring the Quark or fromage frais with chopped herbs or spring onions, spices, a dab of mustard, a bit of ketchup, chutney, salsa or tomato purée. See the dips and spreads section (page 52) for more ideas. ♥

Very Quick Pizza

A speedy pizza makes a fun meal or snack. Make your little pizza with bagels, pitta or tortillas.

1 Split a bagel. Spread it with Classic Tomato Sauce (page 91) or creamed tomatoes (passata), and season with crumbled dried oregano, freshly ground pepper and some crushed dried chillies. Put some shredded half-fat mozzarella cheese on top, and grill until melted.

2 Split a round pitta bread into 2 rounds. Spread with Classic Tomato Sauce (page 91) or passata, top with shreds of half-fat mozzarella cheese, and grill until melted. Or spread with Creamy Pesto (pages 52–3) and a little tomato sauce, and grill. This works on tortillas as well – obviously there is no need to split them first. ❂ Ⓥ ❂

DESIGNER SANDWICHES

These elegant sandwiches (maybe elegant is not quite the word – some of these over-stuffed beauties tend towards the ungainly) are more than a snack or a quickly snatched convenience meal. A great sandwich can be a work of art – enjoy these to the fullest.

Muffuletta

SERVES 4

A slightly juicy (the best sandwiches are somewhat sloppy) rendition of a New Orleans Italian classic. The first time I ate a muffuletta was in New Orleans, standing on the bank of the murky, rushing Mississippi with my beloved. Here is the sandwich: you will have to provide the river, and the beloved.

1 round rustic loaf or
  1 pain de campagne
Grilled Red Pepper Vinaigrette
  (page 58)
lean Italian sliced meats such as Parma

ham and Bresaola (trim off the rim of
  fat with kitchen scissors)
Cherry Tomato and Olive Relish (page
  64) or Cucumber and Cherry Tomato
  Salsa (page 63)

1 Slice the loaf horizontally. Hollow out the top half (save the scooped-out bread for crumbs to use later).

2 Spread the bottom half with the vinaigrette and top with a layer of each of the sliced meats. Heap the relish on top and cover with the top half of the loaf. Press firmly together. Cut into wedges to serve.

CALORIE COUNT 280 Kcal   **FAT CONTENT** 3g   **PER SERVING**

VARIATION

For a more elaborate sandwich, add drained canned artichoke hearts, cut into eighths, and strips of fresh or canned grilled peppers.

Herbed Beetroot Baguette

SERVES 1–2

Beetroot is *good*! It does not have to be doused in bad vinegar and served on pathetic wilted lettuce. Roast your own beetroot (page 119) or buy vacuum-packed 'natural' (no vinegar) beetroot from the supermarket.

250g (8oz) carton of Quark
1 tablespoon chopped fresh parsley
1 tablespoon chopped fresh chives
1–2 dashes of Tabasco sauce
small split baguette
Beetroot Vinaigrette (page 60)
flavourful, ripe tomatoes, sliced

thinly sliced cooked natural beetroot (no vinegar)
green salad with herbs (from a supermarket greengrocery packet)
strips of grilled red pepper (page 32), or use canned or bottled peppers
salt and freshly ground pepper

1 Put the Quark, herbs and Tabasco into the food processor and process until combined.

2 Spread one half of the baguette with some of the herbed Quark, the other half with some vinaigrette.

3 Layer on the tomatoes, beetroot, greens and pepper strips. Grind on some salt and pepper. Press down the top half.

CALORIE COUNT 374 Kcal   **FAT CONTENT** 3g   **PER SERVING**

Tuna Bean and Rocket Sandwich

SERVES 4

A far cry from tuna mayonnaise or tuna and sweetcorn on white sandwich slices, this well-filled sandwich fills crusty bread with tuna and white beans and a gorgeous dressing. A large loaf will feed several people.

1 round pain de campagne or rustic loaf
Grilled Red Pepper Vinaigrette (page 58)

Tuna Bean Salad (page 81)
rocket leaves

1 Prepare the loaf as described in the Muffuletta recipe (page 47). Spread the bottom half with some Grilled Red Pepper Vinaigrette.

2 Pile on the Tuna Bean Salad and top with rocket leaves. Press the top of the loaf down on the tuna. To serve, cut into wedges.

CALORIE COUNT 187 Kcal   **FAT CONTENT** 2g   **PER SERVING**

Grilled Vegetable Sandwich with Grilled Pepper Chilli Spread

SERVES 1–2

The vegetables can be grilled under the grill, on a hob-top grill pan, or – for smoky delight – on a barbecue. Although just a sandwich, this makes a substantial and memorable meal. Use half or a whole baguette per person depending on their appetite.

20cm (8in) baguette
1 tablespoon Grilled Red Pepper Spread (page 56)
warmed grilled vegetables (page 126):
    1 slice aubergine and 3 slices courgette halved, and ½ a pepper cut into strips

chopped fresh parsley
shredded fresh basil
1 tablespoon Herbed Raita (page 55)

1 For each sandwich, halve a baguette lengthwise. Hollow out the top half (save the scooped-out bread for crumbs to use later). Spread the bottom half with some of the Grilled Red Pepper Spread.

2 Layer on some grilled vegetables: first a layer of aubergine, then courgettes and finally a generous amount of peppers. Top with herbs.

3 Spread the inside of the baguette's top half with the Herbed Raita Press down.

CALORIE COUNT 196 Kcal   **FAT CONTENT** 2g   **PER HALF BAGUETTE**

Aubergine Tomato Sandwich

SERVES 1–2

Grilled aubergine has a lip-smacking 'meaty' quality that makes it a natural for serious sandwich-making. Aubergine tenderly bathed in garlicky tomato sauce and tucked into crusty bread is a New York Italian classic; for me, it has nostalgia on its side. But even without the nostalgia, it drips goodness. Half a baguette makes a delicious snack, but if you're feeling hungry a whole baguette will be more satisfying.

20cm (8in) baguette
warm grilled aubergine slices, halved
   (page 126)
warm Classic Tomato Sauce (page 91)

fresh flat-leaf parsley, chopped
fresh basil leaves, torn
half-fat mozzarella cheese, thinly sliced

1 For each sandwich prepare a baguette as described in the previous recipe. Layer on aubergine slices, spread with Classic Tomato Sauce, and top with the herbs and cheese. Press on the top half. For a lower-fat version omit the mozzarella.

CALORIE COUNT 252 Kcal   **FAT CONTENT** 5g   **PER HALF BAGUETTE**

VARIATION

Use Creamy Pesto (page 52) on one half of the baguette, and Grilled Red Pepper Spread (page 56) on the other, instead of the tomato sauce and mozzarella. ✔

Open-faced Mushroom Crostini

MAKES 4

Eat these melted-cheese-filled mushroom toasts with a knife and fork, and a salad of bitter greens on the side. For mushroom lovers, this is a feast.

4 large flat mushrooms
125ml (4fl oz) stock
60ml (2fl oz) dry red wine
dash of teriyaki sauce
2 garlic cloves, crushed
olive-oil-water spray
salt and freshly ground pepper
4 pieces baguette or ciabatta bread (of a size to hold a mushroom)

1 garlic clove, skinned and halved
2 tablespoons chopped fresh parsley and basil
90g (3oz) shredded half-fat mozzarella cheese, or 3 tablespoons grated Parmesan cheese

1 Preheat the grill.

2 Clean the mushrooms, remove and chop the stalks. Combine the stems in a small frying-pan with the stock, wine, teriyaki and crushed garlic. Simmer until tender and the liquid absorbed.

3 Spray the mushrooms on both sides with the oil spray and grill until just cooked, 2–3 minutes on each side. Season with salt and pepper to taste. Set aside on a plate. (Save the juices.)

4 Toast the bread lightly under the grill. Rub the toasted side with the halved garlic. Drizzle some of the mushroom juices on each half, then place a mushroom, gill side up, on the bread. Fill each mushroom with some of the sautéed stalks. Cover with cheese. Grill until melted. Sprinkle with herbs and serve. For a lower-fat version omit the mozzarella and Parmesan.

CALORIE COUNT 280 Kcal   **FAT CONTENT** 6g   **PER SERVING**

CHAPTER 3

Spreads, Dips, Dressings, Salsas...

This chapter is filled with very useful and versatile recipes to be used in sandwiches, on salads, as snacks and light meals, folded into pasta, dipped, spread, swirled, and generally dolloped anywhere. These are recipes to add to your repertoire to be used over and over again; the kind that are particularly good at adding colour, glamour and flavour to quick and simple meals.

Creamy Pesto

MAKES 350ml (12fl oz)

This is a creamy version of the Italian classic which uses Quark or low-fat fromage frais instead of olive oil. Ricotta can be used in place of Quark and low-fat fromage frais – it has 15 per cent fat rather than the 0 per cent fat of Quark and low-fat fromage frais, but the general fat level will still be lower than the classic olive oil version. Because of the pine nuts and Parmesan cheese, this recipe will not do for those who must drastically eliminate *all* added fat. For convenience, measure out the herbs in a measuring jug.

450ml (¾ pint) torn basil leaves
300ml (½ pint) roughly chopped parsley
5 tablespoons freshly grated Parmesan
   cheese
30g (1oz) pine nuts

200g (7oz) carton Quark (or use very
   low-fat fromage frais)
pan braised garlic to taste (page 31) (or
   2–3 cloves of raw garlic if you like it)
salt and freshly ground pepper

1 Combine all the ingredients in the container of a food processor.

2 Process to a thick paste. Scrape into a bowl and refrigerate. If your Quark is very fresh to begin with, the sauce will keep for a week, but be warned – the garlic gets stronger every day.

CALORIE COUNT 23 Kcal **FAT CONTENT** 1g **PER TABLESPOON**

Creamy Spinach Dip

MAKES 600ml (1 pint)

The secret of perfection here is to cook the spinach very briefly, so that it remains bright green and fresh-tasting. Serve as a spread, as a dip with vegetable, pitta or tortilla dippers, with steamed new potatoes or to fill baked jacket potatoes.

1 garlic clove, crushed to a paste
several dashes each of Tabasco and
　　Worcestershire sauce (vegetarians,
　　omit Worcestershire sauce)
125ml (4fl oz) vegetable stock
200–220g (7–8oz) washed baby
　　spinach

250g (8oz) Quark (or ricotta or creamy
　　medium fat goat's cheese)
5 tablespoons no-fat fromage frais
¾–½ teaspoon Sambal Oelek (see page
　　24)

1 Combine the garlic, Tabasco, Worcestershire sauce and stock in a wok, and cook down until the liquid is reduced to about a tablespoon. Rinse the spinach under the cold tap and cram it, still wet, into the wok. Stir and cook over high heat until just cooked (only a minute or so) but still bright green. Drain in a strainer and squeeze very dry with the back of a wooden spoon. Cool for 10 minutes or so, then chop in a food processor. (Pulse the machine so that the spinach is finely chopped, not puréed.) Cool thoroughly (quick-chill by spreading on a plate and putting into the freezer for a few minutes).

2 Put the spinach back into the food processor with the remaining ingredients and process to a green-flecked cream. Scrape into a bowl and refrigerate until needed.

CALORIE COUNT 12 Kcal **FAT CONTENT** 1g **PER TABLESPOON**

Goat's Cheese Spread

MAKES 600ml (1 pint)

This is one of the most useful mixtures I know. Use it in sandwiches, as a dip, swirl or dollop it over soups or stews, mash it into potatoes, and vary it to your taste (see below).

1 × 150g (5oz) tub medium-fat goat's cheese

1 × 500g (1lb) tub low-fat fromage frais

approx. 2 tablespoons Parmesan cheese, grated

1 Place all the ingredients in a food processor and process until very well combined.

CALORIE COUNT 16 Kcal   **FAT CONTENT** <1g   **PER TABLESPOON**

VARIATIONS

• **Blue Cheese Dip:** Instead of Parmesan, mash in 1 tablespoon of soft blue-veined cheese. (Blue-veined cheeses are full-fat cheeses, but a little bit goes a long way!) ✪

• **Lower-Fat Dip:** Substitute Quark for the goat's cheese. ♥

• **Herbed Dip:** Stir in chopped fresh flat-leaf parsley and snipped chives, or chopped coriander, or snipped dill, or whatever seems right. ✪

Herbed Raita

MAKES 300ml (½ pint)

Raita is that refreshing yogurt sauce/relish that cools things down and smooths things out when you are having a spicy and complex Indian meal. At its simplest, chopped herbs are stirred into yogurt, but cucumbers, spring onions, spices and so on can be added as well. Serve it swirled onto vegetable stews (Indian or not – vary the herbs to suit the dish), or as a salad dressing (thinned with a little buttermilk, or use undrained yogurt), or swirled onto soups. If you don't like the sourness of yogurt, use very low-fat fromage frais.

500g (1lb) natural organic very low-fat yogurt	4 tablespoons chopped fresh herbs (coriander, mint and flat-leaf parsley)

1 Line a sieve with a dampened piece of butter muslin or a dampened blue J-cloth, leaving an overhang, and place it over a deep bowl. Pour in the yogurt and fold the muslin over the top. Refrigerate for an hour or so.

2 Pour away the whey, and put the thickened yogurt into a bowl. With a rubber spatula, fold in the chopped herbs.

CALORIE COUNT 14 Kcal   **FAT CONTENT** Neg   **PER TABLESPOON**

VARIATIONS

• **Cucumber Raita:** Stir in peeled, seeded, sliced cucumber (page 134) and sliced spring onion. ♥

• **Herbed Yogurt Dip or Spread:** Drain the yogurt overnight, instead of for a few hours. (Begin with 2–3 times the amount of yogurt called for in the recipe.) ♥

• **Tzatziki:** Marinate a clove of crushed garlic in 1 tablespoon of wine vinegar or balsamic vinegar. Drain 1–2 cartons of yogurt as described above. Stir in the garlic, and 1 cucumber, peeled, seeded, thinly sliced and drained (see page 134). Fold in torn fresh mint leaves and chopped parsley. ♥

Herbed Goat's Cheese Raita

MAKES 175ml (6fl oz)

A goat's cheese raita can be used as described for the previous recipe, or as a dip or sandwich spread.

---

1 × 150g (5oz) pot medium-fat goat's cheese

2 tablespoons fromage frais

2–3 tablespoons chopped fresh mixed herbs (e.g. chives, basil and flat-leaf parsley)

Combine in a food processor and blend until well combined.

CALORIE COUNT 22 Kcal   **FAT CONTENT** 2g   **PER TABLESPOON**

VARIATION

Fold in some shredded smoked salmon and replace the basil with snipped fresh dill. Spread onto lightly toasted bagels or crumpets. ✪

Grilled Red Pepper Spread

MAKES 300ml (½ pint)

Another wonderful, zesty sandwich spread (and the colour!). Swirl it into soups or drizzle it over vegetable stews.

---

2 grilled red peppers (page 32), or 2 bottled roasted peppers

1 rounded teaspoon Dijon mustard

1 rounded tablespoon fromage frais

2–3 dashes each of Tabasco and Worcestershire sauce (vegetarians, omit Worcestershire sauce)

Combine the ingredients in a blender or food processor and blend until smooth.

CALORIE COUNT 4 Kcal   **FAT CONTENT** Neg   **PER TABLESPOON**

OPPOSITE *Muffuletta (page 47)*
OVERLEAF *Couscous Salad with Apricots, Fennel and Tomato and Red Onion Salsa (page 88)*

Rémoulade Sauce

MAKES 500ml (¾ pint)

Rémoulade makes a splendid spread for sandwiches, particularly cucumber, salad, smoked turkey or chicken, or any combination (all of these piled into a sandwich together sounds good to me). Or use it as a dip with steamed prawns (page 145) or as a garnish to Mustard-Yogurt Grilled Fish (page 137) – in fact, anywhere you would use tartare sauce.

500ml (¾ pint) no-fat fromage frais
1½ teaspoons grainy mustard
2 tablespoons drained capers, chopped
2 tablespoons chopped cornichons (small gherkins)
2 tablespoons chopped fresh flat-leaf parsley

1 tablespoon snipped fresh tarragon, or ½ teaspoon crumbled dried tarragon
½ teaspoon paprika (use smoked paprika if you can find it)
3 spring onions, trimmed and chopped
several dashes of Tabasco sauce

Combine all the ingredients and refrigerate. Leave for several hours or overnight for the flavours to develop.

CALORIE COUNT 10 Kcal   **FAT CONTENT** Neg   **PER TABLESPOON**

Spicy Ketchup

MAKES 300ml (½ pint)

Dabble steamed prawns or vegetable crudités into this scarlet sauce. Even better, make a double portion (don't quite double up on the hot ingredients – taste as you go) and serve with oven-fried potatoes.

300ml (½ pint) tomato ketchup
several dashes each of Tabasco and Worcestershire sauce (vegetarians, omit Worcestershire sauce)

½ tablespoon hot mango chutney or Chinese-style chilli sauce
chopped fresh herbs (e.g. flat-leaf parsley, coriander)
squeeze of lemon or lime juice to taste

Combine in a blender and blend to a rough purée.

CALORIE COUNT 18 Kcal   **FAT CONTENT** Neg   **PER TABLESPOON**

Basic Vinaigrette

MAKES 300ml (½ pint)

Salad dressings can be problematic without oil, but I'm pleased with my vinaigrette method; I think that you will find it very useful. Make the base, then use it to make any number of interesting dressings. All of these coat salad leaves very well.

90ml (3fl oz) balsamic vinegar
90ml (3fl oz) lime juice or lemon juice (or a combination)
90ml (3fl oz) orange juice

2 teaspoons teriyaki sauce
several dashes of Tabasco sauce
2 garlic cloves, crushed
1–2 pinches of sugar (to taste)

Put all the ingredients into a screwtop jar, put on the lid and shake well.

CALORIE COUNT 3 Kcal   **FAT CONTENT** Neg   **PER TABLESPOON**

Grilled Red Pepper Vinaigrette

MAKES 300ml (½ pint)

Basic Vinaigrette (see above)
½ grilled pepper (page 32) or ½ canned or bottled pepper, drained

2 teaspoons Red-Pepper-Garlic Provençal mustard or Dijon mustard (bought ready-made)

Combine the ingredients in a blender and blend until smooth.

CALORIE COUNT 7 Kcal   **FAT CONTENT** Neg   **PER TABLESPOON**

Garlic Vinaigrette

MAKES 300ml (½ pint)

Basic Vinaigrette (page 58)
5–6 garlic cloves (or more to taste),
   pan-braised (page 31)

2 tablespoons chopped fresh parsley
2 teaspoons Dijon mustard

Combine the ingredients in a blender and blend until smooth.

CALORIE COUNT 5 Kcal   **FAT CONTENT** Neg   **PER TABLESPOON**

Tomato Vinaigrette

MAKES 300ml (½ pint)

125ml (4fl oz) balsamic vinegar
125ml (4fl oz) strained fresh lemon juice
125ml (4fl oz) strained fresh orange
   juice
2–3 garlic cloves, lightly crushed
3 sun-dried tomatoes, roughly chopped

3 black olives, slivered off their stones
1 tablespoon Dijon mustard
1 canned plum tomato, well-drained
   and seeded
a pinch of sugar

1 Combine the vinegar, juices, garlic, sun-dried tomatoes and olives and leave to marinate for 5–10 minutes.

2 Put into a blender with the mustard, tomato and sugar and blend until almost smooth.

CALORIE COUNT 7 Kcal   **FAT CONTENT** Neg   **PER TABLESPOON**

Beetroot Vinaigrette

Prepare the Tomato Vinaigrette on page 59, but substitute ½ a vacuum-pack, natural (no vinegar) beetroot for the plum tomato.

CALORIE COUNT 5 Kcal   **FAT CONTENT** Neg   **PER TABLESPOON**

Honey Mustard Vinaigrette

MAKES 300ml (½ pint)

Basic Vinaigrette (page 58), without the sugar	2 teaspoons Dijon mustard 1½ teaspoons honey

Combine the ingredients in a blender and blend until smooth.

CALORIE COUNT 96 Kcal   **FAT CONTENT** <1g   **PER TABLESPOON**

Mango Chutney Vinaigrette

MAKES 350ml (12fl oz)

Basic Vinaigrette (page 58) 1 × 1cm (½in) slice of ginger, crushed	2 teaspoons Dijon mustard 1 tablespoon hot mango chutney

Combine the ingredients in a blender and and blend until smooth.

CALORIE COUNT 5 Kcal   **FAT CONTENT** Neg   **PER TABLESPOON**

SALSAS

Salsas are raw relishes made from vegetables, herbs, sometimes fruit, and usually a few chillies as well. They add colour, freshness and pizazz to simple meals.

Mango and Fennel Salsa

MAKES 600ml (1 pint)

If you have a problem with the anise flavour of fennel, use the small inner stalks (leaves and all) of a bunch of celery instead, and add some torn chervil leaves at the end.

1 mango, diced (see page 134)
1 head of fennel, trimmed and diced
1 fresh chilli, trimmed, ribbed, seeded and finely diced
1 tablespoon balsamic vinegar

juice of ½–1 lime (to taste)
salt to taste
3 tablespoons chopped flat-leaf parsley
1–2 tablespoons fresh mint or basil

Combine all the ingredients.

CALORIE COUNT 3 Kcal   **FAT CONTENT** Neg   **PER TABLESPOON**

Tomato and Orange Salsa

MAKES 450ml (¾ pint)

Turn this into a Chinese relish (good with fish or pork tenderloin) by adding a slice of peeled crushed ginger, and substituting rice vinegar for the wine vinegar.

juice and zest from ½ an orange
juice of ½ a lime
1 seedless orange, peeled, sectioned and diced
1 tablespoon wine vinegar
600ml (1 pint) peeled, chopped, ripe, flavourful tomatoes

1 fresh chilli, seeded and finely chopped
2 tablespoons chopped fresh coriander
2 tablespoons chopped fresh flat-leaf parsley
½ cucumber, peeled, seeded (page 134) and chopped

Combine all the ingredients.

CALORIE COUNT 5 Kcal   **FAT CONTENT** Neg   **PER TABLESPOON**

Cherry Tomato and Mango Salsa

MAKES 600ml (1 pint)

1 large ripe mango, diced (page 134)

12 cherry tomatoes, halved

½ –1 fresh chilli, seeded, ribbed and chopped

2 tablespoons chopped fresh coriander

2 tablespoons chopped fresh flat-leaf parsley

juice of ½ a lime

Combine all the ingredients.

CALORIE COUNT 4 Kcal   **FAT CONTENT** Neg   **PER TABLESPOON**

Tomato Salsa with a Hint of the Orient

MAKES 750ml (1¼ pints)

The Oriental hint comes from the fragrant rice vinegar, but you could use balsamic or red wine vinegar instead, or a combination.

2–4 garlic cloves, crushed

1 fresh chilli, seeded, ribbed and chopped

juice of ½ a lime

6 tablespoons rice vinegar

500g (1lb) ripe, flavourful tomatoes, peeled, seeded and diced

1 red onion, chopped

250g (8oz) cucumber, peeled, seeded (page 134) and diced

chopped fresh coriander and flat-leaf parsley

1 In a bowl, combine the garlic, chilli, lime juice and vinegar, and leave to marinate for 10 minutes.

2 Stir in the remaining ingredients.

CALORIE COUNT 4 Kcal   **FAT CONTENT** Neg   **PER TABLESPOON**

Cucumber and Cherry Tomato Salsa

MAKES 1.25 litres (2 pints)

This and the following olive version are glorious in flamboyant sandwiches built in large round loaves – see the Muffuletta on page 47, as an example. They also add sparkle to pasta dishes – I love pasta tossed with a piping hot tomato sauce, then topped with an icy tumble of one of these salsas.

250g (8oz) cherry tomatoes, quartered
1 cucumber, peeled, halved, seeded
   (page 134) and sliced thinly
1 fresh chilli, minced
1½ tablespoons balsamic vinegar
1–2 garlic cloves, crushed (the amount
   depends on your taste – if you hate
   garlic, leave it out)

1 tablespoon small capers
2 teaspoons of the caper brine
juice of ½ a lime
3 spring onions, trimmed and sliced thin
2 tablespoons chopped fresh parsley
2 tablespoons chopped fresh coriander
2 tablespoons shredded fresh mint
freshly ground pepper to taste

Combine all the ingredients. Leave to stand at room temperature, stirring occasionally, until serving time.

CALORIE COUNT 1 Kcal **FAT CONTENT** Neg **PER TABLESPOON**

Cherry Tomato and Olive Relish

MAKES 900ml (1 ½ pints)

Higher in fat than the previous salsa (because of the olives) but much lower in fat than the unbelievably oily original that inspired it.

1–3 garlic cloves, crushed (the amount depends on your taste)
1 ½ tablespoons balsamic vinegar
juice of ½ a lemon and ½ an orange
500g (1lb) firm, ripe cherry tomatoes (use half red, half yellow when available)
2 inner stalks of celery, with leaves
5 green olives

5 black olives
3 spring onions
2 tablespoons chopped fresh flat-leaf parsley
2 tablespoons shredded fresh mint or basil
1 fresh chilli
2 teaspoons olive brine

1 Combine the garlic, vinegar and juices in a small bowl and leave to marinate while you quarter the cherry tomatoes, slice the celery, sliver the olive flesh off their stones, trim and thinly slice the spring onions, chop the parsley, shred the mint and basil, and de-seed and finely chop the chilli.

2 Combine all the ingredients, including the garlic and its marinade, in a large bowl and stir well. Leave to stand at room temperature, stirring occasionally, until you are ready to use it. To keep for more than a few hours, store in the refrigerator.

CALORIE COUNT 3 Kcal   **FAT CONTENT** Neg   **PER TABLESPOON**

Diced Carrot Salad

MAKES 1 litre (1 ¾ pints)

This is a sort of carrot relish, very bracing and refreshing, to serve as a garnish, a vegetable accompaniment, or a snack.

750g (1½lb) carrots, peeled and diced
6 tablespoons orange juice
2 tablespoons lemon juice
¼ teaspoon cinnamon

1 tablespoon rice vinegar
4 tablespoons chopped parsley
salt and freshly ground pepper

Combine all the ingredients and leave to marinate before serving.

CALORIE COUNT 5 Kcal   **FAT CONTENT** Neg   **PER TABLESPOON**

Orange and Red Onion Salsa

MAKES 450ml (¾ pint)

Very refreshing and herby, and lovely nestled next to a spice-rubbed chicken breast or a fillet of poached fish.

2 seedless oranges, peeled, segmented
    and chopped
1 small red onion, finely diced
½–1 fresh chilli, seeded, ribbed and
    chopped

juice of 1 juicy lime
1 tablespoon orange juice
2 tablespoons chopped fresh coriander
2 tablespoons chopped fresh mint
2 tablespoons chopped fresh parsley

Combine all the ingredients.

CALORIE COUNT 5 Kcal   **FAT CONTENT** Neg   **PER TABLESPOON**

Spring Onion Coriander Relish

MAKES 125ml (4fl oz)

A simple little relish to float on top of a soup, like a jewel. Purée the Spicy Sweet Potato Stew on pages 130–1, thin to soup consistency, and float a dab of the relish on top. It would nicely adorn the Red Pepper (page 75) or Borlotti Bean (page 74) soups as well.

1 garlic clove, crushed
1cm (¼in) piece root ginger, peeled and crushed
3 tablespoons rice vinegar

2 bunches spring onions, trimmed and sliced (green and white)
3–4 tablespoons chopped fresh coriander

1 Marinate the garlic and ginger in the vinegar for 15 minutes.

2 Add the marinade to the spring onions and mix in the chopped coriander.

CALORIE COUNT 6 Kcal   **FAT CONTENT** Neg   **PER TABLESPOON**

Peach and Grilled Pepper Salsa

MAKES 450ml (¾ pint)

Peaches, smoky peppers, herbs and chillies make a memorable summery salsa. Fresh mango can be substituted for one or both of the peaches for a change.

2 grilled peppers (1 red, 1 yellow)
2 ripe peaches
¼–1 fresh chilli, seeded, ribbed and chopped
1 tablespoon balsamic vinegar

juice of ¼ a lime
1 tablespoon shredded fresh mint
1 tablespoon chopped fresh flat-leaf parsley
freshly ground mixed peppercorns

1 Dice the grilled peppers and put into a bowl with their juices.

2 Dice the peaches over the bowl so that none of the juices are lost.

3 Stir in the remaining ingredients.

CALORIE COUNT 5 Kcal   **FAT CONTENT** Neg   **PER TABLESPOON**

DIPPERS

The next three methods make no-fat dippers for all of your dips and spreads. Relying on store-bought crisps, tortilla chips and so on piles on the fat Calories – making your own is easy and fun. Every oven is different, so take the timing as a very general guide only. The first time out for these recipes, check them carefully – they may need more time or less.

Pitta Crisps

1 Preheat the oven to 150°C/300°F/Gas Mark 2.

2 With kitchen scissors cut some pitta bread (brown or white) into quarters or eighths, then separate each piece into two. Bake, in one layer, on a non-stick baking tray for 10–15 minutes, until dried out and crisp. ✓ Ⓥ ♥

Tortilla Chips

Maize tortillas are a wonderfully versatile and delicious Mexican food. They resemble chapattis made from maize meal, and contain *no* fat whatsoever. Many supermarkets are now stocking maize tortillas in the packaged bread section.

corn (maize) tortillas

1 Preheat the oven to 150°C/300°F/Gas Mark 2.

2 Bake the tortillas directly on the oven shelf for 15–20 minutes, turning once, until crisp right through (they will break with a clean 'snap'). Break into quarters or eighths and store in an airtight tin. Ⓥ ♥

See the microwave method on the following page.

Microwave Method

1 Put a double layer of kitchen paper on the microwave carousel.

2 Arrange 5 tortillas around the periphery of the paper. They should not quite touch each other. Microwave at full power for 2–2½ minutes.

3 If the towels are wet, replace them. Turn the tortillas over. Microwave at full power for another 2–2½ minutes.

4 Remove to a rack and allow to rest for 5 minutes. Break into quarters or eighths, and store in an airtight tin. ❂

Potato Crisps

1 LARGE BAKING POTATO (approx. 300g/10oz)
MAKES approx. 50 crisps

The timing here is a bit iffy – a little too long and the crisps burn. You'll need to work out the right timing for your oven. Once you've got it, you'll likely make these again and again. Or look for those marvellous microwave gadgets (they look like mini plastic toast racks) that make no-fat crisps in the microwave (see mail order guide, page 213). One large baking potato – approximately 300g (10oz) – will probably fill 2 non-stick trays. Prepare as many as you need.

1 large baking potato (King Edward or Maris Pipers)	oil-water spray salt (optional)

1 Preheat the oven to 180°C/350°F/Gas Mark 4.

2 Slice the potato paper-thin, using a mandoline or the slicing disc of a food processor, or the slicing side of an old-fashioned box grater.

3 Mist a non-stick baking tray lightly with oil spray, and arrange the potato slices in a simple layer. Salt lightly if desired. Bake in the preheated oven for approximately 15 minutes. Re-position the crisps on the trays, and re-position the trays if necessary, and bake for another 3–5 minutes, or until crisp, browned but not burnt.

CALORIE COUNT 23 Kcal   **FAT CONTENT** Neg   **PER 5 CRISPS**

Potato Skins

Potato skins are popular in pubs and wine bars, and are usually served with a creamy dip, or chilli con carne. The skins are invariably deep-fried – total disaster.

large baking potatoes
oil-water spray

1 Preheat the oven to 200°C/400°F/Gas Mark 6.

2 Scrub the potatoes and halve them, lengthwise.

3 With a teaspoon or a melon baller, scoop out the insides, leaving a shell about 5mm (¼in) thick. (Save the scraps for another use – mashed potatoes, for instance.)

4 Spray the shells with oil-water spray, and bake directly on the oven rack for 25–35 minutes, until golden brown and very crisp. Serve at once, filled with a savoury mixture such as Lentil Chilli (page 78) or Grilled Vegetable Ratatouille (pages 126–7) or with dips (pages 52–7).

CALORIE COUNT 70 Kcal   **FAT CONTENT** <1g   **PER HALF POTATO**

CHAPTER 4

Soups

I like soups with texture, character and deep flavour; soups that nourish the body and soothe the soul. I mean that literally – my soups burst with vitamins and minerals, as well as plenty of gorgeous carbohydrate to raise your serotonin levels and calm your mood. The big chunky soups that overflow with vegetables and pasta are more soupy stews than soup, and make wonderful meals in themselves, with just some good bread to mop up all the juices. Make big potfuls of these beauties and eat them throughout the week, or freeze them in individual portions and microwave as needed. The more restrained smooth soups work well as first courses, although they do, in larger quantities, make satisfying informal meals, served with bread, salad, plenty of garnishes, and a great pudding to follow. These smooth soups are like little black dresses – they cry out for jazzy accessories. Plain is nice, but well-garnished is nicer. Garnish your soup with one or more of these:

• Swirls, dollops and salsas chosen from the dips and spreads chapter (page 52)

• Scatterings of chopped, snipped or torn fresh herbs ♥

• Freshly popped popcorn (yes, popcorn makes good croûtons) ♥

• Bite-sized Shredded Wheat (ditto) ♥

• Croûtons of slow-baked, garlic-rubbed bread slices (rye bread is particularly good) ♥

• Cubes of leftover polenta, grilled or not (or cube the ready-cooked shrink-wrapped polenta now available in most supermarkets) ♥

• A spoonful of cooked rice, or wild rice ♥

• A modest scattering of grated Parmesan cheese ◓

Sweet Potato and Smoked Corn Soup with Mushroom Stock

MAKES 1.8 litres (3 pints)

This is a soup of beautiful colour and great character. If you wish, use unsmoked corn (just as it comes out of the tin). You will diminish its character a bit, but it will still have lots of verve. If you want the soup to be perfectly smooth, push the purée through a sieve in step 3. In that case, garnish it to your heart's content, with Spring Onion Coriander Relish (page 66), or one of the salsas (pages 61–6), and a swirl of Grilled Red Pepper Spread (page 56), or Herbed Goat's Cheese Raita (page 56)

1 large red onion, chopped

2 dry-packed sun-dried tomatoes, chopped

2 garlic cloves, crushed

½–1 fresh chilli, seeded, ribbed and chopped

½ teaspoon paprika (use smoked if possible)

150ml (¼ pint) dry red wine

1.5 litres (2½ pints) vegetable stock

2 smoked ears of corn or 1 small can of supersweet corn kernels, drained and smoked (page 131)

500g (1lb) sweet potatoes, peeled and cubed

2 grilled peppers, chopped (page 32) or use bottled or canned peppers

a pinch of sugar

salt and freshly ground pepper

juice of ½ a lime

chopped fresh coriander

1 Combine the onion, sun-dried tomatoes, garlic, chilli, paprika, wine and 300ml (½ pint) of stock. Simmer for 5–7 minutes until the onions are tender and caramelizing a bit (the liquid should be just about gone).

2 Cut the kernels off the corn cobs and add to the pot along with the sweet potatoes and another splash or 2 of stock. Sauté, stirring, for a few moments, then add the remaining ingredients, except the lime juice and coriander and leave to simmer, partially covered, until the potatoes are very tender. Cool slightly.

3 Purée in batches in the blender, until very smooth (hold down the cover). Return to the pot, stir in the lime juice and adjust the seasonings. Serve with a spoonful of Goat's Cheese Spread (page 54) dolloped on to each serving (if you are able to have a dab of fat), and scatter on the coriander.

CALORIE COUNT 144 Kcal   **FAT CONTENT** 1g   **PER ½ PINT**

Intense Mushroom Soup

MAKES 1.5 litres (2½ pints)

The intensity comes from dried mushrooms and their soaking water – add more by shaking in some Shake O'cini in step 2.

30g (1oz) dried porcini (ceps)
1kg (2lb) fresh mushrooms, cleaned and
    quartered
approx. 300ml (½ pint) medium sherry
1–2 dashes of teriyaki sauce
150ml (¼ pint) vegetable stock

1 bunch of spring onions, trimmed and
    sliced
2 garlic cloves, minced
1 teaspoon dried tarragon, crumbled
salt and freshly ground pepper
piece of Parmesan cheese rind (optional
    – see page 22)

1 Rinse the dried mushrooms well under cold running water. Put them in a bowl with hot water to generously cover. Leave to soak.

2 Meanwhile, in a soup pan, combine the fresh mushrooms with the sherry, teriyaki sauce, stock, spring onions, garlic and tarragon. If your pan is too small, do this step in several batches. Simmer until the mushrooms are cooked and almost no liquid remains. Stir frequently and do not let them scorch or brown.

3 Strain the soaking water from the dried mushrooms through a sieve lined with cheesecloth or a coffee filter to eliminate grit and sand. Rinse the mushrooms well under cold running water. Discard any tough stems and chop the mushrooms coarsely. Add the soaked mushrooms and their filtered water (you'll need 1.25 litres (2 pints) – top up with vegetable stock if necessary) to the fresh mushrooms in the pot.

4 Add the salt and pepper, and the Parmesan rind. Bring to the boil, then reduce the heat and simmer, partially covered, for ¾ hour. Discard the cheese rind. Taste and add more salt and pepper if necessary. Cool. In batches, put the soup in the liquidizer. Flick the motor on and off once or twice – you want a rough chopped effect not a smooth purée. Serve piping hot. The soup will keep in the refrigerator for several days and may be frozen. (Omit the Parmesan for an even lower-fat version.)

CALORIE COUNT 37 Kcal   **FAT CONTENT** <0.5g   **PER ½ PINT**

Onion Soup

MAKES 1.8 litres (3 pints)

I like to use a selection of onions in my onion soup – add crushed garlic as well, if you wish. The secret to having a flavourful no-fat onion soup as opposed to a watery one is the caramelization of the onions and the deglazing of the pan in step 1. In step 2, 300ml (½ pint) of the soup is puréed, then stirred back into the remaining soup to produce really good body.

3 red onions (about 500g/1lb)
3 large Spanish onions (about 2kg/4lb)
3 leeks, white part only, split lengthways
   and sliced
1.8 litres (3 pints) stock
about 150ml (¼ pint) dry white wine

4 tablespoons brandy
½ teaspoon teriyaki sauce
several dashes of Tabasco and
   Worcestershire sauce (vegetarians,
   omit the Worcestireshire sauce)
salt and freshly ground pepper

1 Put the onions and leeks into a non-stick wok with 300ml (½ pint) of stock and the wine. Bring to the boil, cover, and boil for 10 minutes. Uncover and simmer briskly, stirring occasionally, until the onions are meltingly tender, and catching and sticking a bit. Pour in a splash of white wine, and stir and scrape up the browned bits from the bottom of the pan. Pour in the remaining stock and season with teriyaki, Tabasco, Worcestershire sauce, salt and pepper. Simmer, uncovered, for 10–15 minutes more. Cool slightly.

2 Ladle out 300ml (½ pint) of the soup and purée in the blender until very smooth. Stir back into the soup and adjust the seasonings.

CALORIE COUNT 214 Kcal   **FAT CONTENT** 1g   **PER ½ PINT**   Ⓥ ✳ 🍎 🍸 ♥

VARIATION

When the soup is done, heat the grill. Ladle the soup, steaming hot, into oven-proof ceramic pots or soup bowls, float a toasted croûton (baguette slice) – rubbed with a halved garlic clove – in each, top with some grated Parmesan and shredded half-fat mozzarella, and grill until the cheese is melted, bubbly and speckled with brown. ◉

Purée of Borlotti Bean Soup with Sherry

MAKES 1.5 litres (2½ pints)

Make an event of this suave and velvety soup by serving it with an array of garnishes. Have each diner add garnishes to the soup in whatever order seems right and according to their own taste.

4 sun-dried tomatoes, chopped
1 large carrot (150–175g/5–6oz), peeled and cut into chunks
2 stalks of celery, sliced
2 large red onions, cut into chunks
1 large red pepper, seeded, peeled and coarsely chopped (page 134)
1 garlic clove, crushed
1 medium fresh chilli, stemmed, seeded and chopped (optional)
½ teaspoon ground cumin
¼ teaspoon ground coriander
1.25 litres (2 pints) stock
120ml (4fl oz) medium dry sherry

2 × 475g (15oz) cans borlotti beans, drained and rinsed
salt and freshly ground pepper

Garnishes
chopped red onion or Orange and Red Onion Salsa (page 65)
chopped fresh coriander and flat-leaf parsley
crumbled, de-fatted chorizo (page 178)
crumbled medium-fat feta or grated Parmesan cheese
white rice
Spring Onion Coriander Relish (page 66)
lime wedges

1 Combine the sun-dried tomatoes, chopped vegetables, garlic, chilli, spices, 300ml (½ pint) of stock and 100ml (3½fl oz) of sherry in a heavy-bottomed pan. Cover, bring to the boil, and boil for 5–7 minutes.

2 Uncover and simmer for approximately 5 minutes more, until the liquid is almost gone and the vegetables are tender and 'frying' in their own juices. As the vegetables begin to catch and brown, pour in a splash of sherry or stock, and scrape up the browned bits with your wooden spoon.

3 Stir in the beans and the remaining stock and simmer briskly for 5–7 minutes more. Remove from the heat and leave to cool for 10–15 minutes.

4 Purée in small batches in the blender (hold the lid down) until smooth and velvety. Return to the pan. Adjust the temperature and the seasonings and serve.

CALORIE COUNT 223 Kcal   **FAT CONTENT** 2g   **PER ½ PINT**

Red Pepper Soup

MAKES 1.8 litres (3 pints)

Red peppers are the jewels of the kitchen, for their colour, flavour, and luscious texture when they have been peeled, sautéed in stock and puréed. I use both smoky grilled peppers and raw peppers that have been peeled with a swivel-bladed peeler. They combine with paprika (a close relative) to make an incandescent soup.

1 red onion, chopped

1 garlic clove, crushed

1 tablespoon paprika (smoked paprika would be lovely)

1.5 litres (2½ pints) stock

5 large red peppers, stemmed, seeded, peeled and coarsely diced (page 134)

1 medium (250g/8oz) potato, peeled and coarsely diced

3 large red peppers, grilled, skinned (page 32) and coarsely diced (bottled or canned peppers may be substituted)

salt and freshly ground pepper

1 Combine the onion, garlic, paprika and 300ml (½ pint) of stock in a heavy-bottomed soup pot. Cover and boil for 4–5 minutes, then uncover the pan and simmer until the onions are tender and gently 'frying' in their own juices.

2 Stir in the chopped raw peppers and an additional 300ml (½ pint) of stock. Simmer for a few minutes, stirring occasionally, until the peppers begin to soften. Stir in the potato and cook for 2–3 minutes more.

3 Stir in the remaining stock, the grilled peppers and salt and pepper. Simmer, partially covered, for about 30 minutes, until the vegetables are very tender. Cool slightly.

4 In small batches, purée half the soup in the liquidizer (avert your face and hold down the lid). Combine the puréed and unpuréed portions. Taste and adjust the seasonings.

CALORIE COUNT 168 Kcal   **FAT CONTENT** 2g   **PER ½ PINT**

Beans, Pulses, Pasta and Couscous

BEANS AND PULSES

If you are serious about a low-fat lifestyle, you should really make beans and pulses a regular part of your diet. I don't mean to make it sound like a chore; beans are versatile, delicious, and fun to cook. Everyone eats tons of beans on toast, but there is so much more – and now that many different beans come in cans, interesting dishes can be ready in almost the time it takes to heat up a can of baked beans. Beans take well to lively seasoning, and they have wonderful texture whether served whole, or in smooth, velvety purées. In fact, if you miss the unctuous forbidden pleasures of peanut butter, you may find that bean spreads provide a similar smoothly rich mouth feel.

Beans and pulses are low in fat and, high in nutrients; their fibre supposedly helps lower cholesterol, and they are high in protein as well, although their complement of amino acids (the building blocks of protein) is not quite complete. If your diet is rich in grains and/or small amounts of animal protein (meat, fish, poultry, dairy products), the complement is rounded out nicely. The cuisines of the world are rich in bean/grain combos: beans with rice, with pasta, with tortillas, indeed even beans on toast – the pairing is natural and very pleasing to eat. Of course beans and grains don't have to be eaten together in the same meal to complement one another. If you regularly eat both, even if on separate days, the proteins will be complemented.

DEALING WITH DRIED BEANS

Lentils and split peas need no pre-soaking, but other dried beans do. If you choose not to use canned beans, soak dried ones in plenty of cold water for at least 6 hours (they can soak overnight in a cool part of the kitchen). Discard any that float to the top. After soaking, drain and cover with fresh water or a combination of water and unsalted stock to cover the beans by a good inch. (Draining and adding fresh liquid reputedly helps reduce the windy quality of the beans.) Boil for 10 minutes, skimming off the foam, then simmer, uncovered, for about an hour, or until they are just tender (timing will vary with the age and type of bean). Add some garlic and onion to the pot in this initial cooking, but no salt or acid ingredients such as wine, lemon or lime juice, or the beans will never soften. And if your water is very hard, use bottled water if you want the beans to get tender. Add liquid as needed to keep the beans covered by 5cm (1in). When the beans are just tender, add salt and whatever other seasonings you wish, and continue simmering gently, covered, until they are very tender but still hold their shape.

You can cut the initial soaking period short by the quick soak method: cover the beans with water and bring to a boil. Remove from the heat and let sit for 1 hour. Then they are ready for cooking as above. The problem with this method is that the beans tend to fall apart; I prefer them whole unless I'm planning to make a bean spread. And the quick soak is reputed to produce windier beans. Talking about wind – if you eat beans regularly this problem will eventually disappear, so introduce them gradually until you are eating them several times a week.

Lentil Chilli

MAKES 900ml (1½ pints)

Canned lentils – my, my, whatever next? They certainly do speed things up: this chilli is ready to eat in less than half an hour. It makes a marvellous family meal – people really seem to enjoy it.

2 red onions, chopped

2 garlic cloves, crushed

2 sun-dried tomatoes, snipped (use scissors)

1–2 pinches of crushed dried chilli flakes (more or less to taste)

125ml (4fl oz) red wine

300ml (½ pint) stock

1½ teaspoons ground coriander

1½ teaspoons ground cumin

½ teaspoon ground paprika (smoked if possible)

salt and freshly ground pepper

2 × 475g (15oz) cans lentils, drained and rinsed

2 × 425g (14oz) cans chopped tomatoes

juice of ½ lime

Garnishes

chopped fresh coriander

chopped fresh flat-leaf parsley

finely chopped Orange and Red Onion Salsa (page 65)

lime wedges

cubes of half-fat feta (optional)

1 Combine all the ingredients except the lentils, canned tomatoes and lime juice in a heavy-bottomed frying-pan. Cover the pan and simmer for 5–7 minutes, then uncover and simmer until the onions are very tender and the liquid is about gone.

2 Stir in the lentils and tomatoes and season with more salt and freshly ground pepper. Simmer, uncovered, for approximately 15 minutes, until thick and savoury. Stir in the lime juice. Remove from the heat.

3 Ladle out ¼–⅓ of the sauce and purée in a processor or liquidizer. Combine the puréed and unpuréed portions. Serve with rice and the garnishes, or in tacos (see opposite).

CALORIE COUNT 227 Kcal   **FAT CONTENT** 2g   **PER ½ PINT**

VARIATION: Lentil Chilli Tacos

Fill a tortilla with an interesting mixture, spray with oil-water spray, bake in a hot oven and presto: a Mexican-style calzone – very quick and easy. The Lentil Chilli above is great, but try Mushrooms with Curry Spices (page 115), one of the bean dishes, Italian-style Stir-fried Courgettes (page 128), grilled vegetables with mozzarella, or whatever else sounds good.

oil-water spray
4 wheat-flour tortillas
8 tablespoons Lentil Chilli (page 78)
60g (2oz) slivered half-fat mozzarella
    cheese
2 tablespoons grated Parmesan cheese

chopped fresh flat-leaf parsley and
    coriander
Classic Tomato or Pepper Sauce (pages
    91 and 95)
fresh salsa (page 61)

1 Preheat the oven to 200°C/400°F/Gas Mark 6. Spray a non-stick baking sheet with oil-water spray. If the tortillas don't seem flexible enough to fold, warm them in the oven, wrapped in foil, for 3–4 minutes, or heat on each side for a few seconds in a hot non-stick frying-pan (no need to oil-spray the pan) – they should be flexible, not toasted.

2 Put a tortilla on the baking sheet. Place about 2 tablespoons of Lentil Chilli on one side, top with 2–3 slivers of mozzarella and a modest shower of Parmesan (about ½ tablespoon), and fold over. (Don't crease it or it will tear.) Repeat with as many tortillas as you wish (one tray will hold 4). Spray the tops of the folded tortillas with oil-water spray.

3 Bake uncovered for approximately 10 minutes, until they are beginning to get crisp but are not scorched or dried out. With a fish slice transfer to warm plates, and spoon a generous strip of Classic Tomato or Pepper Sauce diagonally across each. Nestle a generous spoonful of salsa next to each tortilla, and sprinkle with herbs.

CALORIE COUNT 190 Kcal   **FAT CONTENT** 4g   **PER TACO**   Ⓥ

Bean Cakes

MAKES approx. 8 cakes

These bean cakes are made the way I make beef or pork burgers, with flavour-infused aubergines added to the mixture to give big, round taste and good texture. Serve them on a plate with one of the fruit salsas and a tomato salsa (pages 61–6) a swirl of Grilled Red Pepper Spread (page 56) or Yellow Pepper Sauce (page 95), and a dollop of one of the raitas (pages 55–6). Even better, serve in good rolls with raita spread on one side, the grilled pepper spread on the other, and salsa dolloped on top – a very upmarket beanburger!

Infusion
5 spring onions, sliced
2 dry-packed sun-dried tomatoes, diced
3 black olives, slivered off their stones
¼ teaspoon dried oregano
125g (4oz) peeled aubergine, diced
a pinch of dried chilli flakes
1–2 garlic cloves, crushed
300ml (½ pint) stock

Bean mix
1 × 475g (15oz) can borlotti beans or butter beans, rinsed in a colander and drained
1 tablespoon tomato paste
1 tablespoon fromage frais
1 tablespoon grated Parmesan cheese
1 tablespoon plain breadcrumbs
salt and freshly ground pepper

Coating
5 tablespoons fresh breadcrumbs
2–3 tablespoons Parmesan cheese
salt and freshly ground pepper

1 Preheat the oven to 200°C/400°F/Gas Mark 6.

2 Combine the infusion ingredients in a saucepan. Simmer until the aubergine is very tender and the liquid has been absorbed. Cool.

3 Combine the bean mix ingredients and the cooled infusion in the food processor. Process until smooth. Taste and add salt and pepper if necessary.

4 Mix the coating ingredients together and spread on a plate. Scoop up a heaped tablespoon of the bean mixture, form into a rough ball, and toss it in the crumbs, to coat. Form into a 1cm (½in) thick cake. Place on a non-stick baking tray that you have lightly misted with olive-oil-water spray. Repeat until all the bean mixture has been used.

5 Spray the cakes with oil-water spray. Bake for 10–12 minutes, then carefully, using a fish slice, turn them, spray again and bake for a further 10–12 minutes, until they are crusty and golden.

CALORIE COUNT 88 Kcal   FAT CONTENT 2g   PER CAKE

Tuna Bean Salad

MAKES 900ml (1½ pints)   **SERVES** 2–3

When I moved to England from America fifteen years ago, I experienced a tuna crisis. I grew up on tuna fish sandwiches (albacore tuna, sliced spring onions, chopped celery, lots of Hellman's mayonnaise on Jewish rye). By the time I arrived on these shores, I had given up on mayonnaise, Hellman's or otherwise, but I still loved tuna. The canned tuna here is skipjack rather than the milder albacore, and the first time I opened a can of skipjack I thought I'd brought home cat food by accident; it seemed so strong and fishy. But just the other day I was in my local supermarket and there was albacore – stacks and stacks of cans. If you can find albacore in spring water, try this lovely, mild canned fish in my Italian antipasto-inspired salad. The salad is great in a well-stuffed sandwich (see pages 43–50) as a first course, or as a light lunch, garnished with halved cherry tomatoes.

1 × 200g (7oz) can tuna in brine or spring water, drained

1 bunch of spring onions, trimmed and sliced

2 inner stalks of celery, chopped, leaves and all

1 × 425g (14oz) can cannellini beans, drained and rinsed

1 tablespoon drained capers

2 tablespoons shredded fresh basil

2 tablespoons chopped fresh flat-leaf parsley

Basic Vinaigrette (page 58)

1 Drain the tuna, put it into a bowl, and flake it with a fork. Toss in the spring onions and celery.

2 Mix in all but 2 tablespoons of the beans and fold in the capers and the herbs.

3 Combine the reserved beans with the Basic Vinaigrette (page 58) in the blender. Gently mix 4–6 tablespoons of this vinaigrette into the tuna and beans. Refrigerate until needed.

CALORIE COUNT 273 Kcal   FAT CONTENT 2g   PER SERVING

Unfried Beans

MAKES 900ml (1 ½ pints)

My low-fat version of Mexican refried beans axes the lard but infuses the beans with plenty of flavour. Serve as a dip with tortilla chips or pitta chips (page 67), as a spread for crusty bread, or a topping for tostadas (see variation below). Or serve unpuréed with rice or polenta.

1 red onion, chopped	60ml (2fl oz) dry red wine
3 garlic cloves, peeled and roughly chopped	2 × 475g (15oz) cans pinto or borlotti beans, drained and rinsed
1 fresh chilli, seeded, ribbed and chopped	3–4 tablespoons passata
½ teaspoon ground cumin	salt and freshly ground pepper
½ teaspoon ground coriander	juice of 1 lime
2 black olives, slivered off their stones	1 tablespoon chopped fresh parsley
3 sun-dried tomatoes, chopped	1–2 tablespoons chopped fresh coriander
300ml (½ pint) stock	

1 Put the onion, garlic, chilli, spices, olives, sun-dried tomatoes, stock and wine into a heavy-bottomed frying-pan, saucepan or wok. Simmer until the onions are tender, and the onions and spices are 'frying' in their own juices.

2 Stir in the beans, passata and salt and pepper. Simmer until thick and savoury.

3 Stir in the lime juice and herbs. Cool, then purée roughly with a potato masher.

CALORIE COUNT 19 Kcal   **FAT CONTENT** Neg   **PER TABLESPOON**

VARIATION: Unfried Bean Tostados

Crisp whole maize tortillas in the oven (page 67). Spread with the warmed unfried beans. Top with a spoonful of one of the tomato salsas (pages 61–6), some shredded Cos or Iceberg lettuce, and a tiny scattering of Parmesan cheese (optional). Serve at once.

PASTA

I like quality dried pasta, imported from Italy, for most pasta cooking; it gives far better results than the 'fresh' pasta now available in supermarkets. The one exception is lasagne; the fresh lasagne sheets found in the supermarket chill section are really useful and make a layered dish of lasagne much less stodgy than the dry kind. The sheets can be layered with various sauces and fillings, rolled into cannelloni, or flung together casually on a plate for an informal open ravioli. The number of lasagne sheets used for the following recipes depends on the size of the sheets, so you may need more or less.

Mushroom and Roasted Pepper Lasagne

SERVES 4–6

This is a lasagne made without a creamy cheese layer and with a sprinkling of Parmesan on top. It's very colourful, with lively seasonings, and plenty of creaminess supplied by the mushrooms.

12 fresh lasagne sheets

about ½ recipe Grilled Red Pepper Sauce (page 94)

about ½ recipe Spicy Mushroom Sauce (pages 98–9)

3 tablespoons grated Parmesan cheese

1 Preheat the oven to 180°C/350°F/Gas Mark 4.

2 Cook the lasagne according to the packet directions, then drain, rinse in cold water, spread out on tea towels and blot dry.

3 Spread a few spoonfuls of the pepper sauce on the bottom of a 30 × 20 × 5cm (12 × 8 × 2in) baking dish. Cover with a layer of lasagne sheets, then spread on a layer of mushroom sauce, and top with 3 more lasagne sheets. Spread with pepper sauce, top with lasagne sheets, another layer of mushroom sauce and a final layer of 3 lasagne sheets. Top with pepper sauce and an even sprinkling of Parmesan. Cover with foil, so that the foil does not touch the sauce and cheese. Bake for about 15 minutes, then uncover and bake for another 10 minutes or so, until bubbly. Leave for 5 minutes (if you can wait) before cutting into squares and serving. (For a lower-fat version omit the Parmesan.)

CALORIE COUNT 324 Kcal   **FAT CONTENT** 4g   **PER SERVING**   Ⓥ Ⓨ Ⓞ

Vegetable Lasagne

SERVES 4–6

The creamy layer in this vegetable-laden lasagne is made of a soufflé-like mixture of Quark lightened with beaten egg whites. The lasagne is cooked long enough for the whole thing to puff up; the Quark layer remains creamy. Cook it longer and it sets – I prefer the creaminess.

1 small aubergine, sliced and grilled
2 small courgettes, grilled
2 red or yellow peppers, grilled
600ml (1 pint) Classic Tomato Sauce (page 91)
500g (1lb) Quark
250g (8oz) half-fat mozzarella cheese, drained, blotted dry and shredded

salt and freshly ground pepper
3 egg whites, beaten to firm peaks
6 sheets lasagne (12 × 15cm/5 × 6in), cooked (undercook slightly) according to package directions, spread out and blotted dry (see note below)
4–5 tablespoons Parmesan cheese

1 Preheat the oven to 200°C/400°F/Gas Mark 6.

2 Using kitchen scissors, cut up the grilled vegetables and stir them into the tomato sauce.

3 Combine the Quark, mozzarella, salt and pepper in the bowl of a food processor. Process until well amalgamated. Transfer to a bowl. Stir in one quarter of the beaten egg whites, then fold in the remainder.

4 Put a thin layer of tomato sauce into the bottom of a 30 × 18cm (12 × 7in) baking dish and cover with a layer of 3 sheets of lasagne. Spread on the Quark mixture and 2 tablespoons of Parmesan. Top with 3 more sheets of lasagne, spread on the remaining tomato sauce and finally sprinkle on the remaining Parmesan. (Omit both cheeses for a lower-fat lasagne.)

5 Bake in the oven, covered, for 15 minutes, then uncovered for 15–20 minutes, until puffy and bubbling.

Note: If you want to save time by using packaged no-cook lasagne sheets, make sure the tomato sauce is a bit soupy rather than thick so that the pasta cooks properly during the baking.

CALORIE COUNT 310 Kcal   **FAT CONTENT** 7g   **PER SERVING**

Pasta with Asparagus, Yellow Peppers and Peas

SERVES 2–4

I love to use pasta shells here, because all the lovely vegetable bits get caught in the cavities of the pasta – delightful!

250g (8oz) medium-size pasta shells
1 red onion, coarsely chopped
4 black olives, slivered off their stones
4 sun-dried tomatoes, chopped (use scissors)
4 garlic cloves, crushed
1 fresh chilli, cored, seeded and chopped
about 300ml (½ pint) stock
2 tablespoons dry white vermouth

2 yellow peppers, cored, seeded, ribbed and peeled (see page 134) and cut into 2.5cm (1in) chunks
2 canned plum tomatoes, very well drained and cut into strips
125g (4oz) asparagus tips
250g (½lb) frozen petit pois, thawed
1–2 tablespoons shredded fresh mint
juice of 1 lemon
salt and freshly ground pepper

1 Put salted water for the pasta on to boil. (For speed, boil half the water in the covered pot, and the other half in the kettle, then combine.) Cook the pasta in the boiling water for 11–13 minutes, until al dente.

2 Meanwhile combine the onion, olives, sun-dried tomatoes, garlic, chilli, stock and vermouth in a heavy-bottomed frying-pan. Simmer very briskly for 5 minutes, then stir in the pepper pieces. Continue to simmer, stirring frequently, until the peppers have softened a bit and the liquid is just about gone. Add the tomato strips, and stir and cook for 2 minutes.

3 Stir in the asparagus and a tablespoon or so of additional stock. Bring to a simmer, cover and let steam very gently for 3–5 minutes (don't let the asparagus get mushy!). Add the peas and stir and cook for about 2 minutes more (both the peas and the asparagus should remain bright green). Stir in the mint and the juice of ½ the lemon. Season with salt and pepper.

4 Drain the pasta and put into a warm wide bowl. Add the sauce and toss together. Squeeze on the remaining lemon juice and mix once more. Taste and add more salt and pepper as needed.

CALORIE COUNT 325 Kcal   **FAT CONTENT** 3g   **PER SERVING**

Open Ravioli with Sicilian Vegetable Stew and Grilled Pepper Sauce

SERVES 4

A quick and attractive way to use fresh lasagne sheets is to make open ravioli. This is a method rather than a formal recipe – you can mix and match fillings and sauces to make whatever interesting combinations you like, and you can add vegetables if you like: steamed asparagus spears, roughly chopped grilled courgettes and aubergines, pan-sautéed mushrooms. . . For the pasta layers, you'll need square pieces of lasagne – if the lasagne you bring home is rectangular, simply cut the sheets in half. The plates must be warm, and all the filling ingredients very hot. Work quickly to put it all together, and rush it to the table. Each serving uses 2 squares of the pasta.

---

fresh lasagne sheets
Sicilian Vegetable Stew (page 129)
Grilled Red Pepper Sauce (page 94)

Creamy Pesto, optional (pages 52–3)
chopped fresh flat-leaf parsley
shredded fresh basil leaves

---

1 Cook the lasagne according to the package directions. Drain and blot dry. Quickly put a sheet on to a warm plate.

2 Top with some of the vegetable stew. Top with another sheet, placed at an angle. Pour on the sauce. If you wish, top with a dollop of Creamy Pesto (pages 52–3). Scatter on some herbs. Serve at once.

CALORIE COUNT 170 Kcal   **FAT CONTENT** 2g   **PER SERVING**

VARIATIONS

- Fill with Italian-style Stir-fried Courgettes (page 128) and top with Grilled Red Pepper Sauce (page 94)
- Fill with Spinach (page 41) and top with Piccadillo Tomato Sauce (page 92)

COUSCOUS

Couscous is made from tiny grains of semolina, like tiny nubbins of pasta. Most of the couscous readily available now is precooked, so it just needs to be soaked in boiling liquid; I use stock for flavour. If you have the time and patience, steam it for 10 minutes after soaking – it fluffs it up and puffs it out beautifully. If time is short, though, simple soaking works well.

Couscous Vegetable Salad

MAKES 2.75 litres (4 ½ pints)

This wonderful main dish salad is a spectacular Italianate extravaganza that would feed a crowd at a gala summer party.

1 fresh chilli, seeded, ribbed and chopped

2 garlic cloves, crushed

juice of 1 lime

juice of ½ an orange

3 tablespoons balsamic vinegar

3 peppers (red, yellow, or a combination), grilled, peeled and diced (see page 32)

175g (6oz) ripe tomatoes, peeled, seeded, juiced and diced (see page 134)

1 small head of fennel, trimmed and finely diced

5 spring onions, trimmed – the white part diced, the green part thinly sliced

4 small courgettes, trimmed and finely diced

½ small cucumber, peeled, seeded (page 134) and finely diced

2 carrots, peeled and diced

5 black olives in brine, drained and sliced off the stone

5 tablespoons shredded fresh basil

3 tablespoons chopped fresh flat-leaf parsley

250ml (8fl oz) tomato juice

salt and freshly ground mixed pepper

375g (12oz) couscous

600ml (1 pint) vegetable stock

Garnish

halved cherry tomatoes

chopped fresh flat-leaf parsley

shredded fresh basil or mint

1 In a small bowl, combine the chilli, garlic, citrus juices and balsamic vinegar and leave to marinate while you prepare the vegetables.

2 Put the prepared vegetables into a large bowl. Stir in the garlic mixture, the herbs, and the tomato juice and season well.

3 Put the couscous in a bowl. Bring the stock to the boil and pour over the couscous. Cover and leave to stand for 10–15 minutes. Uncover and fluff with a fork.

4 Fold half the vegetable mixture into the couscous, and mound it on a plate. Scatter the remaining vegetables around the mound. Surround with halved cherry tomatoes, and strew on the herbs.

CALORIE COUNT 155 Kcal   **FAT CONTENT** 1g   **PER ½ PINT**

Couscous Salad with Apricots, Fennel and Tomato and Red Onion Salsa

SERVES 6

A wonderful combo of couscous, crunchy vegetables, dried apricots and fresh mint, to be eaten while the couscous is still slightly warm. For a non-veg version, add lamb meatballs (page 176), Smoked Chicken Thighs (page 157) or Cuban Chicken (page 156). As always, if you don't like fennel, use small inner stalks of celery, leaves and all.

Dressing

2 garlic cloves, crushed

2 tablespoons balsamic vinegar

2 tablespoons fresh lemon juice

3 tablespoons fresh orange juice

juice of 1 lime

Combine all the ingredients and set aside.

Salsa

1 red onion, finely chopped

1 fresh chilli, stemmed, ribbed, seeded and finely chopped

8 ripe vine tomatoes, chopped

2 tablespoons chopped fresh flat-leaf parsley

2 tablespoons torn fresh mint leaves

2 tablespoons dressing (see above)

Combine all the ingredients and set aside.

Couscous

175g (6oz) couscous

300ml (½ pint) well-seasoned stock

Bring the stock to the boil and combine with the couscous. Cover, and leave for 10–15 minutes until the couscous is swollen and tender and the liquid is absorbed. Fluff with a fork.

OPPOSITE *Mushroom and Grilled Pepper Wrap with Salsa (page 99)*
OVERLEAF *Sea Bass and Mussel Stew (page 147)*

Vegetables

½ a cucumber, peeled, halved, seeded (page 134) and sliced

1 head of fennel, trimmed and chopped

6 ready-to-eat dried apricots, chopped (use scissors)

1 tablespoon chopped fresh flat-leaf parsley

1 tablespoon torn fresh mint leaves

3 tablespoons dressing (see above)

Combine all the ingredients in a bowl.

To Assemble

1 Mix the couscous with the vegetables and the remaining dressing. Pile on to a platter.

2 Surround with the salsa. Scatter more herbs over the top.

CALORIE COUNT 128 Kcal   **FAT CONTENT** <1g   **PER SERVING**

CHAPTER 6

Sauces

For low-fat cooking, sauce-making is not as difficult as you may think. In fact, I find it rather exhilarating. I always feel that I'm beating the system when I produce a good sauce without resorting to the traditional butter or oil. The most successful and useful low-fat sauces are made with vegetable purées. The most obvious choices for these nutrient-rich sauces are tomatoes and peppers; when combined with the flavour ingredients of your infusion, they produce finished sauces that resonate with colour, vitamins, flavour and rustic glamour. There are several examples of these useful sauces in this chapter – once you get the hang of it, I'm sure you will think up many more.

All these sauces work extremely well with pasta, but also sauce beautifully those dependable staples of low-fat cooking: fish fillets (try roasting them on a bed of one of the tomato sauces – pages 91–3) chicken breasts and lean steaks (a pan-fried lean steak served with chunky version of the Classic Tomato Sauce (page 91) makes a lovely steak pizzaiola). With a lavish, herby and well-flavoured sauce, these staples are never boring. If you are cutting back on fat, but have no need to cut it out entirely, add a teaspoon of olive oil to the basic infusion/sauté at the beginning of the recipe; it will season the sauce, but won't overload you with fat. (One teaspoon of olive oil will add 40 Calories and 5 grams of fat to the sauce.) Other vegetables can be used in sauces (see Roasted Butternut Squash and Sweet Potato Sauce (page 100) as an example) to produce yet more excitement and colour. I know I do go on about colour, but it's very important to me. Once you start cooking this way, with all these wonderful technicolor lashings of sauces, salsas and vegetables, I'll wager that you will never be able to tolerate an all beige/brown meal again.

Classic Tomato Sauce

MAKES 900ml (1½ pints)

My favourite tomato sauce, with carrots for sweetness, chillies, sun-dried tomatoes and olives for flavour, and plenty of herbs for freshness. It is the most useful sauce I know, worth cooking in quantity and storing in the freezer in small containers. It is cooked quickly to keep it light, and it can be used as it is (chunky), or puréed until smooth (or half and half).

3 red onions, skinned and finely
   chopped
2 carrots, peeled and chopped
2 garlic cloves, crushed
1–2 pinches of crushed red chilli flakes
3 sun-dried tomatoes, chopped
3 black olives, slivered off their stones
175ml (6fl oz) stock

175ml (6fl oz) dry red wine, white wine
   or dry white vermouth
3 × 425g (14oz) cans chopped tomatoes
salt and freshly ground pepper to taste
1 tablespoon tomato paste
1 tablespoon chopped fresh parsley
1 tablespoon shredded fresh basil leaves
1 tablespoon chopped fresh oregano
   (if available)

1 Combine the onions, carrots, garlic, chilli, sun-dried tomatoes, olives, stock and wine in a heavy frying-pan. Cover, bring to the boil, reduce the heat and simmer briskly for 5–7 minutes. Uncover and simmer until almost all the liquid has been evaporated and the carrots are tender.

2 Stir in the tomatoes and season to taste. Simmer, partially covered, for 15 minutes. Stir in the tomato paste and the fresh herbs if you are using them and simmer for 5 minutes more. Taste and adjust the seasonings. For a smooth sauce, purée the tomato mixture in a blender or processor. If you like your tomato sauce chunky, leave it as it is.

CALORIE COUNT 99 Kcal   **FAT CONTENT** 1g   **PER ¼ PINT**

Piccadillo Tomato Sauce

MAKES 900ml (1½ pints)

A Mexican/Spanish inspired variation of tomato sauce, with exceptional freshness because of the celery leaves, and a slightly sweet dimension because of the raisins. Serve on pasta, in lasagne, with polenta, with fish, or with Bean Cakes (page 80).

1 red onion, chopped
2 small stalks of celery with leaves, chopped
2 tablespoons drained capers
2 tablespoons raisins
1 fresh chilli, stemmed, seeded and chopped
½ teaspoon ground cumin
300ml (½ pint) stock
3 × 14oz (425g) cans chopped tomatoes
salt and freshly ground pepper
2 tablespoons tomato purée
1 tablespoon chopped fresh parsley
2 tablespoons chopped fresh coriander

1 Combine the onion, celery, capers, raisins, chilli, cumin and stock in a heavy-bottomed frying-pan. Cover, bring to a boil, and simmer until the celery is tender and the liquid is almost gone.

2 Stir in the tomatoes and season with a bit of salt and pepper. Simmer, partially covered, for 15–20 minutes. Stir in the tomato purée and fresh herbs, taste, and add more salt and pepper if needed.

CALORIE COUNT 71 Kcal   **FAT CONTENT** 0.5g   **PER ¼ PINT**

VARIATION: Moroccan Tomato Sauce

Make the sauce above, using the following flavourings in step 1. Omit the capers and raisins. Add a pinch of sugar as well. Stir in coriander and parsley at the end as above. ♥

2 garlic cloves, crushed
1 teaspoon cumin
2 teaspoons paprika (smoked if possible)

Tomato Aubergine Sauce

MAKES 2.1 litres (3½ pints)

A rich, terracotta-coloured sauce to serve with pasta, in lasagne or with fish fillets.

2 aubergines, peeled and chopped

2 red onions, chopped

8 garlic cloves, crushed

4 black olives, slivered off their stones

¼–½ teaspoon dried chilli flakes (to taste)

1 tablespoon ground cumin

1 tablespoon ground coriander

2 teaspoons ground paprika

1 teaspoon ground turmeric

a pinch of sugar

2 tablespoons lemon juice

175ml (6fl oz) dry red wine

300ml (½ pint) stock

4 × 425g (14oz) cans chopped tomatoes

salt and freshly ground pepper

chopped or shredded fresh coriander, flat-leaf parsley and mint

1 Combine the aubergine, onions, garlic, olives, chilli flakes, spices, sugar, lemon juice, wine and stock in a wok or deep frying-pan. Cover, and simmer briskly for 7–10 minutes. Uncover and simmer until the aubergine and onions are meltingly tender, and the liquid is absorbed.

2 Add the tomatoes and simmer, partially covered, for 15–20 minutes, until thickened. Cool slightly.

3 In small batches, purée in a blender until velvety smooth. The sauce may be prepared to this point and refrigerated or frozen. To continue, bring to a simmer. Add salt and pepper, more lemon juice and a pinch of sugar as needed. Stir in the herbs and simmer for 5 minutes more.

CALORIE COUNT 38 Kcal   **FAT CONTENT** 1g   **PER ¼ PINT**

Grilled Red Pepper Sauce

MAKES 1 litre (1¾ pints)

Grilled peppers impart their smoky sweetness to this version of tomato pepper sauce; to underline it, add ¼ teaspoon of smoked paprika in step 1. Roast fish fillets in this sauce, use it in Vegetable Lasagne (page 84), with pasta or over gnocchi.

1 carrot, about 125g (4oz), peeled and cut into chunks
1 red onion, chopped
2 garlic cloves, crushed
4 sun-dried tomatoes, chopped (use scissors)
pinch of crushed dried chilli flakes (to taste)

300ml (½ pint) stock
125ml (4fl oz) dry red wine
8 grilled red pepper halves, skinned (page 32) and puréed in a blender
2 × 425g (14oz) cans chopped tomatoes
salt and freshly ground pepper

1 Combine the carrot, onion, garlic, sun-dried tomatoes, chilli flakes, stock and wine in a deep frying-pan or non-stick wok. Boil, covered, for 5 minutes, then uncover and simmer briskly until the vegetables are tender, frying in their own juices and the liquid is just about gone. Add a splash more stock during the cooking as needed.

2 Pour in the puréed peppers, the chopped tomatoes, salt and pepper, bring to a simmer, and simmer for 5 minutes. Purée the sauce, in small batches, in the blender.

CALORIE COUNT 61 Kcal   **FAT CONTENT** 1g   **PER ¼ PINT**

Pepper Sauce

MAKES 900ml (1½ pints)

This is a basic method for making a pure pepper sauce (no tomatoes) to use with Bean Cakes (page 80), steamed asparagus, fish fillets, chicken breasts, or Smoked Chicken Thighs (page 158). It dresses up simple food like nobody's business. If you are using dabs of fat and oil here and there (page 5), add a teaspoon of olive oil in step 1. For an impressive celebration dish, make both the red pepper sauce and the yellow (see variation). Make sure that they are both of the same saucelike consistency (they should coat a spoon). Pour carefully and the yellow will coat one side of the plate, the red the other, they will meet in the middle cleanly, and you will feel very clever. Position a poached fish fillet, a smoked chicken thigh or a spice-rubbed pan sautéed chicken breast on the plate, scatter on some roughly chopped herbs, and serve.

---

10 red bell peppers, coarsely chopped
6 spring onions, trimmed and sliced
1 fresh red chilli, stemmed, ribbed, seeded and diced (optional)

½ tablespoon paprika
300ml (½ pint) stock
salt and freshly ground black pepper

---

1 Combine all the ingredients in a deep heavy frying-pan. Bring to the boil, then reduce the heat and simmer for approximately 20 minutes.

2 Season with salt and pepper. Cool slightly.

3 Purée the mixture in batches in a blender or food processor. Strain through a sieve or strainer, rubbing it through with a rubber spatula or wooden spoon. The skins, which are tough, will be left behind. Discard them.

4 Return the sauce to the pan and bring to a simmer. Taste and adjust the seasonings.

CALORIE COUNT 93 Kcal   **FAT CONTENT** 1g   **PER ¼ PINT**   Ⓥ ✳ ♥

VARIATION: Yellow Pepper Sauce

As the sauce above, but omit the paprika and chilli, and use ¼ teaspoon of ground turmeric or ¼ teaspoon of saffron threads and ¼ teaspoon of ground coriander instead. (If you are using a dab of fat, use a teaspoon of butter in step 1.) ♥

Basic White Sauce

MAKES 600ml (1 pint)

Although the classic white sauce preparation, involving a butter-flour roux, and whole milk, or milk and cream, is out of the question for a low-fat lifestyle, you will be able to make a very credible white sauce with infused milk and cornflour. Many variations are possible based on this method.

6 tablespoons skimmed milk powder	approx. 18fl oz (500ml) infused skimmed milk (1 longlife carton) – see note, page 97
3 tablespoons cornflour	
salt and freshly ground pepper	

1 Measure the milk powder and cornflour into a 3½ pint (2 litre), 7in (18cm) top diameter, opaque white plastic jug or in a 7½in (19cm) diameter Pyrex clear glass measuring jug. Sprinkle with salt and pepper.

2 Using a wire whisk, whisk the milk into the dry ingredients. Whisk well – you don't want lumps. And vigorous whisking helps alleviate the chance of volcanic eruptions in the microwave. Cover the jug with a plate.

3 Microwave on full power for 3 minutes. Carefully uncover (avert your face, be careful – the steam is hot), and whisk thoroughly. Re-cover and microwave for another 2 minutes. Carefully uncover, whisk, re-cover and microwave for a final 1½–2 minutes, until boiled, thickened and smooth.

4 Whisk and let stand for 3–4 minutes. Taste and adjust the seasonings if necessary. Store in the refrigerator with a sheet of microwave clingfilm directly over the surface of the sauce.

CALORIE COUNT 133 Kcal **FAT CONTENT** <0.5g **PER ¼ PINT**

Note

This sauce can be made without a microwave, using a bain-marie. Combine the ingredients in a glass bowl. Place over a saucepan of boiling water. Place a plate over the top and heat the sauce for approximately 10 minutes, whisking occasionally. As the sauce begins to thicken, remove the plate and whisk it for a further 3–5 minutes until it reaches the right consistency.

To reheat

If the sauce has thickened too much overnight in the refrigerator, whisk in some skimmed milk to thin it to the desired consistency. Cover the jug with clingfilm and microwave with 30-second bursts, stopping to whisk well (be careful of steam) between bursts, until the sauce is warm and smooth. It is important to follow these directions because a cornflour-bound sauce may break down if overheated.

Note: Longlife milk in cartons has a 'cooked' taste – when you use it in a sauce, that taste is not a problem. Give the sauce lovely flavour by infusing the milk first: put it into a heavy-bottomed non-stick saucepan, and add a bayleaf, 3 spring onions, cut into pieces, 6–7 fresh parsley stalks, a sprig of fresh thyme and 6–7 whole mixed peppercorns. Slowly bring the milk to a slow simmer. Skimmed milk scorches very easily, so do this very slowly – it will take at least 5 minutes. When it reaches simmering point, remove from the heat and leave for a few minutes, then strain and allow to cool. You are now ready to make your sauce.

VARIATIONS

Cheese Sauce: Just the thing for macaroni cheese and cauliflower cheese. With a rubber spatula fold 3–4 tablespoons of freshly grated Parmesan cheese into the warm sauce. Or try half Parmesan, half grated Gruyère cheese.

CALORIE COUNT 153 Kcal   **FAT CONTENT** 2g   **PER ¼ PINT**

Goat's Cheese Sauce: Stir a generous tablespoon or two of medium-fat goat's cheese (in little pots) into the basic sauce.

CALORIE COUNT 144 Kcal   **FAT CONTENT** 1g   **PER ¼ PINT**

Mustard Sauce: Stir 1 tablespoon of Dijon and 1 tablespoon of grainy mustard into the white sauce or, if you can tolerate a little fat, use the cheese sauce.

CALORIE COUNT 144 Kcal   **FAT CONTENT** 1g   **PER ¼ PINT**

Blue Cheese Sauce: Stir in 30–45g (1–1½oz) of crumbled blue-veined cheese. This is fabulous for blanketing steamed broccoli.

CALORIE COUNT 165 Kcal   **FAT CONTENT** 3g   **PER ¼ PINT**

Garlic Sauce: Sieve the purée from 1 head of roasted garlic or pan-braised garlic and stir it into the sauce. The roasted garlic is mild and mellow; the sauce will be absolutely spectacular.

CALORIE COUNT 137 Kcal   **FAT CONTENT** <0.5g   **PER ¼ PINT**

Parsley Sauce: Stir in several tablespoons of chopped fresh parsley.

CALORIE COUNT 135 Kcal   **FAT CONTENT** <0.5g   **PER ¼ PINT**

Spicy Mushroom Sauce

MAKES 1 litre (1¾ pints)

This is a glorified spicy mushroom cream sauce with lots of deep mushroom flavour from the dried porcini. Serve with linguine or potato gnocchi, in tacos (see below), lavished onto squares of polenta, or in a tortilla or wrap.

15g (½oz) dried porcini mushrooms
750g (1½lb) closed cup mushrooms
    (mixed brown and white)
2 tablespoons brandy
1 tablespoon teriyaki sauce
several dashes of Tabasco sauce
    (optional)
½ teaspoon ground paprika
½ teaspoon ground cumin

½ teaspoon crumbled dried oregano
300ml (½ pint) stock
3 tablespoons skimmed milk powder
2 tablespoons cornflour
400ml (14fl oz) skimmed milk
3 tablespoons grated Parmesan cheese
1½ tablespoons Provençal pepper-garlic
    mustard or Dijon mustard
salt and freshly ground pepper

1 Put the dried mushrooms into a sieve and rinse very well under cold running water, then snip into tiny pieces with kitchen scissors. Rinse very thoroughly once more.

2 Combine all the mushrooms (dried and fresh), the brandy, teriyaki, Tabasco, spices and oregano in a non-stick wok. Pour in 150ml (¼ pint) of stock (it will all but disappear) and cook, stirring, on high heat, for about 3 minutes until the mushrooms are well coated with the spices and are starting to soften. Pour in the remaining 150ml (¼ pint) of stock and cook, stirring frequently, on high heat until the mushrooms are cooked but still quite firm, and are swimming in a consider-able amount of their own liquid, about 5–7 minutes more.

3 Meanwhile combine the milk powder and cornflour in a large measuring jug. Whisk in 400ml (14fl oz) of skimmed milk (whisk *very* well to avoid lumps). Slowly stir this mixture into the simmering mushrooms. Stir and cook for a minute or so until the mixture thickens and bubbles. Stir in the grated cheese and the mustard and stir and cook for a few minutes more. If the mixture is too thick, stir in a little more milk. It should be like a silky cream sauce, not a paste. Taste and adjust the seasonings, adding more salt, pepper, grated cheese and mustard as needed. If you are not using the sauce immediately, pour it into a large measuring

jug or other receptacle and store in the fridge with a piece of non-pvc clingfilm directly on the surface of the mushrooms. To make it lower fat omit the Parmesan.

CALORIE COUNT 94 Kcal   **FAT CONTENT** 2g   **PER ¼ PINT**

VARIATION: Mushroom and Grilled Pepper Wraps

oil-water spray	grated Parmesan cheese
wheat-flour tortillas	Grilled Red Pepper Sauce (page 94),
Spicy Mushroom Sauce (page 98),	warmed
warmed	fresh salsa (page 61)
slivered half-fat mozzarella cheese	chopped fresh parsley and coriander

1 Preheat the oven to 220°C/425°F/Gas Mark 7. Spray a non-stick baking sheet with oil-water spray. If the tortillas don't seem flexible enough to bend, heat each one for a few seconds in a non-stick frying-pan. (They should be flexible, not toasted.)

2 Put a tortilla onto the baking sheet. Place about 2 tablespoons of the mushroom sauce on one side, top with 2–3 slivers of mozzarella and a modest shower of Parmesan (about 1 tablespoon), and fold over. (Don't crease it or it will tear.) Repeat with as many tortillas as you wish (one tray should hold 4). Spray the tops of the folded tortillas with oil-water spray.

3 Bake uncovered for 10–15 minutes, until they are beginning to get crisp but are not scorched or dried out. They will probably be oozing a bit – that's fine. With a fish slice transfer the tortillas to warm plates, and spoon a generous strip of the pepper sauce diagonally across each. Nestle a generous spoonful of salsa next to each tortilla, and sprinkle with herbs.

CALORIE COUNT 206 Kcal   **FAT CONTENT** 5g   **PER WRAP**

Roasted Butternut Squash and Sweet Potato Sauce

MAKES (900ml) 1½ pints

Serve spice-rubbed pan-sautéed chicken breasts on this glowing sunset sauce, or serve with roasted mushrooms or roasted cauliflower, or thin it with stock to make a memorable soup, and garnish with a swirl and a dollop: grilled pepper for the former, raita, the latter. I don't want to be boring, but this beautiful recipe – sauce or soup – is bursting with good low-fat nutrition; how satisfying it is when food is colourful, delicious and good for you.

½ a butternut squash, roasted (page 123)

1 orange-fleshed sweet potato (approx. 425g/14oz), peeled and cubed

6 spring onions, trimmed and sliced

2 garlic cloves, crushed

½ fresh chilli, seeded, ribbed and diced

½ teaspoon ground smoked paprika

½ teaspoon ground cumin

½ teaspoon ground coriander

¼ teaspoon ground turmeric

a pinch of ground cayenne

300ml (½ pint) warm stock

3 tablespoons grated Parmesan cheese

salt and freshly ground pepper

lime juice to taste

chopped fresh coriander to taste

1 Prepare and roast the squash (page 123).

2 Steam the sweet potato until very tender (about 15 minutes). Refresh under cold water and drain well.

3 Combine the onions, garlic, chilli, spices and 150ml (¼ pint) of stock in a frying-pan, and simmer until the onions and garlic are tender and the liquid is greatly reduced.

4 Scoop the roasted squash out of its shell. Put the squash and sweet potato into a processor or blender, scrape in the onion-spice mixture, pour in the remaining stock and process until smooth. Sprinkle in 3 tablespoons of grated Parmesan, and process until very smooth. Taste and adjust the seasonings. Mix in some lime juice and chopped coriander. Heat gently, adding a little more stock as needed until it is of sauce consistency. To make this lower fat don't use the Parmesan.

CALORIE COUNT 131 Kcal   **FAT CONTENT** 5g   **PER ¼ PINT**   Ⓥ ✳ ⊘

Delicate Minted Pea Sauce

MAKES 300ml (½ pint)

This is a very pretty sauce, pale green with flecks of darker green mint shreds speckled through it. Serve with new potatoes, with Open Ravioli (page 86), tossed into pasta, or with steamed asparagus.

2 garlic cloves, crushed
3 spring onions, trimmed and sliced
450ml (¾ pint) stock
500g (1lb) frozen petit pois, thawed

juice of 1 lime
salt and freshly ground pepper
1 tablespoon shredded fresh mint leaves

1 Combine the garlic, onions, and 90ml (3fl oz) of stock in a saucepan and simmer until the garlic and onions are tender, and the stock is just about gone.

2 Add the remaining stock, the peas and half the lime juice. Season with salt and pepper, and simmer gently until the peas are just cooked, but still bright green. This takes only a few minutes.

3 Cool slightly, then purée in a blender (in batches if necessary) until smooth and velvety. Taste and add more salt and pepper and the remaining lime juice if necessary. Stir in the mint.

CALORIE COUNT 170 Kcal   **FAT CONTENT** 3g   **PER ¼ PINT**

Red Wine Sauce

MAKES 300ml (½ pint)

This is a gloriously glossy rich wine sauce to use as a pan sauce with lean steaks, roasted pork tenderloin, pan sautéed chicken breasts, and – for vegetarian splendour – roasted mushrooms. For pan-fried lean steaks, for instance, have the sauce ready up to the end of step 2. Spray a non-stick frying-pan with oil-water spray. Pan-fry the steak to your liking, remove from the pan, then pour in the sauce and complete step 3. If you are treating yourself to the occasional dab of fat, swirl in 1 teaspoon of butter now. Return the steak to the pan, heat through, and serve – with Oven-fried New Potatoes (page 106) to make it perfect.

450ml (¾ pint) dry red wine
600ml (1 pint) stock
3 large garlic cloves, peeled and very
   roughly chopped
2 sprigs of fresh thyme
½ bayleaf

2 black olives, slivered off their stones
1 tablespoon Dijon mustard
½ tablespoon tomato purée
a pinch of sugar, to taste
salt and freshly ground pepper

1 Combine the wine, stock, garlic, thyme, bayleaf and olives in a deep saucepan and simmer until reduced by half.

2 Fish out the thyme and bayleaf, pour the liquid into a blender, add the mustard and tomato purée, and blend until smoothish.

3 Return to the pan and simmer for another few minutes until reduced by about a quarter, thickened and glossy. Season with sugar, salt and pepper to taste.

CALORIE COUNT 77 Kcal   **FAT CONTENT** 2g   **PER ¼ PINT**

Gravy

MAKES 1.25 litres (2 pints)

I first developed this recipe so that vegetarians could wallow in the delights of gravy, even though they wouldn't be roasting a joint. Puréed vegetables give the gravy its body (and its nutrients), red wine gives depth. The sieving at the end makes the texture perfect, but if you're pressed for time, and you don't mind the pepper skins, skip this step. Serve this with an enormous heap of mashed potatoes – you really don't need anything else.

4 shallots, chopped, or 1 small onion, chopped
1 large mild onion, chopped
2 stalks of celery, chopped
2 garlic cloves, crushed
2 carrots, peeled and chopped

1.7 litres (3 pints) stock
600ml (1 pint) dry red wine
1 bayleaf
1 × 425g (14oz) can chopped tomatoes
salt and freshly ground pepper

1 Combine the vegetables and 300ml (½ pint) of stock in a heavy-bottomed frying-pan. Cover and bring to the boil. Boil for 5 minutes.

2 Uncover and reduce heat a little. Simmer, stirring occasionally, until the vegetables are tender and the liquid is just about gone.

3 Stir in the wine, bayleaf and tomatoes and simmer briskly, uncovered, for 15 minutes.

4 Stir in the remaining stock and season with salt and pepper. Simmer for 15 minutes, stirring occasionally. Remove the bayleaf.

5 Liquidize until smooth. Sieve into a bowl, rubbing through the solids with a wooden spoon or rubber spatula.

CALORIE COUNT 74 Kcal   **FAT CONTENT** 0.5g   **PER ¼ PINT**

CHAPTER 7

Vegetables

A low-fat lifestyle means changing the balance of your meals: less meat, more grains, more pulses, lots more vegetables. Have vegetarian meals several times a week, and make them really gorgeous: lots of colour, texture, big flavour, plenty of excitement. The grains and pulses chapter has some splendid main dish ideas, and this chapter contains many more vegetable main dishes, plus accompaniments, and includes plenty of old favourites: mashed potatoes, chips, sautéed mushrooms, gratins – all transformed so that they can become dependable and comforting staples in your low-fat life. The happy news is that these are in no way diminished by their lack of fat. An oven-fried potato, for instance, is not a low-fat replica of a conventionally fat-smothered chip; it is a quite new and wonderful thing unto itself. Indulge yourself in vegetables as much as you can – they make low-fat living a great pleasure.

POTATOES

I'm starting with spuds, because they are such a basic and beloved component of almost everyone's diet. A potato is a wondrous and delicious package of low-fat nutrition, one of the most versatile vegetables in the world, and deeply satisfying and filling. Why commit it to a greasy fate, when there are so many superb low-fat techniques? Just remember, one medium potato contains about 90 Calories and 0.2 grams of fat – every tablespoon of oil added piles on an additional 120 Calories and 14 grams of fat.

Chips

Arm yourself with your trusty oil-water spray and a good non-stick baking tray (2 trays are even better), choose some starchy baking potatoes, set your oven to high, and – oh yes – throw away your deep fryer. Oven-frying your chips instead of burying them in boiling oil is one of the most important steps in establishing a low-fat regime. And there are other bonuses as well. No more chip-pan fires, no more vats of over-used fat to deal with, no more frying smell clinging to curtains, clothes, hair. But, of course, the best part is the wonderful, clean, unsullied taste of the chips. How good it is to taste potatoes, instead of a mouthful of grease.

Basic Oven Chips

You will need to fine tune this recipe to suit your oven. Baking time might be a little shorter or longer.

baking potatoes
oil-water spray
salt

1 Preheat the oven to 220°C/425°F/Gas Mark 7.

2 No need to peel the potatoes. Cut the potatoes into 5mm–1cm (¼–½in) slices, then halve the slices, or cut the potatoes into whatever size or shape you prefer for your chips.

3 Spray one or two non-stick baking sheets with oil-water spray. Spread the potatoes on the tray(s) in one layer – they shouldn't touch one another. Spray with oil-water. Pop in the oven and bake for approximately 20 minutes, shaking the trays occasionally to shift the potatoes a bit.

4 Turn the potato pieces with a spatula and – if you have used 2 trays – change their position in the oven. Bake for 10–20 minutes (exact timing depends on the shape of the potatoes, and your oven), until they are browned, crunchy on the outside, and puffy. Sprinkle with salt, and serve at once.

CALORIE COUNT 230 Kcal **FAT CONTENT** 1g **PER BAKING POTATO**

Oven-fried New Potatoes

This is a great favourite in my family. I can never make enough of them. They puff up like little balloons, and 'pop' when you bite into them. It's important to halve the potatoes lengthwise, rather than crosswise, so that the halves are oval-shaped.

oil-water spray
tiny new potatoes, unpeeled, scrubbed
  and dried
salt

1 Preheat the oven to 230°C/450°F/Gas Mark 8.

2 Spray a non-stick baking tray with oil-water spray. Halve the potatoes lengthwise (the halves should be oval-shaped), and spread them on the tray skin side down, in one not-too-crowded layer. Bake for 35–40 minutes (depends on your oven, and on the potatoes) until well speckled with brown, dramatically puffed up, and cooked through. Spread out on a plate, sprinkle with salt, and serve at once.

CALORIE COUNT 214 Kcal   **FAT CONTENT** 1g   **PER 6 NEW POTATOES**

Spicy Oven-fried New Potatoes

Mix Indian spices and lemon juice into tomato purée, and use the mixture to coat new potatoes, baked as in the recipe above. This mixture will coat up to 500g (1lb) of potatoes. Use 2 trays if necessary.

½ teaspoon ground turmeric   juice of ½ a lemon
½ teaspoon garam masala   1 rounded tablespoon tomato purée
¼ teaspoon ground cumin   new potatoes, unpeeled, scrubbed, dried
¼ teaspoon coriander   and halved, as above

1 Preheat the oven to 230°C/450°F/Gas Mark 8.

2 In a bowl whisk together the spices, lemon juice and tomato purée. Tip in the potatoes, and stir with 2 spoons to coat them thoroughly.

3 Oil-water-spray 1 or 2 non-stick baking trays. Spread the potatoes, on the tray(s) skin side down, and bake as in the previous recipe.

CALORIE COUNT 232 Kcal   FAT CONTENT 2g   PER **6 POTATOES**

Extra Crunchy, Spicy Oven-fried Potato Wedges

SERVES 2–4

Egg whites mixed with Mexican spices give potato wedges a very sexy spicy crunch. Serve these with salsa, a creamy dip, or Grilled Red Pepper Spread (page 56).

1 large egg white	¼ teaspoon ground cayenne (to taste)
½ tablespoon Dijon mustard	freshly ground mixed pepper
½ tablespoon tomato purée	500g (1lb) Désirée potatoes, unpeeled,
½ teaspoon crumbled dried oregano	washed and dried
½ teaspoon ground cumin	oil-water spray
½ teaspoon ground coriander	salt

1 Preheat the oven to 230°C/450°F/Gas Mark 8.

2 Put the egg white into a large bowl and beat with the mustard, tomato purée, oregano, spices and pepper.

3 Cut the potatoes into quarters or eighths, depending on the size of the potatoes, and toss them around in the egg-white mixture until very well coated.

4 Oil-spray a non-stick baking sheet and spread the potatoes out on the tray, skin side down. Roast for 40 minutes, until brown, puffed, tender inside, and very crunchy on the outside. Salt, and serve at once, with one of the dips, if you wish.

CALORIE COUNT 210 Kcal   FAT CONTENT 2g   PER **SERVING**

Mashed Potatoes

Where would we be without mashed potatoes? Depressed and despondent, that's where! Mashed spuds are almost magical in their soothing properties, so I say, get rid of the grease and dive in. I like my mash made from baked potatoes; the texture will be wonderful, almost creamy, and you will have the marvellous skins to snack on. Bake large bakers in the oven at 200°C/400°F/Gas Mark 6 for 1½–2 hours. The longer the baking the creamier the potato flesh. To open the potatoes, pierce an X on the top with a fork, then squeeze so that the steaming potato flesh comes surging up through the perforations. I'm adamant about piercing rather than cutting – it results in much fluffier potato flesh. Scoop the potatoes out of their skins into a large bowl and mash with a potato masher for a homely effect (my favourite), or push through a ricer for a more refined, airier effect. Never try to mash potatoes by processing them in a food processor; they will turn horribly gluey. If you have an electric mixer with a wire whip attachment, it works well for beating additional ingredients into the potatoes, otherwise use a wooden spoon to beat in some warmed milk and warmed stock, a spoonful at a time, along with salt and freshly ground pepper, until they are just the way you like them. Alternatively, instead of milk and stock, stir in (by the spoonful) very low-fat fromage frais, or buttermilk, or medium-fat goat's cheese (in little pots). To make the mash truly memorable, beat in the soft sieved pulp from a head of roasted garlic as well. Serve the skins cut into pieces, topped with a little tomato sauce or tomato passata, and a sprinkling of grated Parmesan cheese or shredded mozzarella, and briefly grilled – lovely canapés! Try the mash in mounds, dented on top. Then fill the dent with Gravy (page 103). Life doesn't get much better than this.

An alternate method of preparing the potatoes for mashing is to steam them (in chunks), then drain them very well. I'm giving you a few very fine recipes for mashed potato gratins – the potatoes can be baked or steamed, so use the method that suits your timing and inclination.

Mashed potato possibilities

• Mix half and half with mashed Foil-Roasted Root Vegetables (page 118). ♥

• Serve mash in mounds, dented, with the dent filled to overflowing with a mushroom sauté, or one of the tomato or tomato pepper sauces (pages 91–5). If you love contrast, top with a blob of icy salsa (pages 61–6). ♥

Sweet Potato Mash

MAKES 600ml (1 pint)   **SERVES** 2–3

Baked sweet potatoes make wonderful eating. Here they are mashed with a sherry spice infusion, citrus juices and mustard. They can be eaten as they are in a startlingly orange, spicy heap, or made into an elegant gratin.

1kg (2lb) orange-fleshed sweet potatoes (about 3)
1 red onion, very finely diced
2 garlic cloves, crushed
approx. 125ml (4fl oz) medium sherry
approx. 250ml (8fl oz) vegetable stock
¼ teaspoon ground cumin
¼ teaspoon ground coriander

¼ teaspoon ground turmeric
a pinch (or more to taste) of cayenne pepper
juice of ½ a lime
juice of ½ an orange
1 heaped teaspoon wholegrain mustard
salt and freshly ground mixed pepper corns, to taste

1 Preheat the oven to 200°C/400°F/Gas Mark 6.

2 Prick the sweet potatoes in several places with a thin skewer, and roast for 40 minutes or so, until they are very tender, and spitting caramelized juice. (Put a baking tray on the oven floor to catch the drips.)

3 Meanwhile, combine the onion, garlic, sherry, stock and spices in a frying-pan. Simmer briskly, covered, for 5–7 minutes, then uncover and simmer until the onions are tender and catching and browning. Pour in an additional splash of sherry and stock, then cook, scraping up the browned bits, for a few moments.

4 Skin the sweet potatoes, and mash them in a bowl. Mix in the red onion mixture, squeeze in the citrus juice, and stir in the mustard and salt and pepper.

CALORIE COUNT 496 Kcal   **FAT CONTENT** 2g   **PER SERVING**   Ⓥ 🍸 ♥

VARIATION: Sweet Potato Gratin

Spread the mash in a gratin dish and sprinkle with grated Parmesan cheese. Grill until the cheese is melted. (Or you can refrigerate the gratin for a day or so, then bake uncovered at 180°C/350°F/Gas Mark 4, until it is hot, bubbly and the cheese has melted.) ❷

Roasted Potatoes

As with oven-fries, very low-fat roasted potatoes are not a replica of the high-fat version, but a very satisfying thing unto themselves. Make them with good chicken stock if they are to be served with a roasted bird, but they are good with vegetable stock as well.

olive-oil spray

stock

small new potatoes or medium-sized all-
  purpose potatoes, halved or quartered

salt and freshly ground pepper

1 Preheat the oven to 200°C/400°F/Gas Mark 6.

2 Mist a shallow baking dish with oil spray. Pour stock into the dish to a depth of about 5mm (¼in). Put the potatoes in the dish in one layer. Season with salt and pepper, and stir them around.

3 Roast uncovered for 30–40 minutes, shaking the pan and stirring occasionally. When they are browned and tender, they are done. (Pour a bit more stock into the dish as necessary during cooking.)

CALORIE COUNT 265 Kcal **FAT CONTENT** 2g **PER 6 NEW POTATOES**

Garlic and Lemon Roasted Potatoes

SERVES 4

The garlic will turn soft within its skin – encourage diners to press down with their forks, so that the subtle purée oozes out to be eaten with the pungent potatoes. If you've never tasted roasted garlic cloves, this will be a revelation.

750g (1½lb) waxy, oval potatoes, e.g.
  Charlotte

chicken stock as needed

2 tablespoons lemon juice

1 large, firm head of garlic, separated
  into (unpeeled) cloves

4 sun-dried tomatoes, quartered

4 black olives, slivered off their stones

several dashes of Tabasco sauce

dash of Worcestershire and teriyaki
  sauce (vegetarians, omit the Worcestershire sauce)

oil-water spray

chopped fresh flat-leaf parsley

1 Scrub the potatoes, but do not peel them. Halve them lengthways and spread them out in a shallow roasting pan with the remaining ingredients (use about 60ml (2fl oz) of stock to start). Spray with oil-water spray. Roast, uncovered, for approximately half an hour, stirring occasionally, and adding a bit of stock as needed to prevent burning. The potatoes are done when they are tender, speckled with charred patches, and bathed in scant, thick, syrupy pan juices, and the garlic is tender within its skin. Sprinkle with chopped parsley.

CALORIE COUNT 168 Kcal   **FAT CONTENT** 1g   **PER SERVING**

Aloo Chat

MAKES 1.25 litres (2 pints)   **SERVES** 4

This is Indian inspired; an utterly simple, very bracing dish of lemon saturated potatoes, with a little chilli added to give it a jolt.

500g (1lb) new or Charlotte potatoes

4 tablespoons lemon juice (approx. 2 large lemons)

1 bunch spring onions (approx. 8), thinly sliced

½ a fresh chilli, seeded, ribbed and finely diced

4 tablespoons roughly chopped fresh coriander

salt and freshly ground pepper

---

1 Steam the potatoes until tender but not mushy. Cut into cubes and put into a bowl.

2 Gently toss all the ingredients together. Allow to sit at room temperature for at least half an hour before serving.

CALORIE COUNT 94 Kcal   **FAT CONTENT** 0.5g   **PER SERVING**

Pan-Braised Piri Piri Potatoes

SERVES 4

A most delicious (and quick) method of cooking potatoes is to braise them in a heavy-bottomed frying-pan on the hob. Use small waxy potatoes such as Charlotte, or smallish new potatoes, and braise them in good stock and lemon or lime juice, with lively seasoning, and other flavour ingredients as the mood moves you. The important thing here is to choose a heavy-bottomed pan that will hold the potatoes in one layer. When halving the oval Charlottes, be sure to do it lengthwise, so that the resulting halves are oval-shaped.

500g (1lb) small waxy oval potatoes such as Charlotte or Exquisa	approx. 300ml (½ pint) stock
	2 teaspoons of Piri piri seasoning
juice of 2 juicy limes	salt to taste

1 Halve the potatoes lengthwise and spread in a non-stick heavy-bottomed frying-pan, cut side up. Squeeze in the lime juice, and add approximately 150ml (5fl oz) stock. Scatter in the seasoning. Cover and simmer briskly for 5–7 minutes, shaking the pan and stirring the potatoes occasionally, until they are approximately half done.

2 Uncover and simmer briskly. As the liquid cooks away, the potatoes will catch and brown a bit. Replenish with a bit of stock as this happens, loosening the browned bits with your wooden spoon as you do so. When the potatoes are cooked through (about 10 minutes) they should be glazed, sticky, and wonderfully tender, but not crumbled or broken up.

CALORIE COUNT 108 Kcal   **FAT CONTENT** <0.5g   **PER SERVING**

Lemon-glazed Pan-braised New Potatoes

MAKES 900ml (1½ pints)   **SERVES** 4

This can be made with the new potatoes called for in the ingredients, or with halved Charlotte potatoes.

500g (1lb) small new potatoes, washed but unpeeled

approx. 300ml (½ pint) stock

1 lemon

1–2 dashes of Tabasco and Worcester-shire sauce (vegetarians, omit the Worcestershire sauce)

salt and freshly ground pepper

1 Spread the potatoes out in a 5cm (2in) deep frying-pan that contains them without any crowding. Pour in stock to come half-way up the potatoes. Squeeze in the juice of ½ the lemon and dash in the sauces. Season with a little salt and some freshly ground pepper. Boil, covered, for 5 minutes, uncovering to stir once or twice. Uncover, and simmer very briskly, stirring occasionally, until the liquid is greatly reduced. Pour in 4–6 tablespoons of additional stock, squeeze in a little more lemon juice, cover, and cook until the potatoes are almost done.

2 Uncover the pan, add a few more splashes of stock and drops of lemon juice and cook, uncovered, stirring until the potatoes are very tender (but not falling apart) and beautifully glazed in the syrupy pan juices. Total time will take anywhere from 20–35 minutes depending on the size of the potatoes. If they are of uneven size, remove them as they are done.

CALORIE COUNT 105 Kcal   **FAT CONTENT** <1g   **PER SERVING**

MUSHROOMS

I have a few tried and true tricks that make low-fat mushroom cookery extremely successful. One is the holy trinity of mushroom cookery – stock, wine and a dash of teriyaki or soy sauce to bring out the mushroom flavour. The other is the use of mushroom stock, made by reconstituting dried mushrooms in plenty of water. Use this powerfully wild-tasting stock with bog-standard supermarket mushrooms, and you will drive them wild – they take on a most undomestic flavour. Mushrooms have a toothsome meatiness that makes them very satisfying as a main dish for those all-vegetable days that are so important to a low-fat lifestyle.

Chinese-glazed Mushrooms

SERVES 4

To make this taste as Chinese as possible, make your mushroom stock with dried shiitake mushrooms.

750g (1½lb) button mushrooms
175ml (6fl oz) mushroom stock
  (page 30)
4 tablespoons medium sherry

1 teaspoon sugar
1–3 dashes teriyaki sauce
freshly ground mixed pepper

Combine all the ingredients in a wok. Simmer briskly, stirring occasionally, until the mushrooms are tender and coated in a syrupy glaze. As the liquid cooks down, reduce the heat, so that the mushrooms do not scorch.

CALORIE COUNT 39 Kcal   **FAT CONTENT** 1g   **PER SERVING**

Mushrooms with Curry Spices, Port and Lime

MAKES 1 litre (1¾ pints)   **SERVES** 4

I like port as a cooking wine – it imparts a hint of sweet stickiness that is absolutely marvellous in a low-fat sauté, especially when combined with a wonderful spice mixture.

300ml (½ pint) mushroom stock (page 30) or vegetable stock

2 small red onions, chopped

4 sun-dried tomatoes, chopped

2 garlic cloves, crushed

5mm (¼in) peeled ginger, crushed

a pinch of cinnamon

¼ teaspoon ground cumin

¼ teaspoon ground coriander

½ teaspoon ground turmeric

a pinch of cayenne pepper

750g (1½lb) small button mushrooms

60ml (2fl oz) port

2–3 dashes teriyaki sauce

350g (12 oz) vine-ripened tomatoes, peeled, seeded and chopped (page 134)

juice of 1 lime

1 Combine 175ml (6fl oz) of stock with the onions, sun-dried tomatoes, garlic, ginger and spices in a wok. Simmer briskly until the onions and spices are frying in their own juices.

2 Stir in the mushrooms, port, teriyaki and remaining stock. Simmer briskly, stirring occasionally, until the mushrooms are just about cooked and the liquid is greatly reduced.

3 Stir in the tomatoes and cook, stirring, until they disintegrate into the sauce. Add the lime juice, and a little salt, if necessary.

CALORIE COUNT 89 Kcal   **FAT CONTENT** 2g   **PER SERVING**

GRATINS

A vegetable gratin – meltingly tender, flavour-infused vegetables under a mantle of creamy sauce, with a topping of brown-speckled melted cheese – can brighten the glummest day. A gratin will scintillate but not fatten, made with the low-fat Cheese Sauce (page 97). The vegetables beneath the creaminess must be very tender – this is no place for crunch.

Aubergine Gratin

SERVES 4

Long cooking with onion, garlic and sherry imbues the aubergine with a gentle savour; as always, long baking in flavourful liquid renders the garlic mild and mysterious. The cooking liquid is incorporated into the sauce so that it takes on the lovely nutty sherry flavour.

6 large garlic cloves	salt and freshly ground pepper
1 red onion, chopped	1–2 dashes Tabasco sauce
2 aubergines, about 250g (8oz) each	olive-oil-water spray
300ml (½ pint) stock	Cheese Sauce (page 97)
125ml (4fl oz) medium dry sherry	2 tablespoons grated Parmesan cheese

1 Preheat the oven to 200°C/400°F/Gas Mark 6.

2 Hit the garlic cloves lightly with a kitchen mallet or the side of a wide knife to loosen the skin. Remove the skin. Split each clove and remove and discard the centre shoot. Scatter the garlic halves in a 30 × 20 × 5cm (12 × 8 × 2in) baking dish with the onion pieces.

3 Trim the ends from the aubergines and peel them lengthwise in alternate strips, leaving the aubergines with purple stripes. Cut in 1cm (½in) thick slices, and overlap the slices on the onions and garlic. Pour the stock and sherry over the aubergine. Season and spray the slices with oil-water spray. Roast, uncovered, for half an hour, then, with tongs, turn and rearrange the slices, spray with oil-water spray and roast for an additional 20–30 minutes, until quite tender.

4 Meanwhile, make the cheese sauce, adding a dash or two of Tabasco to taste.

5 When the aubergine is done (it should be meltingly tender, and imbued with the sweetness of the onion and garlic), remove it from the oven and carefully drain the remaining liquid into a small jug. Arrange the aubergine slices evenly in the baking dish. Preheat the grill to high. Whisk the liquid into the sauce. If the sauce has cooled, zap it in the microwave in 1–2 minute bursts, whisking well between bursts.

6 Pour the hot sauce evenly over the aubergine. Sprinkle with the grated cheese. Flash under the grill for 3 minutes or so, until the cheese is melted and the top is bubbly and brown-flecked.

CALORIE COUNT 212 Kcal   **FAT CONTENT** 3g   **PER SERVING**   Ⓥ ✳ ⍦ ◉

Cauliflower Cheese

Cauliflower cheese is an old favourite that never goes out of style. At its simplest, steamed cauliflower florets (steamed until tender, but not mushy) are folded into a well-seasoned cheese sauce, topped with more grated cheese, and baked or grilled until bubbly and speckled with brown. Use the Cheese Sauce on page 97, and you can't go wrong. Recently, I made a batch of the Roasted Cauliflower (page 120) and folded it into the Cheese Sauce, along with some crumbled de-fatted chorizo (page 178) – it was astoundingly good. Or you might want to try enfolding steamed cauliflower in a sherried cream sauce: sauté a large chopped red onion and a crushed garlic clove in 300ml (½ pint) of stock and 90–125ml (3–4fl oz) of medium sherry until the onion is tender and slightly caramelized, and the liquid greatly reduced, then stir into the Cheese Sauce. Ⓥ ◉

ROASTED VEGETABLES

Roasting brings out the sweetness and intense flavour of vegetables like no other technique. Depending on the vegetable, it can be roasted uncovered in an oil-sprayed baking dish, (sometimes with a bit of stock added to the pan) or wrapped in foil directly on the oven shelf. Either way, the oven should be hot.

Foil-Roasted Root Vegetables

Use this easy technique for swedes, white turnips, celeriac, carrots and parsnips. It works as well for chunks of butternut squash, acorn squash and pumpkin. The long enclosed roasting turns the vegetable into tender, caramelized, intense, honeyed chunks that are quite irresistible. The idea is to do batches of these every once in a while, and then keep them in the fridge for later eating. Serve them as they are, with accompanying lemon and lime wedges, or mash or whip them with a little fromage frais (1–2 tablespoons) to give them creaminess, and/or a teaspoon or two of mustard, or a flavour infusion made with curry spices, or sun-dried tomatoes, slivered olives and garlic, or a sherried red onion infusion. The mashed roots are particularly delicious if you combine them with mashed potatoes. With or without the potatoes, they make wonderful gratins. Pile the mashed mixture into a baking dish, smooth the top, drizzle on 2–3 tablespoons skimmed milk, and – if you like – a tablespoon or two of grated Parmesan cheese. Bake until hot, and browned on top.

1 Preheat the oven to 220°C/425°F/Gas Mark 6.

2 Peel the root vegetables you have chosen. Small roots such as white turnips, carrots and small parsnips may be left whole. Large ones such as large parsnips, swedes and celeriac should be cut into quarters. Wrap 2–3 single vegetables or 2 vegetable quarters loosely in foil, shiny side in. Crimp well, so that you have a tightly sealed but roomy pouch. Repeat for the remaining vegetables. Roast for 1–1¼ hours, until the vegetables are very tender and beginning to caramelize on the edges. ♥

Roasted Beetroot

If your memories of beetroot are of vinegar-doused, flabby, faded red slices, leaking their dye over a bed of limp lettuce, then this will surprise you no end. Buy fresh roots, wrap and roast, and marvel at the sweet earthiness of the deep red orbs. Dress them with balsamic, or one of the vinaigrettes (try the Beetroot Vinaigrette on page 60), serve them on a bed of their own fresh, uncooked, well-washed, red-veined leaves topped with a scattering of the sliced deep pink stems from those leaves, and banish all the old acrid beetroot memories. Slices of roasted beetroot are also amazingly good as a sandwich filling (page 48).

To prepare beetroots for cooking, trim off the greens and stems, leaving 2.5–5cm (1–2in) of the stem. Scrub them, but take care not to pierce them or they will 'bleed' as they cook. Leave them unpeeled. Wrap in heavy-duty foil, shiny side in. With smaller beetroot, put 2–3 in a packet. Wrap so that they are in roomy, well-sealed pouches. Roast in the oven at 200°C/400°F/Gas Mark 6 for 1–2 hours (the timing depends on the age and size of the roots). Use a skewer to test for doneness; the skewer should go in easily, but the roots should not be mushy. Also, the skins will give slightly when pressed. Cool slightly, then slip off the skins. ♥

Roasted Beetroot Salad
with Balsamic-Citrus Dressing

SERVES 4

2 large roasted beetroot (save the leaves)   dressing (see below)

Line a pretty plate with washed beetroot leaves. Slice the beetroot and overlap on the greens. Chop 6 of the beetroot stems and scatter over the beetroot. Pour the dressing over (see below). Serve with Herbed Raita (see page 55).

Dressing
juice of ½ a lemon
juice of ½ a lime

juice of ½ an orange
1 tablespoon balsamic vinegar
1–2 garlic cloves, crushed

Stir together, and leave to marinate for at least half an hour.

CALORIE COUNT 44 Kcal   **FAT CONTENT** Neg   **PER SERVING**

Roasted Cauliflower

I got this idea from Nigella Lawson's book *How to Cook* – I can't stop making it, and once made, I can't stop eating it. Serve the charred florets with lemon and lime wedges, or in Cauliflower Cheese (page 117).

oil-water spray
1–2 cauliflowers, trimmed and broken
   into florets

a few good pinches of ground cumin
   and ground coriander
lemon or lime wedges

1 Preheat the oven to 220°C/425°F/Gas Mark 7. Spray a non-stick baking sheet with oil-water spray.

2 Scatter the florets on the tray, spray with oil-water spray, and sprinkle on the spices. Toss them around a bit, then spread them out, well spaced. Roast for 15–20 minutes until tender and lightly charred, and then serve with lemon or lime wedges. ✅ Ⓥ ♥

Roasted Asparagus

During asparagus season, why not eat the exquisite stalks every day? I admit I eat out-of-season, far-flung asparagus all year round, whether it's from Kenya, Chile, Mexico or what-have-you. But the seasonal English stalks? They're another thing entirely. I love the thick stalks trimmed and peeled (see page 134 – and it really is worth peeling them), steamed for 2–3 minutes (depending on size) until they just bend a little, then refreshed under cold running water to stop the cooking and set the colour. Drain and dry them, and serve with a wonderful sauce (Grilled Red Pepper Sauce (page 94) for example) for dipping, or with a poached egg with a perfectly soft yolk (for those who can have the occasional egg). But, for a change, try roasting the spears, until they are softened and slightly charred.

thick asparagus spears, prepared as
   described on page 134

olive-oil-water spray
freshly ground pepper

1 Preheat the oven to 220°C/425°F/Gas Mark 7.

2 Spray a baking dish with the oil-water spray. The dish should be of a size to hold the asparagus in one uncrowded layer. Spread the stalks in the pan, and grind on some pepper. Bake for 10–20 minutes (depending on size), turning once during the baking. ✓ Ⓥ ♈ ♥

Roasted Brussels Sprouts

Roasting turns small Brussels into exquisite browned nuggets. Lay them in an oil-water-misted baking dish, pour in a little bit of stock (about 5mm/¼in depth) and roast at 200°C/400°F/Gas Mark 6, stirring and shaking the pan every once in a while, until the sprouts are browned and tender (but not mushy) when pierced with a thin skewer. Add more stock as needed, but when the sprouts are done, the pan should be just about dry. Ⓥ ♈ ♥

Roasted Fennel

The sweet anise herbal quality of fennel is brought to mellow life by roasting. Trim and quarter several heads (page 134), and spread in an oil-misted baking dish. Pour in stock to 5mm (¼in), and roast at 200°C/400°F/Gas Mark 6, carefully turning occasionally, until tender and speckled with brown. Replace the stock as needed, but when done, the pan should be just about dry. It takes 30–35 minutes all told. If you are adding dabs of fat, the fennel is delicious with a bit of Parmesan sprinkled on half-way through, so that it forms a brown cheesy crust. Heaven! Ⓥ ♈ ♥

Roasted Packet Vegetables

Supermarket packets of ready prepared casserole vegetables (usually various roots, plus Brussels sprouts, plus leeks) or so-called Mediterranean vegetables can be roasted with great success. Mist a baking dish with oil-water spray, pour in stock to a depth of 5mm (¼in), and spread out the vegetables. Roast at 200°C/400°F/Gas Mark 6, stirring occasionally, until they are tender, browned and unbearably aromatic (it smells like a roast dinner, although without the roast). Total time will be half an hour or more, depending on the vegetables. At the end, pour in a little more stock to loosen the browned bits on the bottom of the casserole. When you pour a tablespoon or so of stock into the hot baking dish, it will sizzle like mad. Stir and turn the veg, scraping the bottom of the dish with your wooden spoon, and then serve with lemon wedges. (That is, serve the veg, not the spoon, although if your wooden spoons have seen the same sort of action mine have, they'll probably be delicious.) ⓥ ♥

Butternut Squash Roasted with Hoisin and Ginger

SERVES 4

I'm so delighted that squash, those jewels of the New World, are finally readily available in our supermarkets. Here, Chinese flavours are applied to the North American vegetable. I think it would be a perfect accompaniment to the Christmas turkey.

1 butternut squash	1cm (½in) peeled ginger, crushed
4 tablespoons hoisin sauce	1 garlic clove, crushed
1 tablespoon teriyaki sauce	oil-water spray
2 tablespoons medium dry sherry	

1 Preheat the oven to 190°C/375°F/Gas Mark 5.

2 Halve the butternut squash lengthwise (put a large sharp knife against the squash and tap it with your kitchen mallet) and scoop out the seeds and fibres. Peel (using a swivel-bladed peeler). Slice across into 5mm–1cm (¼–½in) crescents. Put them into a large bowl.

3 Whisk together all the rest of the ingredients except the oil-water spray. Pour over the squash, and mix with 2 spoons to thoroughly coat the slices.

4 Oil-water-spray a non-stick baking sheet. Arrange the slices on the sheet in an uncrowded layer. Roast in the oven for about 40 minutes, turning once, until tender, browned, and slightly charred in places. Serve with lemon or lime wedges.

CALORIE COUNT 283 Kcal   **FAT CONTENT** 1g   **PER SERVING**   Ⓥ Ⓨ ♥

Roasted Butternut Squash Halves

SERVES 2

Serve the burnished squash halves filled with Chinese-glazed Mushrooms (page 114) or Couscous Salad with Apricots (page 88). Fill to overflowing, so that the filling spills out on to the plate. Or use the flesh of the squash in the Roasted Butternut Squash and Sweet Potato Sauce (page 100).

1 butternut squash	several dashes of Tabasco sauce
1–2 tablespoons teriyaki sauce	freshly ground mixed pepper
juice of 1 lime	oil-water spray

1 Preheat the oven to 200°C/400°F/Gas Mark 6. Halve the squash from stem to stern (see step 2, previous recipe) and scrape out the seeds and fibres. Place the squash halves, cavity up, on a baking sheet.

2 Combine the remaining ingredients, except the oil-water spray, and brush over the squash. Mist with the spray.

3 Roast in the oven for 35–45 minutes (the timing depends on the size of the squash). The idea is to bake them long enough for the flesh to become very tender, but not long enough for the shells to collapse. Brush with the teriyaki mixture several times during the roasting.

CALORIE COUNT 283 Kcal   **FAT CONTENT** 1g   **PER SERVING**   Ⓥ Ⓨ ♥

Roasted Tomatoes

Supermarkets now sell something called 'vine tomatoes', which seems strange because all tomatoes are grown on the vine – even the pale pink tennis ball impostors often masquerading as tomatoes in the supermarket greengrocery bins. What makes these different is that they are sold still on the vine, and they are bred for flavour. If you buy them, bring them home, and immediately eat them (a logical progression you may think), you will probably be disappointed. They will need further ripening uncovered on your kitchen counter (or enclosed in a paper bag with a banana) in order for the flavour to develop. Once ripened, the flavour is very good indeed. When you have a glut of over-ripe (too soft for slicing) tomatoes, roast them at 220°C/425°F/Gas mark 7 until they are collapsed, speckled with charred bits, and wafting a sweet, caramelized fragrance through your kitchen (it will take 30–45 minutes). Tip them with their juices into a bowl, and let sit for a while (half an hour or so) for the juices to thicken. Pull off the skins and serve the tomatoes sprinkled with a little balsamic vinegar and strewn with torn fresh basil and flat-leaf parsley leaves as a sort of rough chutney or relish, or tear the flesh into strips and use – with their juices – as part of the quantity of tomatoes in a tomato sauce, or make your own intense tomato purée: purée the tomatoes and push through a non-reactive sieve. Ⓥ ♥

Roasted Tomato Ketchup

MAKES 450ml (¾ pint)

15 very ripe, flavourful, juicy vine tomatoes	125ml (4fl oz) red wine
2 large red onions, finely chopped	90ml (3fl oz) stock
4 garlic cloves, crushed	salt and freshly ground pepper to taste

1 Preheat the oven to 220°C/425°F/Gas Mark 7.

2 Put the tomatoes in one layer on a baking tray. Bake, uncovered, for about half an hour, or until blistered and charred. Cool slightly.

3 While the tomatoes are baking, combine the onions, garlic, wine and stock in a heavy-bottomed, non-reactive frying-pan. Cover and boil for 5–7 minutes.

Uncover and simmer briskly until the onions are tender and beginning to brown, and the liquid is just about gone.

4 When the tomatoes have cooled somewhat, squeeze them out of their skins into the frying-pan. Discard the skins. Simmer the tomato pulp until it is thick, about 20 minutes. Season to taste. Cool slightly.

5 Pour the sauce into a liquidizer and blend until smooth. Rub through a sieve to eliminate the seeds.

CALORIE COUNT 9 Kcal   **FAT CONTENT** Neg   **PER TABLESPOON**

Roasted Tomato Swirl

MAKES 450ml (¾ pint)

olive-oil-water spray	several dashes each of Tabasco and
12–15 flavourful tomatoes	Worcestershire sauce (vegetarians,
2 tablespoons tomato purée	omit Worcestershire sauce)

1 Roast the tomatoes as described in the previous recipe.

2 Pull off the skins, cut out the cores and put into a processor or blender with the remaining ingredients. Purée.

3 Use to swirl or drizzle over soups and stews.

CALORIE COUNT 5 Kcal   **FAT CONTENT** Neg   **PER TABLESPOON**

GRILLED VEGETABLES

If you have an outdoor grill, these vegetables take on a primal smokiness that brings out the caveperson in all of us. If not, a ridged grill pan on the hob is a pretty good substitute, and, of course, they can be done under the cooker grill as well.

Peppers

Peppers are the most remarkable grilled vegetables of all – they emerge from under their blackened skins, supple, smoky, sweet; superb cut into strips and sprinkled with balsamic vinegar, puréed into glorious sauces, or layered into sandwiches (see page 32 for the grilled pepper technique). The grill loves courgettes and aubergines as well. They too are perfect for substantial sandwich-making. I like to keep all of these in the fridge for impromptu snacks – just right for a savoury tooth. Ⓥ ♥

Grilled Aubergines and Courgettes

Choose small courgettes, and slant-cut them crossways, or slice them lengthwise into long paddle shapes.

Choose small aubergines, peel them if you wish (I rather like the purple skin), and slant-cut them crosswise, or slice lengthwise into paddle shapes.

Spray the vegetable slices with oil-water spray, then grill under the cooker grill, or on a ridged grill pan, until tender, and just speckled with brown. Turn once as they grill. Ⓥ ♥

Grilled Vegetable Ratatouille

MAKES 3 litres (5 pints)   **SERVES** 8

Fabulous as a vegetarian main dish (if you wish, top with a little shredded half-fat mozzarella and grill until melted) or as an accompaniment to simply grilled skinless chicken, lean meat, or fish fillets.

Choose one of the tomato sauces (the Classic (page 91) and the Piccadillo (page 92) work especially well here) and mix it with grilled courgettes, aubergines and peppers that you have chopped coarsely (use scissors for speed and convenience). Simmer together, then mix in chopped fresh parsley, shredded fresh basil, and some chopped fresh oregano if you have it. For one quantity of tomato sauce, use approximately 2 aubergines, 6–7 courgettes, and 3–4 peppers, although with this recipe there really are no definite amounts.

CALORIE COUNT 120 Kcal **FAT CONTENT** 2g **PER SERVING**

Caramelized Carrots

MAKES 900ml (1½ pints) **SERVES** 4

Balsamic vinegar and a touch of sugar emphasize the carrot's intrinsic sweetness. Serve these hot or cold.

750g (1½lb) carrots, peeled and sliced	125ml (4fl oz) vegetable stock
3 garlic cloves, crushed	juice of approx. ½ a lemon
1 teaspoon paprika	salt and freshly ground pepper
1 teaspoon sugar	1 tablespoon balsamic vinegar

1 Combine all the ingredients except the salt, pepper and vinegar. Cook, covered, for 10 minutes, then uncover and stir in salt and pepper. Cook for a further 10 minutes until the carrots become tender and start to caramelize.

2 Add a few more drops of lemon juice and stock and 1 tablespoon of balsamic vinegar. Cook and stir for another minute or two until the carrots are lightly browned and caramelized.

3 Pour a tablespoon or so of stock into the pan to dislodge the brown caramelized bits. Stir and scrape up the browned bits, then tip the contents of the pan into a bowl.

CALORIE COUNT 79 Kcal **FAT CONTENT** <1g **PER SERVING**

Italian-style Stir-fried Courgettes

MAKES 600ml (1 pint) **SERVES** 2–4

Use small tender courgettes in this stir-fry, and serve as a vegetable accompaniment. To serve cold, squeeze on some lemon juice.

300ml (½ pint) stock
4 olives, slivered off their stones
4 sun-dried tomatoes, chopped
4 garlic cloves, crushed
pinch of crushed dried chilli flakes
   (to taste)

500g (1lb) courgettes, trimmed
1 tablespoon chopped fresh oregano
1 tablespoon chopped flat-leaf parsley
salt and freshly ground pepper

1 Combine the stock, olives, sun-dried tomatoes, garlic and chillies in a non-stick wok. Boil for 3–5 minutes until a bit more than half the liquid is gone.

2 Meanwhile cut the courgettes in half lengthways, then slice across into 2cm (¾in) chunks. Tip them into the wok and stir and cook on high for about 3 minutes, until they are tender but not mushy, and bathed in syrupy juices. Stir in the herbs and season with salt and pepper.

CALORIE COUNT 106 Kcal   **FAT CONTENT** 2g   **PER SERVING**

VEGETABLE STEWS

For your non-meat days, treat yourself to a vegetable stew – they give much pleasure. These stews are so low in fat, and so full of good nutrition; they are meant to be served in lavish portions on their own, or with couscous, mashed potatoes or polenta.

Sicilian Vegetable Stew

MAKES 1.2 litres (2 pints)

The combination of raisins, chillies, capers and red wine brings sweet, hot pungency to this gutsy stew – the aubergine cubes soak up all that flavour.

4–5 black olives, drained and slivered off their stones

2 tablespoons drained capers

1–2 tablespoons raisins

3–4 garlic cloves, crushed

1–2 good pinches of crushed, dried chillies

400ml (14fl oz) stock

150ml (¼ pint) dry red wine

1 × 275g (9oz) aubergine, peeled and diced

2 × 425g (14oz) cans whole tomatoes, drained and cut into strips

salt and freshly ground pepper

2 courgettes (about 250g/8oz) each, diced

2–3 tablespoons shredded fresh basil leaves

4–5 tablespoons chopped fresh flat-leaf parsley

1 Combine the olives, capers, raisins, garlic, chillies, stock and wine in a large, non-reactive flameproof casserole or saucepan. Cover, bring to the boil, and simmer for 5–7 minutes.

2 Add the aubergine and tomato strips, and season to taste. Simmer, uncovered, stirring occasionally, for 20 minutes. Stir in the courgettes and simmer for 10 minutes, or until the vegetables are tender. Stir in the herbs, and simmer, stirring occasionally, for 2–3 minutes more.

CALORIE COUNT 109 Kcal   **FAT CONTENT** 1.5g   **PER ½ PINT**   Ⓥ ✽ ♥

Spicy Sweet Potato, Grilled Pepper and Sweetcorn Stew

MAKES 3.3 litres (5¾ pints)

More colour, more excitement, more flamboyant seasonings. Serve up this fiesta of a stew in shallow soup bowls, garnished with limes and herbs. There is enough here to eat lavishly now, and freeze more for later.

2 large carrots, about 375g (12oz), peeled and cut into chunks

2 red onions, coarsely chopped

6 garlic cloves, lightly bashed with a kitchen mallet and the skins removed

1½ teaspoons ground cumin

1½ teaspoons ground coriander

1 teaspoon ground turmeric

2–3 pinches dried chilli flakes (or more, to taste)

5 dry-packed sun-dried tomatoes, chopped (use scissors)

2 black olives, drained and slivered off their stones

2.1 litres (3 pints) vegetable stock

approx. 300ml (½ pint) dry red wine

1kg (2lb) orange-fleshed sweet potatoes, peeled and cut into chunks

250g (8oz) sweetcorn kernels

4 red or yellow peppers (or 2 of each), grilled, peeled and coarsely chopped, with their juices (page 32)

1 × 425g (14oz) can chopped tomatoes

1 × 425g (14oz) can whole tomatoes (cut in pieces)

salt and freshly ground pepper

1 × 475g (15oz) can borlotti beans, drained and rinsed

juice of 1 lime

Garnishes

2–3 tablespoons chopped fresh flat-leaf parsley

2–3 tablespoons chopped fresh coriander

lime wedges

1 Combine the carrots, onions, garlic, spices, sun-dried tomatoes, olives, 300ml (½ pint) of stock and the red wine in a heavy-bottomed soup pot. Cover, bring to the boil and simmer briskly for 10 minutes. Uncover, reduce the heat a little, and simmer until the vegetables are tender, the liquid is just about gone and the vegetables are catching a bit. Add a bit more liquid as it cooks if necessary.

2 Add the sweet potatoes and a splash more red wine and stir and cook for a minute or so, scraping up any browned bits with your wooden spoon, until the potatoes are well combined with the onion and spice mixture. Stir in the sweetcorn, the

peppers and their juices, the tomatoes and the remaining stock. Season with salt and pepper. Simmer, briskly, partially covered, for 10 minutes, then stir in the beans and lime juice. Simmer for another 5 minutes. Serve ladled into wide, shallow soup bowls. Sprinkle on the fresh herbs and serve with wedges of lime.

CALORIE COUNT 219 Kcal   **FAT CONTENT** 2g   **PER ½ PINT**   Ⓥ ✳ ◖ ♥

VARIATION: **Creamy Sweet Potato Soup**

Purée in a blender until smooth and velvety. Serve hot with the garnishes. ♥

Smoked Corn

Once only seasonal locally grown sweetcorn was worth eating, and it had to be eaten almost immediately upon picking. Because the sugars in the kernels turned so quickly to starch, peak flavour was ephemeral. Now, sweetcorn is bred for extra lasting sweetness, so it is possible to capture some of that flavour without the old mad rush from the local farmer's field to the pot of boiling water waiting in the kitchen. Even canned corn (look for cans labelled 'tender crisp') and frozen corn manage to capture some of that elusive quality.

Smoking corn over tea by the Chinese method produces something wonderful. The smoked corn makes an intriguing addition to soups and stews. Shuck ears of sweetcorn and remove the silk. Smoke for 5–7 minutes according to the technique on page 28, then steam over boiling water for about 5 minutes, until the kernels are swollen and bursting with juice. Cool, and cut the kernels from the cob. If you wish, save time by smoking canned corn. Simply drain, scatter into the steamer, and smoke as directed. ♥

Tomato-Fennel-Mushroom Stew

MAKES 1.8 litres (3 pints)

Fennel and mushrooms are a wonderful combination (fennel and anything are a wonderful combination!), but you can substitute the small inner stalks (with leaves) of celery if you just hate it. Cooked celery has its own herbal charms, and will add a pleasant dimension to the stew. If you use celery, try to find some chervil and roughly chop the leaves to garnish the stew.

500g (1lb) button mushrooms, cleaned
1 red onion, chopped
1 carrot, chopped
1 stalk of celery, chopped
1 head fennel, trimmed and chopped
4 garlic cloves, crushed
3 sun-dried tomatoes, chopped
4 black olives, slivered off their stones
300ml (½ pint) mushroom stock (page 30)

175ml (6fl oz) dry red wine
dash of teriyaki sauce
1–2 pinches of dried tarragon, crumbled
2 × 425g (14oz) cans chopped tomatoes
salt and freshly ground pepper
snipped fennel fronds
chopped fresh flat-leaf parsley

1 Combine the mushrooms, onion, carrot, celery, fennel, garlic, sun-dried tomatoes, olives, stock, wine, teriyaki and tarragon in a wok or frying-pan. Cover and simmer, briskly, for 8–10 minutes, then uncover and simmer until the vegetables are tender and the liquid is just about gone.

2 Stir in the tomatoes, season with salt and pepper and simmer, uncovered, for 15–20 minutes, until thick and savoury. Stir in the fresh herbs. Serve with polenta, rice, pasta, couscous or other grains.

CALORIE COUNT 73 Kcal   **FAT CONTENT** 1g   **PER ½ PINT**

Vegetable Stew

MAKES 1.25 litres (2 pints)

This is an old-fashioned root vegetable stew that would be wonderful in a pasty. Make a quick cheat's pasty by baking portions of this in a taco (page 99). Wonderful winter food!

1 stalk of celery, sliced into 2.5cm (1in) pieces

2 large carrots, peeled and cut into 3.5cm (1½in) chunks

2–4 garlic cloves, crushed

1 large onion, cut into chunks

2 red peppers, cut into their natural sections, peeled, seeded and cut into 3.5cm (1½in) chunks

750ml (1¼ pints) stock

125ml (4fl oz) red wine

1 tablespoon redcurrant jelly

1 tablespoon Dijon mustard

1 tablespoon tomato purée

a few drops of teriyaki sauce

juice of 1 lemon

1 parsnip, peeled and cut into 2.5cm (1in) chunks

2 small turnips, peeled and cut into eighths

½ a small swede, trimmed, peeled and cut into 3.5cm (1½in) chunks

salt and freshly ground pepper

1 Combine the celery, carrots, garlic, onion, peppers and 450ml (¾ pint) of stock in a large heavy-bottomed frying-pan. Simmer briskly, stirring occasionally, for 5–7 minutes until the vegetables begin to soften. Stir in the wine and cook for 2–3 minutes more.

2 Whisk together the redcurrant jelly, mustard, tomato purée, teriyaki and the juice of ½ a lemon and stir it in. Cover and simmer for 2–3 minutes.

3 Stir in the root vegetables, the remaining stock and a little more lemon juice to taste. Season with salt and pepper and simmer, covered, for approximately half an hour until all the vegetables are tender. Add a bit more stock as needed.

CALORIE COUNT 156 Kcal   **FAT CONTENT** 2g   **PER ½ PINT**

MISCELLANEOUS VEGETABLE TECHNIQUES

To peel and deseed a tomato
Blanch the tomato in boiling water for 10 seconds. (For speed, boil the water in the kettle, then pour it over the tomatoes in a bowl.) Refresh under cold water, then cut out the cores and slip off the skins. Halve the tomatoes and use your fingers to ease out the seeds.

To peel, deseed and drain a cucumber
Peel the cucumber with a swivel-bladed peeler and cut in half lengthways. With a teaspoon, scoop out the seeds from each half and discard them. Cut the cucumber halves into slices about 5mm (¼in) thick. To drain toss with a little salt and leave in a non-reactive colander for 15 minutes.

To peel a pepper
Cut the peppers in half, lengthwise. Remove the stem, the seeds and the ribs. Cut the halves into their natural sections. Peel each piece with a swivel-bladed vegetable peeler. Cut each piece into strips about 1cm (½in) wide.

To peel and cube a mango
1 With a sharp knife, cut straight down the length of the mango, cutting off one 'cheek' but missing the large flat centre stone. Repeat on the other side, with the second 'cheek'.

2 With a small paring knife, score each mango half lengthways and crossways, cutting

through the flesh all the way to, but not through, the skin. Push out the skin as if you were pushing the mango half inside out. The mango flesh will stand out in cubes. Slice these cubes off the skin.

3 Peel the skin from the centre slice left on the stone, and – as best as you can – slice the mango flesh off the stone. Do it over a bowl to save the juices.

To peel asparagus
1 Cut off the tough woody bottom of each stalk. With a paring knife, or with a swivel-bladed peeler, peel each stalk from the bottom up to the buds. Rinse the stalks under cold running water.

2 If you are not going to cook them at once, stand them in a glass of water as if they were a bunch of flowers, cover with a plastic bag, and refrigerate until needed.

To prepare a head of fennel
Trim the tough outer layers, and the stalks and leaves from the bulbs of fennel. (Save the trimmings for stock-making, and save the feathery fronds to use as a herb garnish.) Trim a little off the bottom, but leave the core intact – it keeps the fennel sections together.

To trim and slice a spring onion
1 Wash the onions, and slice off the beard at the end.

2 Thinly slice or chop the white portions, then slice about 5cm (2in) of the green portion. Sometimes the white portion is used in a sauté, and the green for garnish. Sometimes all of it is used in the sauté.

CHAPTER 8

Fish

Fish is a wonderful choice for a low-fat lifestyle; high in quality protein, nutritious, extremely quick and easy to cook. The fat levels in fish range from very low indeed (cod, seabass, mussels) to the fattier (salmon, mackerel, herring), but even the fattiest fish is relatively low in fat and Calories – a 125g (4oz) piece of salmon contains approximately 230 Calories as opposed to 400 Calories in a comparable hunk of steak. And fish fat is high in Omega-3 fatty acids, believed to have a role in preventing heart attacks and strokes caused by blood clots. If – because of a medical condition – you must drastically control your dietary fat levels, then avoid fatty fish, otherwise it really is an important and valuable component of a low-fat lifestyle.

For a long time it was believed that the cholesterol levels in shellfish made them inappropriate for a low-fat, low-cholesterol diet, but the truth is, the levels are (except for squid) not that high: prawns contain 125–160 milligrams per 100g; oysters, 45–55 milligrams; mussels, 45–60 milligrams. Squid is high, with 200–300 milligrams per 100g. (To put things in perspective, an egg has 213 milligrams.) But as I mentioned earlier, the fat levels in shellfish are so low – and though low in fat, high in omega-3 fatty acids – that it is now believed that their consumption will not affect blood cholesterol levels.

Of course, the best thing about fish is how good it is to eat, how quick to cook, how the quality and variety of fish on offer in the supermarkets have improved dramatically over the last few years, how well fish and shellfish respond to the fresh, clean techniques and ingredients of low-fat cooking.

IS THE FISH FRESH OR OVER THE HILL?

The eyes (if the head is attached) should be clear, fresh and bulging. It should smell fresh and clean – of the sea or stream; *never* fishy. Press the flesh with your fingertip – the depression should bounce back.

TIMING

Fish should remain moist – overcooking dries it out. Raw fish is already tender. It just needs to be cooked long enough to coagulate the protein. The rule of thumb is no more than 10 minutes per 2.5cm (1in) thickness. Longer cooking dries fish out and toughens it – a complete waste! Because of the high heat and intense steam within the packet, fish 'en papillote' (page 140) cooks even quicker, so figure a little less than 10 minutes per inch.

The technique of cooking salmon in residual heat (page 142) is quick too; the less than 10-minute rule applies there as well. And grilling, close to the grill, under a coating of mustard-yogurt (page 137) blasts the fish with heat – 3–5 minutes should be enough, depending on the thickness of the fish and the strength of the grill. Exquisite moistness is what you're after, not dry dustiness.

IS IT DONE?

When done, the fish will just be changing from translucent to opaque, and will be beginning to flake.

Mustard-Yogurt Grilled Fish

SERVES 2

Any fish fillet can be grilled under a mantle of mustard-yogurt and breadcrumbs. (A thicker fillet will need an extra minute or so of grilling.) The topping keeps the fish moist.

2 tablespoons Dijon mustard
3 tablespoons very low-fat natural yogurt
about 150ml (¼ pint) plain breadcrumbs
salt and freshly ground pepper

2 plaice fillets (125g/4oz each)
oil-water spray
lemon or lime wedges

1 Preheat the grill to high. Line the grill tray with foil. Put the rack in place and spray with oil-water spray.

2 Whisk together the mustard and yogurt. Season the breadcrumbs very well with salt and pepper and spread out on a plate.

3 Spread the flesh side of the fillets with the yogurt mixture, then sprinkle the crumbs on evenly. Place skin down on the grill rack. Spray with oil-water spray.

4 Grill, close to the heat, for about 3–5 minutes, until golden, and just done. Serve with lemon or lime wedges.

CALORIE COUNT 252 Kcal   **FAT CONTENT** 4g   **PER SERVING**

Halibut Roasted in Piccadillo Sauce with New Potatoes

SERVES 2

Any of the tomato sauces (or the Tomato Aubergine or Grilled Pepper sauces) in the sauce chapter (pages 93 and 94) will work here. For that matter, any fish fillet will work as well; just measure the thickness and time accordingly. This looks amazing – the scarlet sauce, the snowy fish, the scattered green herbs – and I love what happens to the potatoes; they swell within their skins as they roast.

375g (12oz) small Charlotte or new potatoes (about 16)
2 halibut fillets, about 175g (6oz) each, any bones removed with tweezers
salt and freshly ground pepper

600ml (1 pint) Piccadillo Tomato Sauce (page 92)
roughly chopped fresh flat-leaf parsley and coriander

1 Steam the potatoes over boiling water until just done, about 15–20 minutes. Preheat the oven to 230°C/450°F/Gas Mark 8.

2 Season the halibut fillets with salt and pepper.

3 Spread the sauce out in a frying-pan, shallow flameproof casserole or baking dish that will hold the fillets and potatoes in one uncrowded layer. Let it simmer for a few minutes, then set the fillets in the bubbling sauce and nestle the potatoes all around. Immediately put into the oven, uncovered, and let roast for 10 minutes per 2.5cm (1in) thickness, until just done.

4 Scatter the herbs over the top and serve.

CALORIE COUNT 451 Kcal   **FAT CONTENT** 5g   **PER SERVING**

Roasted Fish on Two Pepper Sauces

SERVES 2–4

This is a most impressive dish for a celebration, although it's very easy to make. The sauces can be made several days in advance and reheated when they are needed. It's important that both sauces are the same consistency, so that when you pour them on to the plate, they flow evenly towards the middle. Of course, you could serve this on a bed of just the yellow or just the red sauce, or on one of the tomato sauces.

2 pinches paprika
1 garlic clove, crushed
juice of 1 orange
juice of 1 lime
juice of ½ a lemon
2 tablespoons dry vermouth
2–4 fillets of firm white fish fillets
    (skinned if you wish), e.g. sea bass,
    cod, hake or haddock

oil-water spray
salt and freshly ground pepper
1 quantity each of Red Pepper Sauce
    and Yellow Pepper Sauce (page 95)
torn fresh mint leaves
chopped fresh flat-leaf parsley

1 Combine the paprika, garlic, citrus juices and vermouth. Rub this mixture all over the fish. Set aside while you preheat the oven to 220°C/425°F/Gas Mark 7.

2 Oil-water-spray a baking dish that will hold the fish in one uncrowded layer. Arrange the fish, skin side down, in the dish, season with salt and pepper, and spray with oil-water. Roast for 7–10 minutes until just done. In the meantime, warm the sauces.

3 Have 2 or 4 warm (not hot) plates ready. Put each of the sauces in small measuring scoops of equal size. Hold one in your right hand, one in your left, poise over the plate, then pour. The sauces will each coat one side of the plate, and flow to meet nicely in the centre. If necessary, shake the plate to help them along. Repeat with each plate.

4 Gently lift each fillet out of the baking dish and centre on a plate. Scatter on the herbs and serve at once.

CALORIE COUNT 217 Kcal   **FAT CONTENT** 4g   **PER SERVING**

A NOTE ABOUT FISH 'EN PAPILLOTE'

Any fish fillet can be cooked 'en papillote' with great success. At its simplest, put a fillet in parchment, season with salt and pepper, add a sprinkling of dry white wine (dry vermouth is excellent), a squeeze of lemon or lime, and a spritz of oil-water spray. A scattering of fresh herbs, crushed garlic and sliced spring onions would not be amiss. Fold, crimp and bake as described below. Obviously, this can be endlessly varied, and the results are fresh, delicate and pure. The fish steam-roasts within the packet and swells to bursting with its own goodness. Heavy-duty foil can be used instead of greaseproof paper; make sure the packet is roomy so that the foil doesn't touch the top of the fish.

Rainbow Trout en Papillote

SERVES 2

Rainbow trout fillets roasted en papillote (in greaseproof paper packets) make a dramatic presentation. The three variations below can be used to top any fish fillet en papillote.

2 large garlic cloves	150ml (5fl oz) stock
2 large sprigs of rosemary	2 fillets rainbow trout
125ml (4fl oz) dry red wine	salt and freshly ground mixed pepper

1 Preheat the oven to 230°C/450°F/Gas Mark 8. Put a baking tray in the oven.

2 Combine the garlic, rosemary, wine and stock in a small frying-pan, and simmer briskly until the garlic is tender, and the liquid greatly reduced and syrupy.

3 Tear pieces of parchment, each large enough to enclose a fillet generously, and fold over and crease. Open the paper out again, and place a fillet on each piece, on the bottom half. Season with salt and pepper, and place a sprig of rosemary and some of the garlic-wine mixture on top of each fillet. Spray with oil-water spray.

4 Fold the parchment over the fillet. Crimp the paper closed by folding down one corner. Then start a second fold so that it incorporates some of the first. Continue folding and crimping all around, pressing each fold securely so that no steam or juices will escape. Do make sure that the packets are roomy, so that the paper does not actually touch the surface of the fish .

5 Put the packets on the baking tray, and bake for 5–7 minutes (see Timing, page 136), until the packets are browned and puffed, and you hear serious sizzling.

6 Cut each packet open with scissors and slide the contents into shallow soup plates. Pour the juices from the bag over the fish and serve at once. (Use a leaner fish for a lower fat version.)

CALORIE COUNT 273 Kcal   **FAT CONTENT** 11g   **PER SERVING**

VARIATION: **Tarragon Filling**

4 garlic cloves, crushed
125ml (4fl oz) dry vermouth
150ml (5fl oz) stock
1 generous tablespoon snipped fresh
   tarragon

juice of ½ a small lemon
salt and freshly ground pepper

Combine the garlic, vermouth and stock. Simmer until the garlic is tender and the liquid greatly reduced and syrupy. Stir in the tarragon. Sprinkle the top of the fish with lemon juice, before topping with the tarragon mixture, crimping the parchment and baking.

VARIATION: **Sherry and Ginger**

2 garlic cloves, crushed
3.5cm (1½in) ginger, peeled and
   crushed
6 spring onions, trimmed and sliced

2 tablespoons cream sherry
1 teaspoon teriyaki sauce
1 piece of star anise, broken into 3–4
   pieces

Combine all the ingredients in a pan and simmer until the garlic is tender and the liquid greatly reduced and syrupy. Season the trout with salt, ground mixed pepper and lemon juice. Top with the mixture, squeeze on a bit more lemon juice, and seal into the parchment.

Salmon Fillets with Red Wine Sauce

SERVES 2

Salmon benefits from quick cooking, so that it keeps its sweet moistness. Dried out, over-cooked salmon is a travesty – indeed a tragedy – a horrible waste of exquisite fish flesh. Sear salmon fillets quickly in a heavy-bottomed frying-pan, then cover, remove from the heat and let the cooking finish in the residual heat. The texture will be pearly, succulent and delicate.

300ml (½ pint) dry red wine
300ml (½ pint) fish stock
3 sprigs of fresh thyme
½ bayleaf
2 olives (Kalamata if possible), slivered off their stones

1–2 large garlic cloves, lightly crushed
salt and freshly ground mixed pepper
oil-water spray
2 × 150g (5oz) salmon fillets, any bones removed with tweezers

1 Combine the wine, stock, thyme, bayleaf, olives and garlic in a saucepan and simmer briskly until reduced by half. Remove the thyme and bayleaf. Season with salt and pepper. Keep warm.

2 Season the salmon on both sides with a generous amount of ground mixed pepper and salt. Spray a lidded frying-pan with oil-water spray and heat on the stove. Sear the salmon on both sides, flesh side first, for 1½ minutes in total, until browned.

3 Immediately cover the pan tightly, remove from the heat and leave for 3–4 minutes, until the salmon is just done. The flesh should remain sweetly moist and succulent.

4 Put each salmon fillet on a plate, and drizzle the sauce around it.(For a lower fat meal choose a leaner fish.)

CALORIE COUNT 307 Kcal   **FAT CONTENT** 18g   **PER SERVING**

VARIATION: Salmon with Puy Lentils

MAKES 750ml (1¼ pints)

Nestle the lentils next to the salmon and drizzle some of the red wine sauce over them.

- 1.5 litres (2½ pints) salt-free stock or water
- 2 dry-packed sun-dried tomatoes, chopped (use scissors)
- 2 garlic cloves, crushed
- 6 spring onions, trimmed and sliced
- a pinch of crushed dried chillies
- 3 black olives in brine, drained and slivered off the stones
- 275g (9oz) Puy lentils, rinsed
- freshly ground pepper to taste
- a squeeze of lemon juice, to taste
- Salmon Fillets with Red Wine Sauce (page 142)

---

1 In a saucepan, combine 150ml (½ pint) of stock or water, the tomatoes, garlic, spring onions, chillies and olives. Simmer until the liquid is almost gone.

2 Stir in the lentils and season with pepper. Stir in 1.25 litres (2 pints) of the remaining stock or water. Bring to a boil, and boil for 10 minutes. Reduce the heat and simmer, partially covered, for 30–35 minutes or until tender. Add a bit more salt-free stock or water during this time, if necessary, to prevent scorching. When the lentils are tender, stir in some vegetable bouillon powder if you have used water, pepper and a bit of lemon juice.

CALORIE COUNT 509 Kcal   **FAT CONTENT** 19g   **PER SERVING**

Spicy Mussels

SERVES 2

Farmed mussels make a cheap, easy and companionable meal. This messy feast (noisy too – all that slurping the tender mussels from their shells, and splashing the hunks of bread in the spicy broth) makes a great celebration meal to be shared with those you love, who also love real food, the kind of food you almost have to climb into and wallow.

300ml (½pint) passata
300ml (½pint) tomato juice
300ml (½pint) fish stock
3 red peppers, grilled (see page 32) or use bottled red peppers
oil-water spray
1 red onion, chopped
2 stalks of celery, chopped
½ tablespoon ground cumin
1 teaspoon ground coriander

300ml (½pint) vegetable stock
175ml (6fl oz) dry white wine
4 garlic cloves, crushed
1 fresh chilli, seeded, ribbed and chopped
1kg (2lb) mussels
3–4 tablespoons chopped fresh coriander
2–3 tablespoons chopped fresh flat-leaf parsley

1 Combine the passata, tomato juice and fish stock. Purée the grilled peppers and stir into the tomato mixture. Spray a soup pot or large wok with oil-water spray. Add the onion and celery and stir over low heat until they begin to wilt. Stir in the cumin and coriander and stir for a few seconds until fragrant. Stir in 300ml (10fl oz) of stock, the wine, garlic and chilli, and simmer until the onions and celery are tender and the liquid just about gone. Stir in the tomato-pepper mixture and simmer for another 10 minutes.

2 Scrub the mussels to remove any grit and traces of barnacles, and pull and scrape away their wispy 'beards'. Discard any mussels that are cracked or abnormally heavy. Tap and squeeze any mussels that are not tightly closed; if they do not immediately close tightly, discard them. Swish the mussels around in a big bowl of cold water, drain, and repeat once more.

3 Stir the herbs into the liquid, then tip in the mussels and clap the cover on the pan. Simmer for 4–6 minutes, until they open. With oven gloves, pick up the pan half-way through and give it a good shake. At the end of cooking, discard any mussels that have not opened.

4 Divide the mussels and broth (if it seems gritty, strain it through a sieve) between two big bowls. Have plenty of paper napkins on hand, and roll up your sleeves! (Place an extra bowl on the table for discarded shells.)

CALORIE COUNT 355 Kcal   **FAT CONTENT** 6g   **PER SERVING**

Prawns

Perfectly cooked prawns are a rare treat – just a few seconds too much turns them mealy. *Just* done, served with a dipping sauce (dunk and eat with your fingers), they are incomparable. Serve with Rémoulade Sauce (page 57), Spicy Ketchup (page 57), or Grilled Pepper Spread (page 56), or a selection of dips (pages 52–4), or serve tossed into one of those nifty packs of precooked Japanese Udon noodles with Mango Chutney Vinaigrette (page 60). Scatter in cubed mango and roughly torn fresh coriander, mint and flat-leaf parsley leaves.

Rinse peeled, deveined tiger prawns under cold running water. Lay the wet prawns in one layer in a heavy-bottomed non-stick pan. Put the lid on the pan, turn the heat to high and steam for 3–4 minutes (stir them once, half-way through), until just done (they will turn pink and begin to curl). Immediately spread the prawns on a cold plate, and put the plate on a rack to cool slightly. Don't chill them – eat them at once, when they are at their juicy best.

Tiger Prawns in Garlic and Parsley Sauce

MAKES 600ml (1 pint)   **SERVES** 4

The prawns are stir-fried briefly in a sort of semi-Asian rémoulade (very Fusion) until just done. The mustard stabilizes the yogurt, so that it does not curdle.

4 large garlic cloves, peeled and roughly crushed

300ml (½ pint) fish stock (or vegetable or chicken stock)

1 bunch (8–9) spring onions, trimmed and cut into 2.5cm (1in) lengths

3 sun-dried tomatoes, roughly chopped

3 black olives, slivered off their stones

½–1 tablespoon Sambal Oelek (page 24)

2 tablespoons chopped fresh flat-leaf parsley

1 tablespoon Dijon mustard

1 tablespoon very low-fat yogurt

500g (1lb) peeled tiger prawns (thaw overnight in the fridge if frozen)

salt and freshly ground pepper

juice of ½ a lemon

1 Put the garlic and 150ml (¼ pint) of fish stock into a non-stick wok and simmer briskly until the garlic is tender, and the liquid about gone.

2 Put the onions, sun-dried tomatoes, olives, Sambal Oelek, parsley (stems and all), mustard and yogurt into a food processor or blender and blend to a rough purée. Put the prawns into a bowl, scrape in the purée, and toss with 2 spoons to combine very well. Season with salt and pepper.

3 Pour the remaining stock and half the lemon juice into the wok containing the garlic. Boil for 1 minute, then scrape in the prawns and all the purée. Stir and cook over high heat until the prawns are *just* cooked, about 3 minutes. They are done when they turn pink and begin to curl, but taste one to be sure. Don't let them overcook; half a minute too much turns them mealy. Squeeze in the remaining lemon juice, stir, and serve.

CALORIE COUNT 133 Kcal   **FAT CONTENT** 2g   **PER SERVING**

Sea Bass and Mussel Stew

SERVES 4

The fish is simmered on a bed of flavour-infused potatoes – mussels are added at the last minute – they open in no time at all.

---

1 large red onion, cut in half and sliced into thin half-moons

3–4 garlic cloves, crushed

2–3 sun-dried tomatoes, diced (use scissors)

2–3 black olives, slivered off their stones

a pinch of crushed dried chillies, or more to taste

300ml (½ pint) stock

4 small potatoes, each weighing about 60g (2oz), peeled and sliced 5mm (¼in) thick

salt and freshly ground pepper

2 large ripe flavourful tomatoes, peeled, seeded and chopped (see page 134)

1–2 tablespoons shredded fresh basil

1 bayleaf

a 7cm (3in) strip of orange zest

approx. 300ml (½ pint) stock, brought to the boil

2 × 150g (5oz) sea bass fillets, skinned if you wish

2 dozen mussels

chopped fresh flat-leaf parsley for garnish

---

1 Combine the onion, garlic, sun-dried tomatoes, olives, chillies and 300ml (½ pint) of stock in a heavy-bottomed flameproof casserole or wok. Cover and bring to the boil. Boil for 5 minutes, then uncover and cook, briskly, until the onion is tender and the liquid almost gone.

2 Spread the onions evenly over the bottom of the pot. Arrange the sliced potatoes over the onions. Season with salt and pepper. Spread the tomatoes over the potatoes. Add the basil, bayleaf, and orange zest. Sprinkle on a little more salt and pepper and pour in enough boiling stock to just cover the vegetables.

3 Cover the pot and simmer for 20 minutes, or until the potatoes are almost tender. If the liquid is gone, pour in another few fluid ounces of hot stock to come halfway up the potatoes and prevent them from sticking and burning. Lay the fish, skin side down, on the potatoes. Sprinkle with some more salt and pepper, cover, and simmer gently for 3 minutes. Then uncover and scatter in the mussels. Cover again, and simmer briskly for 2–3 minutes more until the fish is just done, and the mussels have opened. Sprinkle with parsley.

CALORIE COUNT 222 Kcal   **FAT CONTENT** 4g   **PER SERVING**

CHAPTER 9

Poultry

L ean poultry means no skin – ever. Well – almost never. It means no goose fat, duck fat, chicken fat, all that classic schmaltz so beloved by the traditionalists. Rather than fretting about their loss, think about how fresh, clean and vibrant poultry will taste without the usual blunting cloak of fat. Chicken breast fillets are very lean, and skinless chicken thighs and skinless duck breasts are relatively lean. All three are exciting blank canvases for all sorts of interesting spicy sauces and garnishes.

CHICKEN BREASTS

Boneless skinless chicken breast fillets are blameless: low in fat, cholesterol and calories, perfect for a low-fat lifestyle, but they can be so boring! Avoid boring yourself to distraction by making sure that you don't overcook the delicate morsels, and spice and sauce them cleverly to make the most of their creamy texture and delicate taste. Trim them very well of all bits of fat, skin and gristle before beginning the recipe.

Grilled Chicken Breasts Peperonata

SERVES 2–4

A ridged grill pan for use on the hob enables you in a sense to barbecue indoors, a very good way to add flavour to the bland breasts. Rub them with a spiced marinade, grill, and then finish off on a bed of richly flavoured vegetables.

Peperonata

6 red peppers (or 3 red and 3 yellow), seeded, ribbed and peeled (page 134) and cut into 1cm (½in) strips
1 large red onion, skinned, halved and sliced into thin half-moons
2 black olives, slivered off their stones
2 garlic cloves, crushed
4 sun-dried tomatoes, chopped
60ml (2fl oz) dry white vermouth
juice of 1 lemon
175ml (6fl oz) stock
salt and freshly ground pepper
1 tablespoon drained capers (optional)
2 tablespoons chopped fresh flat-leaf parsley

1 Combine the peppers, onion, olives, garlic, sun-dried tomatoes, vermouth, half the lemon juice, and the stock in a heavy-bottomed pan. Season with salt and pepper. Bring to the boil, reduce the heat, and simmer until the vegetables are very tender and 'frying' in their own scant juices. Stir in the capers, if you wish, and the parsley. Stir and cook for a few minutes more, then set aside.

Chicken

4 garlic cloves, crushed
juice of 1 lemon
juice of ½ an orange
2 tablespoons balsamic vinegar
2 dashes of teriyaki sauce
2–4 chicken breasts, well trimmed
salt and freshly ground pepper
oil-water spray
60–90ml (2–3fl oz) stock

1 Combine the garlic, citrus juices, balsamic vinegar and teriyaki. Put the chicken breasts in a baking dish and rub with the mixture. Turn to coat them thoroughly, then leave to marinate for about 15 minutes.

2 Heat a grill pan. Season the chicken with salt and pepper and spray with oil-water spray. Shake any garlic pieces off the chicken, and grill for 2–3 minutes on each side, until marked with grill marks. Add the chicken to the peperonata.

3 Add a little stock and bring to a simmer, turning the chicken once or twice, until it is just cooked through, approximately 7–8 minutes. Serve the chicken breasts with the peperonata alongside.

CALORIE COUNT 343 Kcal   **FAT CONTENT** 4g   **PER SERVING**

Chicken Paprikash

SERVES 4

My favourite Hungarian flavour principles without the traditional lard, and with ricotta standing in for the usual sour cream.

Paprikash

1 large red onion, chopped
1 garlic clove, crushed
2 carrots, peeled and chopped
2 red peppers, seeded, ribbed and peeled (page 134)
2–3 sun-dried tomatoes, chopped

1 tablespoon paprika
450ml (¾ pint) stock
125ml (4fl oz) dry white vermouth
150ml (¼ pint) passata
salt and freshly ground pepper
45g (1½oz) ricotta cheese

1 Put the onion, garlic, carrots, peppers, sun-dried tomatoes, paprika and 300ml (½ pint) of stock and vermouth in a heavy-bottomed frying-pan or casserole. Cover and bring to the boil. Simmer briskly for 5–7 minutes. Uncover, reduce the heat and simmer until the vegetables are gently 'frying' in their own juices.

2 Stir in the passata and 60–90ml (2–3fl oz) of stock. Season with salt and pepper. Simmer for 10–15 minutes, until the carrots are tender.

3 Stir a few tablespoons of the pan liquid into the ricotta, then blend in a blender, or with an immersion blender, or with a wire whisk. Stir this creamy mixture back into the vegetables.

Chicken

2–4 chicken breast fillets
a couple of pinches of paprika

salt and freshly ground pepper
oil-water spray
1 tablespoon chopped fresh marjoram

1 Rub the chicken with paprika and plenty of ground pepper. Season with salt and spray on both sides with oil-water spray.

2 Heat a ridged grill pan. Grill the chicken for 3–5 minutes on each side, until just done.

3 Bring the vegetable mixture to a gentle simmer. (Don't boil or it may separate.) Add the chicken to the vegetables and turn to coat with the creamy sauce. Strew with marjoram.

CALORIE COUNT 296 Kcal   **FAT CONTENT** 7g   **PER SERVING**   ♈ ⊘

VARIATIONS

You could also make the grilled chicken with the following:

• **Roasted Butternut Squash and Sweet Potato Sauce** (page 100) ⊘

• **Grilled Vegetable Ratatouille** (pages 126–7) ♥

• **Mushrooms with Curry Spices** (page 115) ♥

• **Sicilian Vegetable Stew** (page 129) ♥

• **Italian-style Stir-fried Courgettes** (page 128) ♥

Creamy Chicken Curry

MAKES 1 litre (1¾ pints)   **SERVES** 4

Because the yogurt is drained (pages 29–30), it does not curdle when you add it to the pan in step 6. But be sure not to boil it at that stage, or it may not behave. If you want your curry to be hotter, leave a few seeds on the chilli. Serve this with rice, Cucumber Raita (page 55), roasted tomato chutney (page 124) and Cherry Tomato and Mango Salsa (page 62).

1 teaspoon ground turmeric,
1 teaspoon ground cumin
1 teaspoon ground coriander
½ teaspoon ground cinnamon
oil-water spray
2 medium red onions, cut into 8 wedges each
300ml (½ pint) chicken stock
2 tablespoons tomato purée

2 garlic cloves, minced
½–1 fresh chilli, seeded, ribbed and chopped
4 boneless, skinless chicken breasts, cut into strips 2.5cm (1in) wide
salt and freshly ground pepper
3 tablespoons drained very low-fat yogurt (see pages 29–30)
chopped fresh coriander

1 Combine the ground spices. Oil-spray a heavy-bottomed non-stick frying-pan. Heat.

2 Separate the onion pieces and spread in the pan. Stir until the onions are wilted and sizzling (2–3 minutes). Add the spice mixture, and stir until fragrant, about 1 minute.

3 Combine the stock and tomato purée and stir in, along with the garlic and chilli. Simmer briskly for 3–4 minutes, until the onions are tender, and the liquid is somewhat reduced (it should still be quite soupy).

4 Stir in the chicken and season with salt and pepper. Stir-fry (use 2 wooden spoons to keep it constantly moving) for 2–3 minutes, until the chicken pieces are almost cooked through.

5 Off the heat, stir in the yogurt, one tablespoon at a time. Stir until completely amalgamated. Return to a *low* heat, and stir and cook until the chicken is *just* done (cut a few pieces across with scissors to be sure). It should retain a creamy texture – if overcooked it becomes stringy. Let the sauce simmer gently, it must not boil.

6 Sprinkle with chopped coriander and serve at once.

CALORIE COUNT 181 Kcal   **FAT CONTENT** 2g   **PER SERVING**

Roasted Orange Chicken Breasts

MAKES 4 pieces

Orange and basil join that dependable duo, Worcestershire and teriyaki. Both sauces are salty, so you'll need hardly any extra salt.

4 boned skin-on chicken breasts	salt and freshly ground pepper
juice of 1½ large oranges	250ml (8fl oz) dry vermouth
1 teaspoon Worcestershire sauce	250ml (8fl oz) chicken stock
1 teaspoon teriyaki sauce	orange wedges
4 large fresh basil leaves	watercress
2 slices of orange	

1 With kitchen scissors trim the fat from the chicken. Loosen the skin on the breasts so that it is attached on one side only. Fold the skin flaps back and squeeze on the juice of ½ an orange. Combine the Worcestershire and teriyaki and rub into each chicken breast. Put a basil leaf and ½ an orange slice directly on to the flesh of each breast. Season with pepper and cover with the skin flap. Leave to marinate while you preheat the oven to 200°C/400°F/Gas Mark 6.

2 Choose a baking dish that will hold the chicken with room to spare, and that will work in the oven *and* on the hob. Choose a grill rack that will fit the dish. Put the chicken in or across on the rack, boned side down. Season with salt and pepper. Roast in the lower third of the oven for 15 minutes, then, using a fish slice, carefully turn each breast over (be careful to keep the skin flap, herb leaves and orange slices intact), and roast for another 15–20 minutes, until the chicken is just cooked through, plump and bursting with juice. Remove to a plate, skin side up, and cover loosely with foil to keep warm.

3 Pour the fat out of the pan and set the pan on the hob. Pour in 250ml (8fl oz) each of dry vermouth and chicken stock. Boil down, stirring up all the lovely, sticky deposits in the pan, until thick, dark and syrupy (about 5 minutes). Remove the skin flaps, herb leaves and orange slices from the chicken. Quickly dredge them in the syrupy juices, arrange on a platter and spoon any extra juices over them. Garnish with orange wedges and watercress and serve at once.

CALORIE COUNT 184 Kcal   **FAT CONTENT** 4g   **PER SERVING**

OVERLEAF *Grilled Turkey Burger (page 162)*
OPPOSITE *Lamb in Mustard, Red Wine and Redcurrant Sauce (page 166) with Sweet Potato Mash (page 109)*

CHICKEN THIGHS

Chicken thigh fillets (boneless, skinned) are now sold regularly in the supermarket; if you can't find them, they are easy enough to do yourself. Whether DIY or store-bought, trim away all vestiges of fat, skin and gristle. Chicken thighs have tons of flavour, and are much more robust than the pale, delicate breasts.

Chicken, Potatoes and Mushrooms in Smoky-Yogurt Sauce

SERVES 6

Yogurt, mustard and grilled pepper combine to make a suave, smoky sauce to coat pan-braised chicken thighs. Mushroom stock brings the mushrooms to life.

6 skinless and boneless chicken thighs, well trimmed
salt and freshly ground pepper
150ml (¼ pint) drained natural very low-fat yogurt (pages 29–30)
½ a grilled pepper, diced (or use a bottled or canned pepper)
2 tablespoons French mustard
several dashes each of Tabasco and Worcestershire sauce
oil-water spray
1 teaspoon paprika (smoked would be perfect)
2 garlic cloves, crushed
4 spring onions, trimmed and finely sliced

about 300ml (½ pint) dry white wine or vermouth
about 300ml (½ pint) mushroom stock (page 30)
2 all-purpose potatoes, about 175g (6oz) each, peeled and diced
60g (2oz) small button mushrooms, halved
60g (2oz) small chestnut mushrooms, quartered
5g (¼oz) soaked, dried mushrooms, chopped
dash of teriyaki sauce
2 teaspoons fresh thyme leaves
1 tablespoon snipped fresh tarragon leaves

1 Season the chicken thighs with salt and pepper and set aside.

2 Combine the yogurt, grilled pepper, mustard, Tabasco and Worcestershire sauce in a blender and blend until smooth. Set aside.

3 With oil-water spray, spray a non-stick frying-pan that will hold the chicken in an uncrowded layer. Heat, and when it sizzles sear the chicken, turning with tongs for 1–2 minutes. Add the paprika, garlic and spring onions and pour in 60ml (2fl oz) each of wine and mushroom stock (it will bubble furiously). With the tongs, turn the chicken in the liquid until just cooked through and glazed, about 5–7 minutes in all. Add a little more stock or wine as needed. Put the chicken on a clean plate and set aside.

4 Put the potatoes, all the mushrooms and the teriyaki into the pan, along with 150ml (5fl oz) each of wine and mushroom stock. Season with salt and pepper. Simmer, briskly, stirring occasionally, until the liquid has cooked down considerably, and the mushrooms and potatoes are tender. Stir in the herbs and 60–90ml (2–3fl oz) additional stock and simmer for another 2–3 minutes.

5 Stir in 4 tablespoons of the yogurt mixture, a tablespoon at a time. Simmer gently for 2 minutes or so, until thickened. Taste and add more Tabasco, Worcestershire sauce, salt and pepper as needed. Return the chicken to the pan and turn it a few times to heat through.

CALORIE COUNT 160 Kcal   **FAT CONTENT** 3g   **PER SERVING**

Cuban Chicken

MAKES 4 pieces

If you don't have saffron, and don't feel like buying it for the tiny bit called for here (it's always used in small amounts), use turmeric instead. Serve this with rice.

4 skinless, boneless chicken thighs	2 garlic cloves
juice of 1 lime	400ml (14fl oz) stock
1 teaspoon ground cumin	125ml (4fl oz) dry white wine
1 teaspoon ground paprika	⅛ teaspoon saffron
1 red onion	olive-oil-water spray
1 medium carrot	salt and freshly ground pepper
1 canned plum tomato, well drained and torn into strips	2 tablespoons chopped fresh flat-leaf parsley

1 Trim the thighs (use kitchen scissors for ease) of any scraps of fat, skin and bone. Put them in a shallow dish and squeeze the lime juice over them. Combine the spices and sprinkle evenly over the chicken. Turn the thighs to coat them well. Put aside to marinate.

2 Meanwhile, chop the onion, and peel and roughly chop the carrot. Combine all the vegetables and garlic in a frying-pan with 300ml (½ pint) of stock and the wine. Crumble in the saffron and stir. Simmer briskly, covered, for 5 minutes, and uncovered for about 5 minutes, or until the vegetables are tender and the liquid just about gone. Scrape into a bowl and set aside.

3 Spray the pan with oil-water spray. Season the chicken with salt and pepper. Sear it on both sides, turning with tongs, for 1–2 minutes. Pour in about 100ml (3½ fl oz) of stock (it will bubble furiously). With tongs, turn the chicken in the liquid, over high heat, until *just* cooked through and glazed (5–7 minutes in all). Add a splash of stock, as needed. Stir in the vegetables and heat through. Serve sprinkled with parsley.

CALORIE COUNT 130 Kcal   **FAT CONTENT** 3g   **PER PIECE**

Smoked Chicken Thighs

MAKES 6 pieces

Wok-smoking (pages 28–9) is so much fun. It is particularly successful with poultry, and infuses it with a mysterious and subtle smokiness that I find quite compelling. If you wish, use these smoked chicken pieces to make fajitas: slice the thighs across at a slight angle, and serve with tortillas, beans, and a selection of salsas and rice. Fill the tortillas with various combinations of these ingredients and eat with gusto.

6 boneless, skinless chicken thighs, very well trimmed

1–2 good pinches of ground ginger and ground paprika

salt and freshly ground mixed peppercorns

smoking mixture (see page 28)

oil-water spray

lime wedges

Garlic Vinaigrette or Mango Chutney Vinaigrette (pages 59 and 60)

watercress and cherry tomatoes for garnish

1 Rub the chicken thighs with the spices and ground mixed peppercorns to taste. Leave for 15 minutes or so.

2 Arrange the wok and steamer for smoking as described on page 28. Put the chicken, well spaced, on the steamer rack and smoke on high for 7 minutes, and low for 7 minutes. Turn the heat off and leave in the covered wok for a final 7 minutes.

3 Spray a ridged grill pan with oil-water spray and heat. Grill the chicken, turning, until just done – it should be gloriously juicy, not dry and stringy. Serve at once, with lime wedges, and vinaigrette for dipping. Garnish with watercress and halved cherry tomatoes.

CALORIE COUNT 94 Kcal　**FAT CONTENT** 3g　**PER PIECE**

Smoked Chicken Thighs in Tomato Gravy

MAKES 4 pieces

Add some roasted tomato purée (page 124) for extra flavour if you wish. Serve these on a bed of pasta shapes, with plenty of fresh herbs.

4 boneless, skinless chicken thighs, very well trimmed
smoking mixture (page 28)
oil-water spray
2 garlic cloves, crushed
2 black olives, slivered off their stones
1 red onion, chopped
2 sun-dried tomatoes, chopped
1 fresh chilli, seeded, ribbed and chopped
150ml (¼ pint) chicken stock

175ml (6fl oz) dry red wine
15 'vine' tomatoes, roasted, peeled, cored, seeded and chopped (page 134) or ½ a 425g (14oz) can of chopped tomatoes
salt and freshly ground pepper
a good handful of shredded fresh basil leaves
2–3 tablespoons chopped fresh flat-leaf parsley

1 Smoke the chicken thighs according to the recipe on page 157, up to the end of Step 2. Set aside on a plate.

2 Oil-spray a frying-pan that will hold the chicken pieces in one uncrowded layer. Heat the pan and throw in the chicken, tossing it about for just a minute or so. Return to the plate and add the garlic, olives, onion, sun-dried tomatoes, chilli, stock and wine to the pan. Cover and simmer for 4–5 minutes, then uncover and simmer for a few more minutes until the onions are tender, and the liquid is almost gone. Stir in the tomatoes and simmer for 3–4 minutes, until thickened.

3 Return the chicken pieces to the pan, season with salt and pepper, and simmer, stirring and turning the chicken pieces until they are just cooked through. Stir in the herbs and serve.

CALORIE COUNT 143 Kcal   **FAT CONTENT** 3g   **PER PIECE**

Chicken with Masses of Garlic

MAKES 6–8 pieces

I once had an angry letter from a reader about one of my roasted chicken recipes which called for an entire head of garlic; some of the cloves were used for the sauce, some to flavour the chicken. 'I didn't use all of the garlic because I was sure it would make us ill,' she wrote. How wrong she was. Garlic, used in quantity and cooked long and slow, is mellow and mild, and quite exhilarating. It's reputed to help all sorts of ills from blocked arteries to bacterial infections. I don't know about that, but I do know that it is delicious, and it makes me feel terrific.

If you must drastically curtail your fat, drain the pan juices into a jug and place in the freezer for 15–20 minutes so that the fat can rise to the top. (Cover the chicken and garlic so it doesn't dry out.) Skim off and discard the fat, stir the juices back into the pan, and reheat.

---

2 large, firm heads of garlic
oil-water spray
6–8 chicken thighs (on the bone), skinned and trimmed of all fat and gristle
300ml (½ pint) chicken stock

300ml (½ pint) dry white vermouth
1 teaspoon dried tarragon
¼ teaspoon ground allspice
⅛ teaspoon ground cinnamon
salt and freshly ground pepper
several tablespoons chopped parsley

---

1 Preheat the oven to 200°C/400°F/Gas Mark 6. Put the separated garlic cloves into a saucepan, add boiling water just to cover, and boil for 2 minutes. Refresh under the cold water tap, and peel the cloves.

2 Choose a shallow casserole or a frying-pan that works on the hob *and* in the oven, spray it with oil-water spray, and heat on the hob. Sear the chicken pieces just to seal, a minute or so on each side, and set aside on a plate.

3 Pour the stock and wine into the pan and bring to the boil. Boil down, stirring and scraping up any brown bits with a wooden spoon, until reduced by about half.

4 Remove from the heat and stir in the chicken, garlic, tarragon and spices. Season with salt and pepper. Cover tightly, and put into the oven for ¾–1 hour, until the chicken is falling off the bone, the garlic is melting and the fragrance is astounding. Scatter on the parsley. Serve in shallow soup plates with plenty of crusty bread to soak up the juices.

CALORIE COUNT 99 Kcal   **FAT CONTENT** 2g   **PER PIECE**

DUCK BREASTS

Duck breast fillets are now sold in most supermarkets, so if you want to cook this meaty, rich cut at home, you don't have to buy the whole duck. I've even seen them sold without the skin, but if not, it's very easy to strip off the skin, with the help of a small, sharp knife. It is very important to get rid of the skin if you have a desire for any sort of low-fat lifestyle at all; duck breast with the skin has 4 times as much fat as without. And the rest of the duck just oozes fat. The skinned breast makes very good eating; it can be smoked, grilled in a hob-top grill pan, or roasted.

Smoked Duck Breast with Two Orange Salsas

SERVES 4

The rich red beefsteak-like flesh of a duck breast takes beautifully to tea-smoking. Smoke first, then grill until cooked but still pink and juicy.

1 tablespoon teriyaki sauce
1 tablespoon each of orange and lime juice
4 duck breasts, skinned and trimmed
salt and freshly ground pepper

smoking mixture (page 28)
oil-water spray
Tomato and Orange Salsa (page 61)
Orange and Red Onion Salsa (page 65)
lime wedges

1 Rub the teriyaki and citrus juices into the duck breasts and season with plenty of salt and freshly ground mixed pepper.

2 Prepare a wok for smoking (page 28). Smoke the duck for 5 minutes on high, 5 minutes on low, then remove from the heat and leave to sit, covered, for 5 minutes more.

3 Heat a ridged grill pan and spray it with oil-water spray. Grill the duck breasts, turning once or twice. They are best served pink, and may take anything from 2 to 6–7 minutes, depending on their size, your hob, and the grill pan. (They are done when they feel firm yet springy when poked with your finger.) Slice at an angle across the grain and overlap the slices on each plate. Nestle some of each salsa on each side of the slices. Garnish with lime wedges.

CALORIE COUNT 233 Kcal   **FAT CONTENT** 9g   **PER SERVING**

Grilled Duck Breast with Cherry and Cranberry Chutney

SERVES 2–4

Grilled duck breast doesn't need that much embellishment: a little chutney or salsa nestled next to it sets it off nicely without obscuring it.

Chutney: Makes 450ml (15fl oz)
1 fresh chilli, seeded and chopped
2 garlic cloves, crushed
2.5cm (1in) root ginger, peeled and crushed
3 sun-dried tomatoes, roughly chopped
1 large red onion, very roughly chopped
125ml (4fl oz) red wine
300ml (½ pint) stock
juice of ½ a lime, ½ a lemon and ½ an orange
1 tablespoon Worcestershire sauce
several dashes each of teriyaki and Tabasco sauce

1 tablespoon balsamic vinegar
90g (3oz) dried sour cherries
90g (3oz) dried cranberries
1 teaspoon ground cumin
½ teaspoon ground coriander
a pinch of sugar

Duck
2–4 duck breasts, skinned
salt and freshly ground pepper
oil-water spray
1–2 tablespoons chopped coriander
1–2 tablespoons chopped fresh parsley

1 Combine all the chutney ingredients in a non-stick frying-pan and simmer until thick and syrupy. Add a bit more lemon juice or sugar as needed. Leave in the pan.

2 Sprinkle the duck breasts with salt and a generous amount of freshly ground pepper. Spray a ridged grill pan with oil-water spray and heat. Sear the duck breasts on both sides, then reduce heat a bit and cook for approximately 3 minutes on each side. The duck should remain quite rare inside.

3 Add the duck breasts to the chutney. Simmer, turning the duck in the pan, until it is nicely glazed (3–4 minutes) and cooked the way you like it. (For best results it should remain pink inside. It will feel firm yet springy when pressed with your finger.) Put the duck on to a board and slice crossways on the diagonal. Put a few spoonfuls of the chutney on a warm plate, arrange the slices on the chutney, and scrape on any duck juices from the board. Sprinkle with the herbs and serve.

CALORIE COUNT 411 Kcal   **FAT CONTENT** 11g   **PER SERVING**

Grilled Turkey Burgers

MAKES 4–6 burgers

The leanest possible burger is made out of turkey instead of red meat. Many supermarkets are now carrying minced turkey, or turkey stir-fry strips. Turkey meat is very low in fat, so if you must keep the fat levels very low indeed you might want to try this out. I prefer the stir-fry strips, minced by pulsing briefly in the processor – the texture is better than the pre-minced turkey, and it won't have the little bits of skin and gristle I've seen in the pre-minced variety. With minced turkey, it is very important that the burgers be cooked right through. Serve in baps or rustic rolls with Rémoulade Sauce (page 57) on the bottom, and Cranberry-Apple Sauce (page 206) on top.

375g (12oz) turkey stir-fry pieces, pulsed in the processor until minced

3 rounded tablespoons tomato purée

½ tablespoon very low-fat fromage frais

1 garlic clove, crushed

chopped pulp from a 250g (8oz) roasted aubergine (see page 30)

1–2 tablespoons breadcrumbs

several dashes of Worcestershire sauce

6 spring onions, trimmed and very finely chopped

2 tablespoons finely chopped fresh parsley

salt and freshly ground pepper

1 Preheat the grill to high. Combine all the ingredients and blend together very well. Fry a tiny piece in a non-stick frying-pan and taste for seasoning. Add more salt and pepper as needed. Form the mixture into 4–6 oval burgers. Add more bread crumbs if the mixture seems too loose.

2 Line the grill tray with foil and put the rack on the tray. Spray with oil spray. Place the burgers on the rack and grill, close to the heat, for 5–7 minutes on each side, or until cooked right through.

CALORIE COUNT 136 Kcal   **FAT CONTENT** 2g   **PER BURGER**

Meat

Meat is much leaner than it used to be, but it still tends to be too high in fat to be a regular part of a low-fat lifestyle. The answer is to eat it occasionally – 3–4 times a week – surrounded by and bulked out with vegetables. Mince is wonderful for this kind of eating – buy the leanest, combine it with roasted aubergine and use it to make burgers, sausage patties, shepherd's pies, etc. Occasionally buy lean cuts of meat – small sirloin steaks, pork loin steaks, lamb leg steaks – and trim the rim of fat off (with scissors) before cooking. (Lamb is higher in fat than the others, so save it for special occasions only.) Buy pork tenderloin as well; it's one of the leanest cuts of meat there is (if you trim off any outside fat), and it makes good eating when marinated or spice-rubbed and then roasted, or sliced into medallions and pan-fried. But the bulk of your diet should be grains, pulses, vegetables, fish and the occasional skinned poultry

If you are cutting back on fat but not cutting out fat, try the following: buy meat with minimum fat marbling and cut off any surrounding fat; use oil-water spray to pan-sauté meat; and chill stews, daubes, ragoûts etc. so that the fat rises to the top and hardens, then scrape it off and discard.

Thai-inspired Beef Salad

SERVES 2–4

A vibrant example of how a small amount of meat can be eked out with vegetables.

2–4 sirloin or tenderloin steaks, well trimmed (125g/4oz each)

Marinade
juice of 1 juicy lime
1½ teaspoons teriyaki sauce
5mm (¼in) ginger, crushed
1 garlic clove, crushed
ground mixed pepper

Dressing
juice of 2 juicy limes
¼ teaspoon Chinese chilli sauce
5mm (¼in) ginger, crushed
1 garlic clove, crushed
a pinch of sugar
2 teaspoons Thai fish sauce (nam pla)

¼ teaspoon teriyaki sauce

Cucumber relish
1 long cucumber, peeled, halved, seeded and sliced thin
1 fresh chilli, cored, seeded, and sliced very thin
⅛ teaspoon Teriyaki sauce
a pinch of sugar
2 tablespoons rice vinegar

Salad
1 packet of washed baby spinach leaves
sliced small radishes
halved cherry tomatoes
sliced spring onions
chopped fresh coriander

1 Combine the marinade ingredients in a non-reactive dish. Dredge the steaks in the mixture and leave to marinate for 15 minutes or so.

2 Combine the dressing ingredients in a screwtop jar, shake well, and set aside. Then toss together the cucumber relish ingredients in a small bowl. Set aside.

3 Heat a ridged grill pan. Remove the steak from the marinade and shake off the garlic and ginger. Grill 3–5 minutes on each side. Turn once and brush with the marinade. Remove from the pan to a waiting plate and let rest for a moment.

4 Spread the spinach leaves out on a platter. Slice the beef across slightly at an angle and put the slices into a bowl. Add any juices that have accumulated under the beef to the dressing, and then pour the dressing over the beef slices. Mix with 2 spoons to coat the beef with the dressing. Arrange the beef slices over the leaves – make sure all the dressing is used. Surround with the cucumber relish, radishes and tomatoes. Strew on the sliced spring onions and coriander. Serve at once.

CALORIE COUNT 207 Kcal   **FAT CONTENT** 6g   **PER SERVING**

Beef Steak in Red Wine Mustard Sauce

SERVES 2–4

With any small steak (beef, pork, lamb) my basic technique is to sear it in a pan until well sealed and browned. Set aside while you make a quick sauce in the pan (usually with stock and some sort of wine – red wine, sherry, port, madeira). Then slice the meat crossways and return to the sauce in the pan. Finally stir and cook for a few minutes until the meat is just done to your taste and coated with the rich-tasting sauce. When the sauce is made in the pan, all the crusty browned bits are incorporated into it, giving deep, gorgeous flavour. Serve the sauced slices with a grain (rice, couscous, bulghur), a salsa, and a scattering of chopped or shredded herbs. For a wonderful presentation, press the just-cooked grains into a small ramekin or teacup, then immediately unmould on to individual plates. Tip and scrape the sautéed meat across the mound.

oil-water spray	2 large garlic cloves, crushed (optional)
2–4 sirloin steaks or fillet steaks	150ml (5fl oz) dry red wine
(125g/4oz each), trimmed of all fat	150ml (5fl oz) stock
salt and freshly ground pepper	½–1 tablespoon Dijon mustard

1 Spray a non-stick pan with oil-water spray and heat. Season the steaks with salt and pepper.

2 Sear the steaks on both sides, 2–3 minutes in all. When they are well browned on the outside, but still quite rare, set aside on a waiting plate.

3 Pour the wine and stock into the pan and add the garlic, and boil, stirring and scraping up the brown bits with your wooden spoon. When reduced by about half, stir in the mustard, and simmer briskly for a few moments. Pour in any juices that have accumulated under the steaks.

4 Quickly slice the steaks, crosswise, slightly on the diagonal. Stir the slices into the simmering sauce. Stir and cook for a minute or two, until cooked the way you like it. Serve at once, with oven-fried potatoes or rice with an accompanying salad or salsa nestled next to it on the plate, or on lightly toasted, garlic-rubbed ciabatta bread.

CALORIE COUNT 190 Kcal   **FAT CONTENT** 8g   **PER SERVING**

Lamb in Mustard, Red Wine and Redcurrant Sauce

SERVES 2–4

The thick clinging sauce that coats these lamb slices is almost indecently rich and delicious. You'll swear that it's fattening!

Marinade

2 large garlic cloves, crushed

3 tablespoons roughly chopped fresh thyme

2 tablespoons roughly chopped fresh rosemary

freshly ground mixed peppercorns, to taste

350ml (12fl oz) dry red wine

2–4 well-trimmed lamb leg steaks (125g/4oz each)

oil-water spray

Sauce

90–125ml (3–4fl oz) chicken stock

1 teaspoon wholegrain mustard

1 teaspoon Dijon mustard

1 teaspoon redcurrant jelly

a few drops lemon juice

salt

watercress

Couscous

Makes 1.5 litres (2½ pints)

250ml (8fl oz) well-seasoned vegetable stock

175g (6oz) couscous

3–4 tablespoons chopped fresh parsley

3–4 tablespoons shredded fresh mint

freshly ground pepper to taste

Dressing

300ml (½ pint) vegetable stock

1½–2½ tablespoons balsamic vinegar

1–2 limes

2 garlic cloves, crushed

½ teaspoon ground cumin

1–2 pinches of cayenne pepper

1 Combine the marinade ingredients in a non-reactive container. Put the lamb into the marinade and leave for at least 2 hours.

2 Oil-water-spray a heavy-bottomed non-stick frying-pan and heat. Sear the steaks on both sides so that they are sealed and well browned, but still quite rare. Remove to a waiting plate.

3 To make the sauce, strain the marinade into the frying-pan (press down on the solids and then discard them). Pour in the stock. Boil until reduced by about a

third. Whisk in the mustards, the redcurrant jelly, a few drops of lemon juice and salt to taste. Boil for a minute or so more, until thickened.

4 Slice the lamb across, slightly on the diagonal, and add to the sauce. Stir and cook for 2–3 minutes until cooked the way you like it.

5 Pack the couscous (see below) into 2–4 small ramekins, then unmould on to individual plates. Tip and scrape the lamb and all the syrupy juices across the mounds of couscous and surround with watercress. Alternatively serve the lamb with Sweet Potato Mash (page 109). (Choose lean beef or pork instead of lamb to bring down the fat content.)

To make the Couscous

1 Bring the stock to the boil and add to the couscous in a large bowl. Cover with clingfilm and leave for 10 minutes. Uncover and fluff with a fork.

2 Add all the remaining ingredients including the dressing to the couscous and mix with 2 spoons. Taste and add more seasonings, vinegar and lime juice if necessary.

To make the Dressing

1 In a small frying-pan, combine half the stock, ½ tablespoon balsamic vinegar, the juice of ½ a lime, the garlic, cumin and cayenne. Cover and boil for 5 minutes. Uncover and simmer briskly until the garlic is very tender and the liquid has cooked down to a syrupy glaze.

2 Add the remaining stock and boil until reduced by about half. Stir in 1 additional tablespoon of balsamic vinegar and the juice of ½ a lime or more to taste.

CALORIE COUNT 199 Kcal   **FAT CONTENT** 10g   **PER SERVING**

Pork Steaks with Port-Lime Red Onions

SERVES 2–4

Pork loin steaks are very lean. Jazz up their blandness with a spice rub, and a sauce of lime, red onions and port.

2–4 boneless loin pork steaks, about
    1.5cm (¾in) thick
coarsely ground black pepper
½ teaspoon each of ground cumin,
    coriander and paprika
oil-water spray
salt
1 large red onion, halved and thinly
    sliced

300ml (½ pint) ruby port
300ml (½ pint) chicken or vegetable
    stock
juice of ½–1 juicy lime
1 teaspoon tomato purée
Couscous (see page 167)
chopped fresh coriander and flat-leaf
    parsley
Orange and Red Onion Salsa (page 65)

1 Trim the pork of fat, then rub on both sides with the pepper and other spices. Leave for 15–20 minutes.

2 Oil-water-spray a heavy-bottomed non-stick frying-pan and heat. Season the pork with salt and sear on both sides for a minute or so, until well browned and sealed but not cooked through. Set aside on a waiting plate.

3 Tip the onion into the pan with the port, stock and the juice of ½ the lime. Bring to the boil, reduce the heat and simmer briskly until the onions are wilted.

4 Return the pork to the pan with any rendered juices. Cook, turning the pork in the onions, until the meat is cooked through and glazed, and the onions are tender. Remove the pork, then stir in the tomato purée and more lime juice, salt and pepper, to taste. Slice the pork crosswise, slightly on the diagonal, and put back into the pan. Stir to combine everything well.

5 Pack the couscous into 2–4 ramekins, then unmould on to individual plates. Tip the pork and onions across the couscous, with all the juices. Scatter on the herbs and garnish with salsa.

CALORIE COUNT 217 Kcal   **FAT CONTENT** 5g   **PER SERVING**

PORK TENDERLOIN

Pork tenderloin is very lean, just about the leanest cut of meat available. Overcooking dries it out woefully. Cook until just done (155–160°F internal temperature) so that it remains juicy. Marinate, roast (steam-roast on a rack over boiling water), slice and eat – what could be simpler?

Chinese-inspired Roasted Pork Tenderloin

SERVES 4

Serve this with Chinese-glazed Mushrooms (page 114), rice and Spring Onion Coriander Relish (page 66).

1 pork tenderloin, well trimmed (about 375g/12oz)

Marinade
4 tablespoons teriyaki sauce
2 tablespoons tomato ketchup

3 tablespoons hoisin sauce
2 tablespoons medium dry sherry
2 tablespoons lemon shred marmalade
2 tablespoons soft brown sugar
juice of ¼–½ lemon (to taste)

1 Whisk together all the marinade ingredients. Put the pork in a plastic food bag, pour in the marinade, squeeze out the air, seal, put into a baking dish and refrigerate overnight.

2 Preheat the oven to 240°C/475°F/Gas Mark 9. Line a shallow roasting tin with foil, shiny side up, and place a rack in the tin. Pour water into the roasting tin to a depth of 1cm (½in). Spray the rack lightly with the oil-water spray, and place the pork on the rack. Roast in the oven for 20–25 minutes, turning once half-way through, and basting with a little of the marinade. Let rest for 5 minutes.

3 While the pork is cooking, tip the marinade into a non-reactive frying-pan and simmer for 5 minutes (add a little stock or water if needed).

4 Slice the pork crosswise, slightly on the diagonal. Mix the slices with the marinade. Serve with rice.

CALORIE COUNT 183 Kcal   **FAT CONTENT** 4g   **PER SERVING**

Honey Spice Roasted Pork

SERVES 2

The honey mustard gives this roasted pork a beautiful glaze. Serve with Sweet Potato Gratin (page 109), and Honey Mustard Vinaigrette (page 60) as a dipping sauce for the slices.

3 garlic cloves, crushed
½ tablespoon chopped fresh ginger
4 spring onions, chopped
salt and freshly ground pepper to taste
a generous pinch of ground cumin
a pinch of ground coriander
a pinch of ground paprika

½ tablespoon soy sauce
juice of ½ a lemon
1 tablespoon Dijon mustard
1 tablespoon honey
1 pork tenderloin (300–375g/
   10–12oz) trimmed of all fat

1 Combine all the ingredients except the pork in a liquidizer and purée. Rub the mixture all over the pork. Put the pork and the mixture in a plastic bag and seal. Put into a baking dish. Marinate in the fridge for at least 4 hours. (It may marinate overnight.) Turn the bag occasionally.

2 Preheat the oven to 240°C/475°F/Gas Mark 9.

3 Put the pork on a rack in a shallow roasting pan. Pour in boiling water to a depth of 1cm (½in). Roast for 20–25 minutes, turning once half-way through and brushing occasionally with the marinade until done (the internal temperature will be 155–160°F). Leave for 5 minutes, then slice on the diagonal.

CALORIE COUNT 114 Kcal   **FAT CONTENT** 4g   **PER SERVING**   ☗

SAUSAGES

Make your own little sausage patties out of very lean mince, puréed roasted aubergine (page 30), and whatever herbs and spices you like. The plump, juicy little patties are very good to eat, although they are not – obviously – real sausages; no casings, no lashings of fat. The same technique can be used to make meatballs or burgers; it's all in the size and shape. So use these recipes however you want to.

Sausages: form the mixture into little patties and grill or gently pan-fry in an oil-water-sprayed non-stick frying-pan.

Meatballs: form the mixture into little balls, then grill or pan fry as above, followed by a brief simmering in a tomato or pepper sauce (pages 91–5) if you wish.

Burgers: form into larger burger shapes and grill or pan-fry as above. Serve in rolls or baps with a creamy spread (pages 52–6) on the bottom and Spicy Ketchup (page 57), Grilled Red Pepper Spread (page 56) or mustard on top. Add a dollop of salsa, or some sliced flavour-ripe tomatoes, and a few slivers of red onion. Believe me, one of these burgers, with a side dish of one of the oven-fried potatoes, makes a meal to cherish.

Aubergine note

The amount of roasted aubergine needed will vary with the moisture in the meat, *and* the aubergine. Add less than the whole amount at first, then a little more as needed. You want a sausage, meatball or burger that will not fall apart in the cooking, yet is moist and juicy. If the mixture seems too loose, add a little bit (a tablespoon or so) of breadcrumbs – but the meat must be lean, because breadcrumbs will hold on to fat.

Moroccan-inspired Sausage Patties

MAKES approx. 25 sausage patties

The garlic in these spicy little meatballs will be strong; if you'd rather tone it down, marinate the crushed cloves in the lemon juice, then continue with the recipe. Serve these on a bed of Classic Tomato or Grilled Red Pepper Sauce (pages 91 and 94), or even better, Roasted Butternut Squash and Sweet Potato Sauce (page 100). Add a mound of Couscous (page 167) and garnish with Tomato and Orange Salsa (page 61) and roughly chopped fresh mint and flat-leaf parsley. Or serve the sausages with Roasted Vegetables (page 118), or a Vegetable Stew (page 133) and Couscous.

3 garlic cloves, crushed
juice and grated zest of ½ a small lemon
500g (1lb) lean lamb mince
pulp of a 250g (8oz) roasted aubergine (page 30)
approx. 2 tablespoons each chopped fresh mint and parsley

1 tablespoon tomato purée
2 teaspoons ground cumin
1 teaspoon ground coriander
½ teaspoon ground allspice
1 fresh chilli, cored, seeded, ribbed and finely chopped
salt and freshly ground pepper

1 Preheat the grill to its highest setting. Line the grill tray with foil, shiny side up. Put the rack on the tray, and spray lightly with oil spray.

2 Combine all the ingredients very well. Fry a tiny piece in a non-stick frying-pan and taste for seasoning. Adjust the seasoning as needed.

3 Form the mixture into plump little patties: 500g (1lb) of mince will yield approximately 30–35 plump little patties. (I think this size is best – the sausage is delicate, and several on a plate with sauce, garnishes and vegetable accompaniments look enchanting.) Space the patties on the grill rack so that they are not touching each other (you'll have to do this in batches), and grill with the rack in the upper position (close to the heat) for 3–4 minutes on each side. The idea is to cook them through, so that they are *just* done, and not dried out. They should be quite juicy. You will soon get the hang of it for your particular grill.

4 Line a platter or shallow baking dish with kitchen paper, and put the patties on them in one layer to blot up any rendered fat. (They most likely will not all fit, so put one layer of patties in the dish, cover with more kitchen paper, top with another layer of patties and so on.)

5 The cooked sausage patties may be served at once, or refrigerated for later. To reheat, put stock in a large frying-pan or flameproof casserole to the depth of 1cm (½in). Add the patties in one layer. (You may have to do this in two batches.) Cover, bring to a bare simmer, and simmer *very gently* for 10 minutes or so, or until heated through. If you plan to serve them with a sauce, simmer them gently in the sauce to reheat them. They may also be frozen, either as they are, or in a tomato sauce. Bring the fat down by choosing extra lean pork or beef mince instead of lamb.

CALORIE COUNT 33 Kcal   **FAT CONTENT** 2g   **PER PATTY**

Paprika Meatballs

MAKES 30–35 meatballs

If you have some smoked paprika, use it here. Serve the meatballs in Piccadillo Tomato Sauce (page 92) with flat ribbon noodles, or serve in the Paprikash (pages 150–1) or Peperonata (page 149) mixtures.

500g (1lb) extra lean minced beef	juice of ½ a lemon
chopped pulp from a 250g (8oz)	1 tablespoon paprika
roasted, peeled aubergine (page 30)	salt and freshly ground pepper to taste

1 Preheat the grill to its highest setting. Line the grill tray with foil, shiny side up. Put the rack on the tray, and spray lightly with oil spray.

2 Combine all the ingredients very well. Fry a tiny piece in a non-stick frying-pan and taste for seasoning. Adjust the seasoning as needed.

3 Form the mixture into little balls: 500g (1lb) of mince will yield 30–35 walnut-sized meatballs. Space the meatballs on the grill rack so that they are not touching each other, and grill as described on page 172.

4 Continue with steps 4 and 5 as in the previous recipe, pages 172–3.

CALORIE COUNT 24 Kcal   **FAT CONTENT** <1g   **PER MEATBALL**

Mexican Sausage Patties and Beans

MAKES 750ml (1¼ pints) beans, 30–35 sausage patties   **SERVES** 6

All the components (beans, sausages) can be made well in advance, and refrigerated for a day or so or frozen for months. Serve with tortillas, rice and salsa.

Beans

1 large red onion, chopped

2 large garlic cloves, crushed

1 fresh chilli, seeded, ribbed and
  chopped

½ teaspoon dried oregano, crumbled

½ teaspoon chilli powder

¾ teaspoon ground cumin

¾ teaspoon ground coriander

175ml (6fl oz) stock

1 teaspoon Dijon mustard

475g (15oz) can borlotti beans, drained
  and rinsed

475g (15oz) can pinto beans, drained
  and rinsed

425g (14oz) can chopped tomatoes

salt to taste

2 tablespoons chopped fresh parsley

1 tablespoon chopped fresh coriander

1 In a large frying-pan combine the onion, garlic, chilli, herbs and spices and stock. Simmer until the onions are tender, the spices have lost their raw taste and the liquid is almost gone.

2 Stir in the mustard, beans, tomatoes and salt. Simmer gently, stirring occasionally, for 15–20 minutes until thick and savoury. Stir in the parsley and coriander.

Sausages

500g (1lb) very lean minced pork

chopped pulp from a 250g (8oz)
  roasted aubergine

2 spring onions, chopped

1 tablespoon chopped fresh mint

1 tablespoon chopped fresh coriander

½ teaspoon cumin

½ teaspoon ground coriander

salt and freshly ground pepper to taste

juice and grated rind of ½ a lime

1 tablespoon tomato paste

several dashes Tabasco sauce

1 Preheat the grill. Line the grill tray with foil, shiny side up. Place the grill rack on the tray.

2 Combine all the sausage ingredients in a bowl. Mix well until well blended. Fry a tiny piece in a small non-stick frying-pan (use no fat!) and taste. Adjust the seasonings to your taste.

3 Form the mixture into tiny patties, or meatballs a little smaller than walnuts, and arrange on the grill rack. Grill close to the heat as described in the previous recipe.

To assemble

stock
1 tablespoon Parmesan cheese

1 Preheat the oven to 180°C/350°F/Gas Mark 4.

2 Spread the beans on the bottom of a shallow baking dish and add enough stock to make a slightly soupy mixture. Place the sausages on the bean mixture, pushing them in as you do so. Sprinkle the Parmesan over everything. Cover the dish.

3 Bake for 30–35 minutes, until hot and bubbly.

CALORIE COUNT 310 Kcal   **FAT CONTENT** 5g   **PER SERVING**

Kofta Curry

MAKES 30–35 meatballs   **SERVES** 6

Little lamb meatballs, nestled into a curry sauce, with plenty of interesting garnishes – it's my favourite kind of meal. Lots of different colours, textures and tastes on one plate.

Meatballs
2–3 garlic cloves, crushed
chopped pulp from a 250g (8oz)
   roasted aubergine (see page 30)
500g (1lb) very lean ground lamb (lean
   beef can be used too, if desired)
½ teaspoon ground cinnamon
a pinch of ground cloves
1cm (½ in) fresh ginger, crushed
salt
4 tablespoons chopped fresh coriander
4 tablespoons chopped fresh parsley

Sauce
2 large red onions, cut into eighths

½ teaspoon ground turmeric
½ teaspoon ground cinnamon
2 teaspoons ground coriander
a pinch of cayenne pepper (or to taste)
500ml (16fl oz) stock
2 garlic cloves, crushed
3 tablespoons tomato purée
salt

Garnish
chopped fresh coriander and flat-leaf
   parsley
Cucumber Raita (page 55)

1 Preheat the grill to its highest setting.

2 In a large bowl, combine all the meatball ingredients and mix with your hands until thoroughly amalgamated. Fry a tiny piece in a small frying-pan (use no fat!) and taste. Adjust seasonings to your liking. Form the mixture into small balls, a little smaller than walnuts.

3 Line the grill tray with foil, shiny side up. Place a rack on the tray and arrange the meatballs on it. Grill as described on page 172. Set aside.

4 To make the sauce, put the onion pieces in an oil-water-sprayed heavy, non-reactive frying-pan. Cook, stirring, for a few minutes, until the onions are sizzling, and beginning to wilt. Add the spices and stir for a few seconds.

5 Stir in 300ml (10fl oz) of stock and add the garlic and let it bubble up, stirring up the browned deposits with a wooden spoon as it bubbles. Simmer gently, stirring all the while, until the mixture is very thick (not at all soupy). Taste the mixture and cook very gently for a few more minutes if necessary.

6 Stir in the tomato purée and the remaining 175ml (6fl oz) stock and season to taste. Place the meatballs in this sauce. Simmer gently, covered, for 15–20 minutes, until the sauce is very thick and rich. (If they don't all fit in your pan, put into a baking dish and simmer in the oven at 180°C/350°F/Gas Mark 4. Add more stock as needed.) Serve with Aloo Chat (page 111), Mushrooms with Curry Spices (page 115), rice, and Orange and Red Onion Salsa (page 65). Serve at once, or cool and refrigerate until needed. This tastes good on the second or third day, so do not hesitate to make it in advance. Add more stock when reheating. To serve, strew with herbs and pass the raita. (Use extra lean pork or beef mince in place of lamb to bring down the fat.)

CALORIE COUNT 169 Kcal   **FAT CONTENT** 7g   **PER SERVING**

Commercial Sausages

I love sausages, if only they weren't so greasy – not at all the thing for a low-fat lifestyle. My little sausage patties (page 171) are really marvellous, but as any diehard sausage-lover knows, they are not *real* sausages. A real sausage is stuffed into a casing made out of animal intestine and has that wonderful sausageness that a little meatball, however exquisite, can never achieve. So here's how to rid a real sausage of some of its fat.

First of all buy continental sausages rather than British ones (sorry!). British sausages contain rusk, and rusk stubbornly holds on to fat. Find fresh Italian or French sausages in natural casings in delis and speciality food shops. It's worth searching these out for a special occasion meal. Then:

1 Spray a non-stick pan (of a size to hold your sausages without crowding them) lightly with oil-water spray and heat. Put in the sausages and sear all over. Prick with a thin skewer or cake tester and let them cook in their own fat, turning occasionally with tongs, until browned and sizzling.

2 With tongs, remove the sausages to a plate lined with kitchen paper. Blot them. Blot the frying-pan with kitchen paper but do not wipe out the lovely browned bits. You want to get rid of the grease, not the flavour. Return the sausages to the pan, and pour in 60–90ml (2–3fl oz) each of stock and red wine or port. Let it bubble up, then simmer briskly, turning the sausages, until they are cooked through, gorgeously glazed and sticky, and the liquid is about gone. Serve with garlic mashed potatoes, red wine sauce (page 102) and mustard. ☻

VARIATION: **Sausages and Lentils**

To serve one of the most magnificent dishes known to man and woman:

1 Chop a red onion coarsely and add it to the pan along with a crushed garlic clove as in step 2 above, just before you return the sausages to the pan. Pour in the wine and stock, and simmer, scraping up the browned bits with your wooden spoon, until the onions are wilted.

2 Add the sausages and continue as in step 2 above until they are almost cooked, then add the lentils see page 78 (or a can or two of drained cooked lentils) and another 60–90ml (2–3fl oz) of stock. Leave to cook until the sausages are done. Strew on some chopped fresh flat-leaf parsley and serve.

• To make an onion pan sauce to serve with the sausages (no lentils), put onions and garlic in the pan as in step 1, above. When the onions are tender, add 90ml (3fl oz) of additional wine and boil for a moment. Stir in 6 tablespoons of stock and 1 tablespoon of Dijon mustard. Simmer until reduced somewhat and thickened. ✪

Chorizo

To de-fat Spanish chorizo (the highly spiced sausage used in cooking, not the sliced deli chorizo for sandwiches), prick the sausages with a skewer, put them – in one layer – in a baking dish, and roast, uncovered, in a 200°C/400°F/Gas Mark 6 oven for approximately 10 minutes, until they are swimming in their own fat (to save time you could cut the sausage into chunks before roasting – they will cook faster). Drain away the fat (into a glass jar, not down the sink, unless you love your plumber and want to give him lots of money). Blot the sausage, crumble, and use in omelettes and frittatas and to garnish soups, bean dishes and vegetable stews. ✪

Sweets and Treats

Really good low-fat desserts are not nearly as difficult as you may think. I'm always running into people who go all misty-eyed when they see me, because they are reminded of a chocolate roulade, or a bread pudding, or a cheesecake or a tiramisu (Oh, that tiramisu!) that I've fed them at some point. Your desserts can be memorable yet low-fat; it's simply a matter of stocking up on the right ingredients, and learning a few simple techniques.

INGREDIENTS FOR LOW-FAT DESSERTS

Oil-water spray – You'll need one for desserts, filled seven-eights with water, and one eighth with a tasteless oil: safflower or sunflower, for instance.

Sweeteners – Sugar of course, is essential for dessert-making, so it's wise to stock caster sugar, icing sugar, and various brown sugars. I particularly like coarse granulated brown sugar as a seasoning: sprinkled on fruit desserts at the last minute, it imparts a heavenly texture – if made to wait, the sugar melts and you lose that childishly satisfying crunch. And chocolate icing sugar (sold in boxes) is convenient: a mixture of cocoa and icing sugar. If you can't find it, make your own by sifting together equal parts of icing sugar and low-fat cocoa powder. Keep other sweeteners on hand as well, for interesting depths of flavour: maple syrup, honey, and my favourites – jams, conserves and marmalades. These three are wonderful in low-fat puddings – they add sweetness along with splendid flavour. Look for jars of French no-added-sugar high-fruit spreads and conserves: they come in all sorts of flavours, and are extraordinarily useful.

Wines and spirits – Liqueurs (Cointreau, Kahlua, Cassis, Tia Maria, Crème de Pêche) along with dark rum, sherry and red vermouth, add richness, colour and glamour. In some cases the alcohol is cooked off, in some cases not.

Citrus fruits – Oranges, lemons, limes, for their juice, and their aromatic zest. The zest is the skin without the bitter pith beneath; buy a zester (a handy little gadget with a perforated stubby blade) to easily sliver it into your recipes. Use unwaxed fruit, or scrub before using.

Vanilla extract – Absolutely essential, not only for its exquisite fragrance, but for its ability to enhance other dessert flavours – chocolate for instance. Buy the real thing; ersatz vanilla essence is a very poor substitute (see mail order guide page 213). Natural almond extract is useful too, although it should be used in moderation – it can be very strong.

Chocolate extract – Chocolate extract is a no-fat essence of chocolate; very powerful and intense. It is available by mail order (see page 213) if you can't get it locally.

Amaretti biscuits and Grape Nut cereal – A seemingly odd Italian American duo that I use together to make crumble toppings and crumb crusts for cheesecakes. Choose the Amaretti that are flavoured with apricot kernels rather than high-fat almonds (they come in pairs in pretty paper wrappers).

Sunsweet Lighter Bake and Whitworths Apri Lite – Two superb commercial products used for low-fat baking. Lighter Bake is a prune-apple purée; Apri Lite is an apricot purée. Both are used as fat substitutes in traditional cake (not pastry) making. The rule of thumb is: omit the fat from your cake recipe, and substitute half the amount of Lighter Bake or Apri Lite. One tablespoon of Lighter Bake equals 20g (¾oz); One tablespoon of Apri Lite equals 15g (½oz). The results will not be identical to your original recipe, but they will be very good indeed.

Chocolate – What would life be without it? Use what my son calls industrial strength chocolate – in other words, dark, plain, high cocoa solid (60–70 per cent) chocolate. It's powerful stuff – you'll need very little to add a real chocolate whammy to your special desserts. Depend on low-fat cocoa powder as well (dark, rich, deeply chocolaty). Both are available by mail order (see page 213).

Instant espresso powder – For flavouring mocha-flavoured cakes.

Eggs – Egg whites are virtually no-fat and are used in cakes, meringue, clafoutis and bread puddings. The whole egg is useful too, of course, but do try to limit yourself to 4–5 a week at the most. To cut back on eggs, you can use egg whites instead of whole eggs in many traditional cakes: for every 2 eggs called for in the recipe, use 3 egg whites.

Dairy products – Use the following in place of whole milk, cream, whipped cream, crème fraîche, cream cheese, and mascarpone.
• Quark
• Very low-fat fromage frais
• Very low-fat yogurt
• Ricotta cheese
• Very low-fat soft cheese (6 per cent fat)
• Skimmed milk
• Skimmed milk powder
• Sweetened condensed skimmed milk

ANGEL CAKES

I've written about these classics before, but no low-fat lifestyle cookbook would be complete without them, so you *must* have them here. An angel cake has no added fat *at all*. No egg yolks. No butter or oil. No oil-water spray. It is as pure, blameless, and fatless as the driven snow. It's actually rather like a dense soufflé made with added flour, and must be baked in a special, removable-bottomed angel-cake tin (easily obtained – see mail order, guide, page 213). I'm giving you all the angel cake possibilities, plus ideas for dressing them up.

Vanilla Angel Cake

MAKES 12 slices

125g (4oz) plain flour
275g (9oz) caster sugar
10 egg whites, at room temperature

pinch of cream of tartar
1½ teaspoons natural vanilla extract

1 Preheat the oven to 190°C/375°F/Gas Mark 5.

2 Sift the flour and 100g (3½oz) of sugar together into a bowl and set aside.

3 Put the egg whites into a large bowl and beat with an electric mixer until foamy. Add the cream of tartar and beat until the egg whites hold soft peaks. Continue beating, adding the remaining 175g (5½oz) sugar, 2 tablespoons at a time, until the sugar is dissolved and the whites are stiff and glossy. Fold in the vanilla.

4 A little at a time, sprinkle the sifted flour/sugar mixture over the egg whites and fold in gently but thoroughly.

5 Gently spoon and push the meringue into an ungreased 25cm (10in) diameter, 10cm (4in) deep angel-cake tube tin. Bake for 30–35 minutes. When it is done the top will most likely have cracked like a soufflé. The cake will spring back when gently pressed with your finger, and a cake tester will come out clean when inserted gently into the cake.

6 Cool *upside down* by inverting the cake (in its tin) over a bottle (the neck of the bottle should come right up through the tube), or on an inverted funnel. (Some angel-cake tins have small 'feet' around the rim on which to stand the upside-down tin while the cake cools.) Leave for at least 1 hour.

7 Use a long palette knife to loosen the cake gently around the sides and bottom of the tin, and around the tube. Gently shake, and turn out on to a plate. To serve, cut gently, using a sawing motion, with a long, sharp, serrated knife.

CALORIE COUNT 133 Kcal   **FAT CONTENT** <0.5g   **PER SLICE**

VARIATIONS

Spiced Angel: Sift a small amount (⅛–¼ teaspoon) of ground spice into the flour in step 2. Choose nutmeg, cinnamon or mixed spice. ♥

Citrus-Scented Angel: Fold some grated orange, lemon or lime zest into the beaten egg whites. ♥

Chocolate Angel Cake: Reduce the amount of flour to 90g (3oz) and in step 2, sift in 6 tablespoons of unsweetened low-fat cocoa with the sugar and flour. ♥

Other Possible Flavours: Use almond extract or rose water in place of the vanilla extract. ♥

To serve

Serve slices of the angel cake with scoops of ice-cream or sorbet (pages 199–200), with a tumble of fresh berries. Cubes of angel cake can be used in trifles.

Angel Sheet Cakes

SERVES 8

Any angel cake can be baked flat, filled and rolled into a roulade. Use one of the creams on pages 201–2 to fill the roulade, and it will taste very rich and fattening – not at all like a low-fat dessert.

(a) Vanilla Angel Sheet Cake	**(b) Chocolate Angel Sheet Cake**
60g (2oz) plain light flour	45g (1½oz) plain flour
140g (4½oz) caster sugar	3 tablespoons unsweetened low-fat cocoa
5 egg whites, at room temperature	140g (4½oz) caster sugar
pinch of cream of tartar	5 egg whites, at room temperature
1½ teaspoons natural vanilla extract	pinch of cream of tartar
	1 teaspoon natural vanilla extract

1 Preheat the oven to 180°C/350°F/Gas Mark 4. Line a 33 × 23cm (13 × 9in) Swiss roll tin with baking parchment.

2 Sift the flour (and cocoa for the chocolate version) and 75g (2½oz) of sugar together into a bowl, and set aside.

3 Put the egg whites into a large bowl and beat with an electric mixer until foamy. Add the cream of tartar and beat until the egg whites hold soft peaks. Continue beating, adding the remaining 60g (2oz sugar), 2 tablespoons at a time, until the sugar is dissolved, and the whites are stiff and glossy. Fold in the vanilla.

4 A little at a time, sprinkle the sifted flour/sugar mixture over the egg whites and fold in gently but thoroughly.

5 Gently spoon the meringue into the prepared tin and bake for 10–15 minutes until done. Leave to cool in the tin on a wire rack, then flip over on to a clean tea-towel and peel off the greaseproof paper.

6 To fill, spread the cake with one of the creams, leaving a 1cm (½in) border around the edges. Starting with a long edge, carefully roll the cake, using the tea-towel to help you along. The cake may crack, but it won't matter. Carefully transfer to a platter. To decorate the cake, sift on some icing sugar, or icing sugar sifted with cocoa, or pipe on rosettes of one of the creams on pages 201–2.

CALORIE COUNT (Vanilla) 102 Kcal   **FAT CONTENT** Neg   **PER SERVING**

CALORIE COUNT (Chocolate) 103 Kcal   **FAT CONTENT** 0.5g   **PER SERVING**

Chocolate Roulade

SERVES 8

A chocolate soufflé baked flat on a baking sheet makes an intense, rich base for a roulade. Choose a filling from the list on pages 201–2.

9 tablespoons caster sugar	pinch of cream of tartar
9 tablespoons unsweetened low-fat cocoa	1½ teaspoons natural vanilla extract
9 egg whites, at room temperature	1½ teaspoons dark rum
	icing sugar

1 Preheat the oven to 180°C/350°F/Gas Mark 4.

2 Line a non-stick baking sheet measuring 33 × 23cm (13 × 9in) with silicone baking paper. Set aside.

3 Sift together all but 2 tablespoons of the sugar with all of the cocoa. Set aside.

4 In an electric mixer, beat the egg whites with the cream of tartar until foamy. At highest speed, continue beating, adding the remaining 2 tablespoons of plain sugar a little at a time, until the whites hold stiff peaks.

5 With a rubber spatula, fold the sugar-cocoa mixture into the beaten whites. Fold in the vanilla and rum.

6 Gently and evenly spread the mixture on to the prepared baking sheet. Bake for 20–30 minutes (a toothpick should test *almost* clean). Cool the pan on a rack.

7 Spread a clean tea-towel on your work surface. Cover with a sheet of waxed or greaseproof paper. Sprinkle evenly with icing sugar. When thoroughly cooled, turn the roulade base out on to the paper and peel off the baking paper.

8 To fill, spread with your chosen cream (see pages 201–2). Starting from the long edge, roll the roulade base like a Swiss roll. Use the tea-towel to help you roll it. It may crack a bit, but it doesn't matter. Chill until needed. Serve in slices.

CALORIE COUNT 10 Kcal   **FAT CONTENT** <1g   **PER SERVING**

OVERLEAF *Spicy Plum Crumble (page 195)*
OPPOSITE *Chocolate Layer Cake with Mocha Cream Filling and Chocolate Glaze (page 187)*

Layer Cake

MAKES 12 slices

This is a basic cake recipe using Lighter Bake (page 180), the prune/apple purée fat substitute. Fill the layers with one of the creams on pages 201–2, and top with Marmalade Glaze (see below) or Buttermilk Glaze (page 191).

4½ tablespoons Lighter Bake	grated zest of 1 orange and 1 lemon
175g (6oz) caster sugar	175g (6oz) self-raising flour, sifted
3 eggs	

1 Preheat the oven to 180°C/350°F/Gas Mark 4. Line the base and sides of two 18cm (7in) sandwich cake tins with baking parchment.

2 Whisk together the Lighter Bake, sugar, eggs and zest until foamy, then fold in the flour. Divide the mixture between the two prepared tins. Bake in the oven for 12–15 minutes until the cakes are pale golden and spring back when lightly touched. Turn out and leave to cool on wire racks.

CALORIE COUNT 138 Kcal   **FAT CONTENT** 2g   **PER SLICE**

Marmalade Glaze

Melt some marmalade or jam in a frying-pan or small saucepan with a little orange-flavoured liqueur (Cointreau or Grand Marnier) or water. Use a pastry brush to brush it on to the cake layers.

Chocolate Layer Cake with Mocha Cream Filling and Chocolate Glaze

MAKES 12 slices

A celebration cake that will satisfy the deep chocolate-loving corners of your soul.

90g (3oz) plain light flour

6 tablespoons unsweetened low-fat cocoa powder

275g (9oz) caster sugar

10 egg whites, at room temperature

pinch of cream of tartar

1½ teaspoons natural vanilla extract

2 teaspoons chocolate extract (see mail order guide, page 213)

45g (1½oz) high-cocoa-solid chocolate, grated

Mocha Syrup (page 188)

Mocha Cream (page 188)

Chocolate Glaze (page 188)

1 Preheat the oven to 180°C/350°F/Gas Mark 4. Line two 20cm (8in) cake tins with silicone paper.

2 Sift together the flour, cocoa and 100g (3½oz) of sugar. Beat the egg whites until foamy. Add the cream of tartar and beat until they hold soft peaks. Continue beating, adding the remaining 175g (5½oz) of sugar, 2 tablespoons at a time, until the sugar is dissolved, and the whites are stiff and glossy. Fold in the vanilla, chocolate extract and 30g (1oz) of grated chocolate. A little at a time, sprinkle the sifted flour/sugar mixture over the batter and fold in gently but thoroughly.

3 Gently spoon the meringue into the prepared cake tins. Smooth the top. Bake for approximately 15 minutes, until the top springs back when gently pressed. Cool on a rack, then gently remove from the tins and peel off the baking paper. Be careful – the layers are very fragile.

4 Put one of the cake layers on a plate. Prick it in several places with a fork or skewer. Pour half of the Mocha Syrup over the cake, and tilt the plate to distribute evenly. Sprinkle with the remaining 15g (½oz) of grated chocolate. Chill for an hour or so.

5 Spread the cake with half the Mocha Cream. Top with the second layer (make sure that the more attractive side is on top). Pour on the Chocolate Glaze and spread it evenly with a palette knife. Chill until needed. Serve with the remaining Mocha Cream, to be dolloped over each slice (over-kill!).

CALORIE COUNT 271 Kcal   **FAT CONTENT** 7g   **PER SLICE**

Mocha Syrup

1 tablespoon espresso coffee powder

120g (4oz) demerara sugar

120ml (4fl oz) boiling water

45g (1½oz) finely grated high-cocoa-
solid chocolate

Combine the espresso powder, sugar and water. Stir to dissolve the sugar. Slowly pour the mixture over 1oz of the chocolate (in a bowl), stirring until the chocolate is smooth and melted. Set aside to cool.

Mocha Cream

2 × 250g (8oz) cartons ricotta

½ quantity Mocha Syrup (see above)

Put the ricotta in a food processor (or use a bowl and a hand-held electric mixer). Pour half the cooled Mocha Syrup over the ricotta, and process until very well blended.

Chocolate Glaze

2 tablespoons chocolate icing sugar

½ teaspoon pure vanilla extract

½ teaspoon chocolate extract

approx. 1 tablespoon buttermilk

Put the sugar into a bowl. Using a hand-held electric mixer, beat in the extracts and the buttermilk, a dribble at a time. Beat until the mixture is of a thick pouring consistency.

CALORIE COUNT 271 Kcal **FAT CONTENT** 7g **PER SLICE**

VARIATION: Mocha Roulade

Spread the cake mixture on to a 37 × 25cm (15 × 25in) baking sheet lined with parchment paper, and bake for 10–12 minutes. Allow to cool slightly, then turn out on to a clean tea-towel. Pierce the cake in several places with a tester and sprinkle over one-third of the Mocha Syrup. Fill with the Mocha Cream and roll. Mix the remaining syrup with 1 tablespoon of finely grated dark chocolate and spread over the cake. Refrigerate overnight. Before serving, trim a thin slice off each end to neaten it.

Chocolate Chestnut Layer Cake

SERVES 10

Another celebration, with chocolate chestnut cream rather than mocha. Deeply, sensual chocolate and, again, not at all what you would expect from a lower-fat cake.

90g (3oz) plain light flour	1 teaspoon natural vanilla extract
6 tablespoons unsweetened fat-reduced cocoa powder	1 teaspoon chocolate extract (see mail order guide, page 213)
275g (9oz) caster sugar	45g (1½oz) high-cocoa-solid chocolate, grated
10 egg whites, at room temperature	
pinch of cream of tartar	Chocolate Chestnut Spread (see over)

1 Preheat the oven to 180°C/350°F/Gas Mark 4. Line two 20cm (8in) cake tins with silicone baking paper.

2 Sift the flour, cocoa powder and 100g (3½oz) of sugar into a bowl and set aside.

3 Put the egg whites into a large bowl and beat with a hand-held electric mixer until foamy. Add the cream of tartar and beat until the egg whites hold soft peaks. Continue beating, adding the remaining sugar, 2 tablespoons at a time, until the sugar is dissolved and the whites are stiff and glossy. Fold in the vanilla, chocolate extract and 30g (1oz) of grated chocolate.

4 A little at a time, sprinkle the sifted flour/sugar mixture over the egg-white mixture and fold in gently but thoroughly.

5 Gently spoon the meringue into the prepared tins and smooth the tops. Bake in the oven for 15–20 minutes until the tops spring back when gently pressed with your finger, and a cake tester inserted in the centre of each cake comes out clean.

6 Leave to cool in the tins on a wire rack, then gently remove from the tins and peel off the baking paper. Be careful – they are very fragile. With a sharp serrated knife, split each one in half to form 4 layers.

7 Put a cake layer on a plate, slather with Chocolate Chestnut Spread, and top with another layer. Continue until all the layers are stacked. Top with more of the spread and sprinkle with the remaining grated chocolate. Cover and refrigerate until needed.

CALORIE COUNT 326 Kcal   **FAT CONTENT** 8g   **PER SERVING**   Ⓥ Ⓨ Ⓞ

Chocolate Chestnut Spread

MAKES 250ml (8fl oz) **SERVES** 10

125g (4oz) unsweetened chestnut purée (available in cans)

60g (2oz) high-cocoa-solid dark chocolate, melted

1 tablespoon low-fat unsweetened cocoa powder

3 tablespoons condensed sweetened skimmed milk

1 tablespoon vanilla extract

200g (7oz) carton very low-fat soft cheese

Put all the ingredients in a food processor and process until perfectly smooth. Transfer to a bowl, cover and chill until required.

CALORIE COUNT 10 Kcal **FAT CONTENT** 4g **PER TABLESPOON**

Poppy Seed and Sherry Banana Loaf

SERVES 10

The poppy seeds give this tea loaf a nice crunch, and the banana and cream sherry flavours contribute a perception of great richness. This improves with age – wrap in foil, and hide it for a day or so.

2 bananas, well ripened, peeled and mashed

250ml (8fl oz) cream sherry

juice of ½ a lemon

150g (5oz) soft brown sugar

300g (10oz) self-raising flour

pinch of salt

2 tablespoons poppy seeds

2 egg whites, lightly beaten

oil-water spray (page 180)

Buttermilk Glaze (see below)

1 Preheat the oven to 170°C/325°F/Gas Mark 3.

2 Mash the bananas and mix with the sherry and lemon juice.

3 Sift the sugar, flour, and salt into a bowl, scatter on the poppy seeds and add the banana mixture and the egg whites. Mix together and incorporate well.

4 Line a 20cm (8in) non-stick cake tin with greaseproof paper. Spray with oil spray. Transfer the mixture to the tin, smooth the top, and bake in the oven for approximately 1 hour.

5 When the cake is risen and golden brown, check that it is done by inserting a metal skewer or toothpick into the centre. When it comes out clean the cake is done.

6 Cool on a rack for a few minutes. With a palette knife, loosen carefully all around the sides and turn out. Peel off the greaseproof paper. Cool thoroughly. Store, wrapped in foil. (This is best on the second day: the flavour develops beautifully, and seems to improve with age!) When you plan to serve it, glaze, then let it sit for about a half an hour for the glaze to set. For a lower-fat cake simply omit the poppy seeds.

Buttermilk Glaze
3 tablespoons icing sugar

½ teaspoon pure vanilla extract
approx. 1 tablespoon buttermilk

Put the icing sugar in a bowl. With a handheld electric mixer, beat in the vanilla and dribble in the buttermilk. Beat until the mixture is of a thick pouring consistency. Pour evenly in a strip across the top of the cake, from one end to the other. Tilt one way, then the other, to encourage the glaze to flow and drip down the sides.

CALORIE COUNT 166 Kcal   **FAT CONTENT** 2g   **PER SERVING**

FRUIT

Fruit is the obvious choice for low-fat, high-nutrition puddings and sweets, but do be sure that the fruit is the best, ripest, juiciest, sweetest it can be (see pages 8–9). A very simple fruit combo can be unbelievably satisfying and refreshing. For instance, halve a ripe Galia melon, scoop out the seeds, and fill the hollow with perfect raspberries. Over-fill, so that the berries spill out on to the plate. Sprinkle with 1½ teaspoons of coarse granulated brown sugar, and eat *at once*, while the sugar is crunchy. Really, how can you improve on such bounty?

Fruit Salad

MAKES about 1.25 litres (2 pints)

Fruit salads should always be made with the best of the season. The following recipe is only one idea. Try berries and peach or nectarine cubes in fresh orange and lime juice with a dash of vanilla and Crème de Pêche. Or try fresh orange segments in orange and lime juice with some of the grated zest, and Cointreau. Or halved, perfectly ripe strawberries with lemon juice, a bit of sugar, and a dash of balsamic vinegar.

1 medium ripe melon (Galia or Canteloupe)	1 teaspoon syrup from ginger jar
	juice of ½ a lime
1 ripe mango	juice of ½ an orange
1 ripe papaya	1–3 tablespoons orange liqueur
1 ripe pineapple	1 tablespoon banana jam or ginger
1 piece of stem ginger	preserves

1 Peel, seed, trim and generally prepare the fruit, and cut it all into 3.5cm (1½in) cubes. Chop the ginger into tiny pieces.

2 Combine the fruit with all the remaining ingredients. Using 2 spoons, mix together until the jam is dissolved and everything is well combined. Refrigerate until needed.

CALORIE COUNT 205 Kcal   **FAT CONTENT** <1g   **PER ½ PINT**

Berry Cream

SERVES 2

Any berries or combination of berries can be used here. Soft sugar is sprinkled on top, and allowed to 'melt' (the acid in the berries and the fromage frais caramelizes it). No 'crunch' this time, but lovely flavour.

125g (4oz) ricotta
2 tablespoons no-fat fromage frais
1 teaspoon natural vanilla extract
approx. ½ tablespoon wild blueberry
   conserve, raspberry jam, strawberry
   jam or orange marmalade (to taste)

250g (8oz) blueberries, raspberries or
   hulled, quartered strawberries
1 teaspoon soft brown sugar

1 Combine the ricotta, fromage frais, vanilla and conserve in the food processor and process until well mixed and fluffy. Scrape into a bowl and fold in the berries, then divide between two 275ml (9fl oz) wine goblets.

2 Evenly sprinkle the sugar over the surface of the contents of each goblet. Set aside for 5–7 minutes for the sugar to 'melt'. To make a lower-fat version use Quark or no-fat fromage frais in place of the ricotta.

CALORIE COUNT 155 Kcal   **FAT CONTENT** 7g   **PER SERVING**

Pear Clafoutis

SERVES 6

A clafoutis is a puffy, oven-baked fruit-filled pancake, very like a sweet, fruity Yorkshire pudding. This low-fat version is packed with pears, dried cherries and dried apricots.

Batter
oil-water spray
100g (3½oz) light plain flour
100g (3½oz) light brown sugar
3 tablespoons skimmed milk powder
300ml (½ pint) skimmed milk
6 tablespoons very low-fat natural yogurt
4 egg whites
2 teaspoons vanilla extract

Fruit
675g (1lb 6oz) pears, peeled, cored
  and coarsely diced
3 tablespoons dried cherries
6 dried apricots, diced
a pinch each of cinnamon and ground
  mace
½ tablespoon lemon juice
½ tablespoon lime juice
¼ teaspoon demerara sugar

1 Preheat the oven to 190°C/375°F/Gas Mark 5. Oil-water spray a 25cm (10in) non-stick flan tin.

2 Sift the flour, sugar and milk powder into a bowl. Whisk together the milk, yogurt, egg whites and vanilla. Pour into the flour mixture and stir until just mixed, with no lumps.

3 Combine the fruit and juices (but not the demerara sugar).

4 Pour the batter into the flan tin, and scatter the fruit and its juices over the top, leaving a 2.5cm (1in) border all around. Sprinkle on the demerara sugar and bake for 30–40 minutes until set, lightly browned and puffed. Cool on a rack. Serve warm or at room temperature.

CALORIE COUNT 257 Kcal   **FAT CONTENT** <1g   **PER SERVING**

Spicy Plum Crumble

SERVES 4–6

I love old-fashioned puddings: crumbles, bread puddings, all that warming, comforting mother food. The addition of ground pepper may seem odd, but it brings the plums (especially less than brilliant supermarket plums) to life, and adds to the spiced character of the crumble.

Compote

1.625kg (3¼lb) plums, stoned and cut into wedges

1 tablespoon natural vanilla extract

⅛ teaspoon ground allspice

¼ teaspoon ground cinnamon

⅛ teaspoon ground ginger

a pinch of salt

1 tablespoon cornflour

juice of 1 large juicy orange

3 tablespoons lemon shred marmalade

1 tablespoon dark rum

a good grinding of mixed peppercorns

Topping

90g (3oz) Grape Nuts cereal

6 pairs Amaretti biscuits

1 whole egg

2 egg whites

1 teaspoon natural vanilla extract

1 Combine all the compote ingredients in a saucepan or non-stick wok. Simmer, stirring frequently, until the plums are tender but not mushy, and coated in a glossy, syrupy sauce. This takes 7–10 minutes. Pour the compote into a baking dish.

2 Combine the Grape Nuts and Amaretti in a food processor or blender, and process to crumbs. Pour in the egg, the egg whites and vanilla, process to a mush, then spread evenly over the plums, leaving a 1cm (½in) border all around.

3 Bake the crumble in a 200°C/400°F/Gas mark 6 preheated oven for 7–10 minutes, until the top is set and the juices are bubbling.

4 Serve the crumble warm. Choose one of the fruit-flavoured cream toppings on pages 201–2 to serve alongside.

CALORIE COUNT 425 Kcal   **FAT CONTENT** 3g   **PER SERVING**

CHEESECAKES

I grew up in New York City, so I think cheesecake is the ultimate dessert. It's not really a dessert but an entity in itself, to be eaten for celebrations, emotional crises, family and friends get-togethers, and Sunday brunch. I wrote about cheesecake extensively in my *Low-Fat Desserts* book, and I was (and still am) extremely elated to have finally created a good low-fat version of the real New York thing.

In this collection, I'm going to give you a marvellous Chocolate and Banana Cheesecake. You'll need a crumb crust, but the usual digestive biscuit and butter base would ruin the cheesecake's low-fat profile. Haul out your Amaretti and Grape Nuts (page 180) and make this low-fat version.

Chocolate Crumb Crust

150g (5oz) Grape Nuts
150g (5oz) Amaretti biscuits
½ teaspoon cinnamon
¼ teaspoon allspice

1 tablespoon chocolate extract
4 egg whites
oil-water spray

1 Preheat the oven to 180°C/350°F/Gas Mark 4.

2 Put the biscuits and cereal into a blender or processor and process to coarse crumbs. Add the cinnamon, allspice and chocolate extract.

3 Lightly beat the egg whites and mix with the crumb mixture until thoroughly combined.

4 Lightly spray a 25cm (10in) round spring-form tin with oil spray. Scrape the crumb mixture into the pan. With the back of a serving spoon, spread it evenly over the bottom and up the sides.

5 Bake for 7–10 minutes, then cool on a rack.

CALORIE COUNT 1217 Kcal **FAT CONTENT** 9g **PER CRUST**

Chocolate and Banana Cheesecake

SERVES 12

Bananas give their rich texture and intense sweetness to this cheesecake. The banana tastes so rich and fattening, yet is virtually non-fat.

500g (1lb) very low-fat soft cheese
175g (6oz) caster sugar
1 tablespoon lime juice
1 tablespoon vanilla extract
1 whole large egg
4 large egg whites
1 teaspoon each of grated rind of lemon,
  lime and orange

250ml (8fl oz) very low-fat fromage frais
3 medium-sized ripe bananas (mashed)
45g (1½oz) grated dark chocolate
25cm (10oz) Chocolate Crumb Crust
  (see opposite)

1 Preheat the oven to 180°C/350°F/Gas Mark 4.

2 Beat together the cream cheese, sugar and lime juice. Add the vanilla. Beat in the whole egg and the egg whites, one at a time. Beat in the citrus rind, the fromage frais and bananas. Fold in the chocolate. Pour into the crumb crust.

3 Bake for 1 hour, then turn off the oven and leave in the cooling oven for 1 hour. Cool on a rack, then refrigerate overnight before removing the sides of the tin.

CALORIE COUNT 377 Kcal   **FAT CONTENT** 5g   **PER SERVING**

Rum Raisin Cheesecake Mousse

SERVES 4

Deconstruct a cheesecake, then put it back together in a glass, for an easy and pretty creamy dessert. Amaretti, Grape Nuts and egg whites are baked into little biscuits; Quark, ricotta and orange marmalade are whipped into a creamy mousse, enriched with a heady rum and raisin infusion.

65g (2½oz) Amaretti biscuits	5 tablespoons orange juice
65g (2½oz) Grape Nut cereal	zest of 1 orange and ½ a lemon
2 egg whites	250g (8oz) Quark
oil-water spray	250g (8oz) ricotta cheese
6 tablespoons raisins	approx. ½ tablespoon orange
4 tablespoons dark rum	marmalade (to taste)
1 teaspoon natural vanilla extract	

1 Preheat the oven to 180°C/350°F/Gas Mark 4. Break up the biscuits into a food processor, add the Grape Nuts and process to fine crumbs. Lightly whisk the egg whites and process into the crumbs. Spray a non-stick baking sheet with oil-water spray. With a tablespoon measure, spoon equal amounts of the crumb mixture on to the tray and shape with the back of the spoon and your fingers into 5cm (2in) diameter rounds. You will have 10 biscuit rounds in all. Bake in the oven for 5–7 minutes until set. Cool, then loosen with a flexible palette knife.

2 Meanwhile combine the raisins, rum, vanilla, juice and zest in a small frying-pan. Simmer until the raisins are plump and the liquid is almost gone. Cool. (You can fast-chill them by spreading them on a plate and putting them in the freezer for 10–15 minutes.)

3 Combine half of the thoroughly cooled raisin mixture with the Quark and ricotta in the food processor. Process for a moment or so. Taste, and sweeten to your taste with orange marmalade. Process until fluffy. By the time you have finished processing, the raisins will just be flecks in the snowy cheese.

4 Place one biscuit in the bottom of each of four 9cm/3½in diameter, 175ml/6fl oz dessert goblets. Divide the creamed raisin cheese between each of the glasses and top with a spoonful of the reserved raisins. Chill for several hours or overnight. The cheese mixture will thicken during this time. Cut 4 of the remaining biscuits

in half and set aside. At serving time, set 2 biscuit halves into each mound of mousse at a jaunty angle, like gaufrettes in a scoop of sorbet. (The two remaining biscuits are for a private nibble. Enjoy them.)

CALORIE COUNT 438 Kcal   **FAT CONTENT** 8g   **PER SERVING**

VARIATION: **Cranberry Port Cheesecake Mousse**

Substitute dried cranberries and cherries for the raisins and port for the rum. (And to make it lower fat substitute fromage frais or Quark for the ricotta.)

175ml (6fl oz) orange juice

175ml (6fl oz) ruby port

grated zest of ½ an orange

a few drops of lemon juice

1 cinnamon stick

a mixture of dried cranberries and dried cherries (90g/3oz each)

1 teaspoon natural vanilla extract

a pinch of ground ginger

Combine all the ingredients in a small frying-pan. Simmer until the fruits are plump and the liquid just about gone. Combine with the cheese mixture as in step 3 above.

PROCESSOR ICE-CREAMS AND SORBETS

This is certainly the handiest low-fat dessert technique there is, perfect for instant gratification. Because the sorbets and ice-creams are almost pure fruit, they are very nutritious as well. Keep frozen fruit in the freezer so that you can make this at a moment's notice. Freeze cubed fruit (or whole berries, or sliced, peeled bananas) flat on baking trays, then – when solidly frozen – gather into plastic bags and keep frozen until needed. When you're ready, knock the bag on the counter to break up the frozen pieces, then tip into the processor with a bit of marmalade or conserve and 1–3 tablespoons of buttermilk, yogurt, or fromage frais. For very tart fruits (raspberries for instance), use 1–3 tablespoons of sweetened, condensed skimmed milk. (This makes an exceptionally velvety ice-cream.) Add a dash of vanilla extract, a squeeze of lemon or lime juice, process (stopping to scrape down the container as needed) until gorgeously creamy and serve *at once*. It will take less than 5 minutes. The ice-cream won't freeze well (it becomes too icy, grainy and hard), so eat while it's perfect, just after it is finished. To make sorbet instead of ice-cream, use fruit juice in place of the buttermilk, fromage frais, etc.

Banana Ice-Cream

MAKES 900ml (1½ pints)

Frozen bananas make the creamiest instant ice-cream you can imagine; it tastes very indulgent.

6 ripe bananas (approximately 625g (1¼lb), peeled, cut into slices and frozen (see page 199)

1–2 tablespoons very low-fat fromage frais

1–2 tablespoons Chiquita banana drink or orange juice

1 teaspoon natural vanilla extract

splash of rum or Cointreau

a few drops of lime juice

1 Put the *still frozen* banana pieces into the container of your food processor, along with 1 tablespoon fromage frais, 1 tablespoon drink/juice, the vanilla extract and the optional liqueur. Turn the machine on.

2 Add another ½ tablespoon of fromage frais and the lime juice and process. Stop and scrape down the sides occasionally, then start the machine again. When it forms a super-creamy, smooth (no ice crystals), soft ice-cream consistency, it is done. Add a bit more fromage frais and juice if necessary to reach that state.

CALORIE COUNT 102 Kcal   **FAT CONTENT** <0.5g   **PER ¼ PINT**   ♥

Blueberry Ice-Cream or Sorbet

MAKES 450ml (¾ pint)

When fresh blueberries are in season, freeze them for future ice-cream moments, otherwise look for frozen ones in the supermarket.

250g (8oz) carton of frozen blueberries

1 tablespoon blueberry conserve

3 tablespoons buttermilk or fromage frais

approx. 1 tablespoon fresh strained

orange juice

approx. 1 tablespoon fresh strained lemon juice

fresh blueberries for garnish (optional)

1 Put the blueberries (do not thaw them) into the food processor with half the blueberry conserve. Process to coarse icy crumbs. With the machine still running, dribble in 1 tablespoon of buttermilk. When well mixed in, stop the machine and taste for sweetness. Add up to ½ tablespoon more conserve, to your taste.

2 Turn the processor on again and dribble in 1 more tablespoon of buttermilk. Stop to scrape down the sides as needed. Squeeze in a few drops of orange and lemon juice. When the mixture forms a smooth, creamy ice-cream, and when the taste pleases you, it is ready to eat. Add up to 1 additional tablespoon of buttermilk and a few more drops of citrus juice as needed, for texture and taste. Serve at once in glass goblets. Garnish each serving with a scattering of fresh blueberries, if available.

CALORIE COUNT 88 Kcal   **FAT CONTENT** <0.5g   **PER ¼ PINT**

CREAM TOPPINGS AND FILLINGS

Ricotta cheese (14 per cent) is my choice for a whipped cream, mascarpone, crème fraiche substitute. The substitute is no compromise at all; it is good enough to serve to any one – even the fat eaters – without fear of disappointment. The ricotta can be cut half and half with Quark, fromage frais or drained yogurt (page 29) to cut the 14 per cent fat level in half or – for those who must avoid fat entirely – use just fromage frais, Quark or yogurt, or a combination, will do nicely.

To make a delectable creamy topping, or a filling for roulades, put the ricotta in the processor with 1–3 tablespoons, to taste, of marmalade, jam or conserve, and a dash or two of vanilla extract. Process until fluffy.

Orange Cream

MAKES 450ml (¾ pint)

500g (1lb) Quark (or ricotta cheese or a combination)

2 heaped tablespoons orange marmalade or no-added-sugar, high-fruit orange spread

1 teaspoon natural vanilla extract

1 tablespoon orange liqueur (Grand Marnier or Cointreau)

Put all the ingredients in a food processor and process until well mixed and fluffy.

CALORIE COUNT 17 Kcal   **FAT CONTENT** Neg   **PER TABLESPOON**

Substitute other marmalades, jams, conserves or spreads for the orange, for instance: • wild blueberry conserve • black cherry conserve • apricot no-added-sugar, high-fruit spread • peach conserve • Lemon Shred marmalade

Honey or Maple Vanilla Cream

MAKES 550ml (18fl oz)

1 vanilla pod	500g (1lb) very low-fat fromage frais (or
2 tablespoons runny honey or maple	ricotta cheese, or a combination if
syrup	you can take a little fat)

1 With a small, sharp knife, split the vanilla pod lengthwise. With the tip of the knife, scrape the soft pulp from each half into the fromage frais or ricotta. (Save the scraped pod to store in a canister of caster sugar or to simmer in dried fruit compote.)

2 Whisk the honey into the fromage frais. (Or, if you are using ricotta, process in a food processor with the honey.) Stir so that the black vanilla bean specks are evenly distributed through the fromage frais. Store in the refrigerator.

CALORIE COUNT 10 Kcal   **FAT CONTENT** Neg   **PER TABLESPOON**

Banana Cream

MAKES 450ml (¾ pint)

275g (9oz) carton of ricotta	juice of ½–1 lime (to taste)
200g (7oz) carton of Quark	1½ teaspoons vanilla extract
1 tablespoon banana preserves or jam	

Combine everything in a processor, and process until well combined and fluffy.

CALORIE COUNT 20 Kcal   **FAT CONTENT** <0.5g   **PER TABLESPOON**

CHAPTER 12

Celebrations

All celebratory recipes have been marked with a special symbol, so if you are having a birthday, an anniversary, any sort of special occasion blowout, you will be able to celebrate in low-fat style. Because of the nature of these recipes your guests will not feel as if they are depriving themselves for the sake of your low-fat lifestyle. The biggest, most abandoned (as far as healthy eating principles are concerned) celebration of the year is Christmas. More damage has been done to health, lifestyle and waistline in the name of this holiday than any other I can think of.

CHRISTMAS

Christmas doesn't have to be a time of fat-laden disaster. If you have learned to cook lavish and delicious low-fat food during eleven and half months of the year, why not extend that savvy to the Christmas period as well? The problem with living a low-fat lifestyle most of the year, and then sliding back into the fatlined pit for the holiday season, is several-fold. The celebration food isn't all that enjoyable – too greasy, rich and heavy – and leaves you feeling bilious and bloated (and guilty); the resulting weight gain can be shocking and depressing; and the feeling of not being in control of your life, of being at the mercy of dogmatic tradition and outmoded gastronomic rules and regulations, can be demoralizing and destructive. Of course tradition is not all bad, and can be a great comfort. Keep the comfort of Christmas: the joy of a golden, crackly turkey, a mincemeat-laden Christmas dessert, a chocolate-slathered, cream-filled chocolate log, and all the rest of it. But fiddle around with it so that the comfort, the celebration, the good taste and the fun remain, only the fat dimension is missing.

TURKEY TACTICS

Turkeys are lean birds and are usually roasted with plenty of butter to keep them moist. Slipping mushrooms or onion slices under the breast skin and roasting in foil is one way to keep a turkey moist without resorting to butter or other added fats, but there are other options too, should you want to adapt your own favourite roasted turkey recipe to a low-fat version.

1 Avoid pre-basted turkeys, they contain added fat.

2 The breast meat dries out very quickly. Keep it moist by roasting breast down for a while, then on one side, then the other. Finish breast up so that the breast skin can turn golden brown.

3 Baste the turkey with non-fat stock or a combination of stock and white wine, white vermouth or brandy, instead of a buttery mixture. When the turkey is breast up, and as golden as it should be, yet not quite done, drape the bird with dampened buttermuslin and baste through the cloth.

4 Slice a few onions into the roasting dish along with the turkey. Add a few carrots, and some chopped red peppers and whole garlic cloves too if you like them. When the turkey is done, strain the juices, de-fat them, simmer briefly with more stock and wine, then purée the juices with the roasted vegetables and push through a sieve to make a rich gravy.

5 Another gravy option is to make the gravy base on page 103. When the turkey is done, de-fat the pan juices and use, with extra stock if necessary, to finish the gravy.

Christmas Cracker Sausage Rolls

MAKES 12

Filo pastry, filled with the meatball mixture on page 173, can be used instead of fatty puff pastry. Twist the ends into a Christmas cracker shape. Use pure oil spray (available in supermarkets) rather than oil-water spray here, or the sausage rolls will be soggy.

1 packet of frozen filo pastry, thawed overnight in the refrigerator	sausage filling (page 173) pan-sautéed (see below)
1 egg or 1 egg white, lightly beaten	oil-water spray (page 28)

1 Preheat the oven to 200°C/400°F/Gas Mark 6.

2 Unwrap and unroll the filo. Put a piece of clingfilm on your work surface. Put the stack of filo (a packet will probably contain about 12 sheets) on the clingfilm and cover well with another piece of clingfilm. (The pastry will dry out quickly if left uncovered.)

3 One at a time, remove a single sheet of filo, and spread it flat. Lightly brush it with beaten egg or egg white, leaving a 2.5cm (1in) border all around. Spread 1 table-spoon of the filling in a strip where the egg wash begins at the right-hand short edge. Roll the pastry in a cylinder, from right to left, around the filling. Crimp and twist the ends to form a Christmas cracker shape. Don't wrap too tightly, because the filling will expand in the baking. Put seam side down, on to a non-stick baking tray that you have lightly misted with oil spray. Mist the top of the cracker lightly with oil spray. Repeat until the filo is used up.

4 Bake in the preheated oven for 10–15 minutes until golden brown, sizzling and puffed. Check once during baking: shake the tray, and if any seem to be sticking, loosen with a fish slice or palette knife and change their position.

Note

These may be prepared up to the end of step 3 and frozen. To bake from the frozen state, add 5 minutes to the baking time.

CALORIE COUNT 128 Kcal   **FAT CONTENT** 3g   **PER ROLL**   ✳ 🍸

VEGETARIAN VARIATION

For the filling use one of the pan sautéed mushroom recipes (page 114).

Sausage Mix

Choose the meatball mixture from the meat chapter (page 173). Sauté the meat in a non-stick frying-pan with the seasonings called for in the recipe, breaking up any lumps as you cook it. Drain off any fat, then stir in the roasted aubergine pulp. Taste and adjust the seasonings.

Cranberry-Apple Sauce

MAKES 600ml (1 pint)

An old American favourite that makes a glorious accompaniment to turkey, roast pork, cold meats and game. Cranberry Sauce is more of a relish or a chutney than a sauce. Cranberries are now available in most supermarkets during the late autumn and winter months. Buy them in bags or plastic boxes and freeze, so you have them on hand when you want them. Cook them from frozen – there is no need to thaw them first. A brilliant, jewelled red (like edible rubies), the berries are almost frighteningly sour, tasted raw. But cooked with sugar, apples and spices until they pop, they form a wonderful sweet and sour relish. All in all, perfect for Christmas.

2 × 275g (9oz) cartons of fresh cranberries	¼ teaspoon ground cinnamon
200g (7oz) caster sugar	⅛ teaspoon ground cloves
3 tart eating apples (i.e. Granny Smith), peeled, cored and diced	⅛ teaspoon ground allspice
	slivered zest of 1 orange and 1 lemon, parboiled and drained

1 Stir together all the ingredients in a heavy-bottomed saucepan. Cover the pan and cook over medium heat until the mixture comes to a boil. (It is not necessary to add liquid – the apples and berries will render sufficient juice.)

2 Simmer over medium heat for 7–10 minutes until most of the berries have popped, and the mixture has thickened.

3 Cool and refrigerate.

Note

If you can take the fat calories, add 60g (2oz) of very roughly chopped walnuts at the end of step 2. Although high in fat, the good news is that walnuts have the highest percentage of unsaturated fats of any nut.

CALORIE COUNT 25 Kcal   **FAT CONTENT** Neg   **PER TABLESPOON**

MINCEMEAT

A low-fat mincemeat is simply a compote of chopped dried fruit made with wine or liqueurs. It keeps for weeks, well covered, in the fridge, and can be used in all sorts of Christmassy low-fat puds. Several versions of low-fat mincemeat follow, along with some excellent puddings to put them into.

Mincemeat Turnovers

These turnovers make wonderful substitutes for mince pies. The fat and calories saved are significant, but the bursting-with-fruit, crisp turnovers pack a good dose of Christmas satisfaction. Thaw the filo overnight in the refrigerator. (The number of turnovers yielded depends on the number of filo leaves in the package you buy.) For a savoury version, fill with one of the sausage or meatball mixtures on pages 172–7, or with the spinach mix on page 41 (add a dab of feta) or with ratatouille, or another vegetable stew.

---

1 packet of frozen filo pastry, thawed	1 egg or 2 egg whites, lightly beaten, or
Mincemeat (see over)	oil spray

---

1 Preheat oven to 190°C/375°F/Gas Mark 5.

2 Put a sheet of clingfilm on your work surface. Unwrap the filo, unfold it, and place it on the clingfilm. From top to bottom, with a sharp knife, cut the stack of pastry down the centre. Immediately cover with another sheet of clingfilm.

3 Take one piece of filo from the stack. Keep the rest well covered (it dries out very quickly). Spread the sheet out on a clean surface. With a pastry brush, lightly coat it with the egg or egg white, or spray with oil spray. Fold the top third down and then the bottom third up as if folding a business letter. Place a generous tablespoon of mincemeat on the lower right hand corner. Fold up to form a triangle. Brush with egg or spray. Fold back down to form a new triangle. Continue folding up and down until you have formed a compact, many-layered triangle. Brush the finished triangle lightly with egg or spray with oil spray and place on a *non-stick* baking dish. (At this point, the turnovers may be refrigerated for a day or two, or frozen for months.)

4 Bake the turnovers in the oven for 20–30 minutes, or until puffed up and golden. If baking from frozen, add an extra 5 minutes to the baking time. Serve at once.

CALORIE COUNT 89 Kcal   **FAT CONTENT** <1g   **PER TURNOVER**

Mincemeat

MAKES 1.5 litres (2½ pints)

This mincemeat can be prepared in the microwave or the conventional oven. It will keep for weeks, well covered, in the fridge.

500g (1lb) packet of cake fruit (finely minced mixed dried fruit); the mix you choose should include sultanas, currants, orange and lemon peel

275g (9oz) packet of dried apricots, coarsely chopped with scissors or in the food processor

150g (5oz) packet of dried apple chunks or rings, coarsely chopped with scissors or in the food processor

½ teaspoon each of ground cinnamon, allspice and nutmeg

1 vanilla pod

60ml (2fl oz) medium sherry

60ml (2fl oz) brandy

60ml (2fl oz) Cointreau

125ml (4fl oz) water

Microwave method

1 Combine all the ingredients and mix well.

2 Pour into a 1.8 litre (3 pint) glass measuring jug. Cover with a plate. Microwave on high for 4 minutes. Uncover carefully (stand back and avert your face) and stir. Re-cover and microwave for 2–3 minutes more. Repeat, if necessary, until the fruit is tender, and of sticky mincemeat consistency. Remove the vanilla pod before using the mincemeat.

Conventional oven method

1 Preheat the oven to 180°C/350°F/Gas Mark 4.

2 Combine all the ingredients in a baking dish. Cover tightly and bake for about an hour, until the fruit is tender and of sticky mincemeat consistency. Remove the vanilla pod before using the mincemeat.

CALORIE COUNT 23 Kcal　**FAT CONTENT** Neg　**PER TABLESPOON**

Christmas Mincemeat Bread Pudding

SERVES 6

My favourite mincemeat recipe, this custardy pudding is good warm or at room temperature. It makes a lovely Christmas pud, or a festive holiday breakfast.

175g (6oz) unsliced bakery white bread, several days old

2 eggs

3 egg whites

3½–4 tablespoons caster sugar

500ml (16fl oz) skimmed milk

1 teaspoon natural vanilla extract

1–2 pinches of cinnamon or mixed spice

175g (6oz) Mincemeat (page 208)

1 Cut the bread into 1.5–2.5cm (¾–1in) chunks. Put them in a 20cm (8in) square, 2.5–5cm (1–2in) deep baking dish.

2 Beat the eggs and whites with the sugar. Beat in the milk and flavourings. Stir in the mincemeat. Pour the mixture over the bread. Use a broad spatula to push the bread into the liquid. Cover the dish and refrigerate for several hours if you have the time.

3 Remove the dish from the refrigerator, and leave at room temperature while you preheat the oven to 180°C/350°F/Gas Mark 4. Put the kettle on to boil.

4 Choose a baking dish larger than the one with the bread. Put it into the preheated oven. Put the bread dish inside the larger dish. Pour boiling water into the larger dish to come about half-way up the sides of the smaller dish. Bake for 30–40 minutes, until puffed and firm. (A knife inserted near the centre will emerge clean.)

5 Cool the bread pudding on a rack. Serve warm or at room temperature.

CALORIE COUNT 198 Kcal   **FAT CONTENT** 3g   **PER SERVING**   Ⓥ 𝖄

Celebration Menus

Just about all of the recipes in this collection can be put together in one way or another to form a celebration feast – it depends on the nature of the celebration and the tastes and habits of your friends and family. Here are a few suggestions: I'm sure that you will have fun thinking up your own festive combinations.

Christmas Menu

This is as colourful, lavish and celebratory a Christmas as you will ever see, yet the fat has been drastically reduced. I love the idea of having two kinds of potatoes; it is *so* indulgent.

Christmas Cracker Sausage Rolls or Turnovers
(pages 204–5)

*

Intense Mushroom Soup (page 72)

*

Roasted Turkey (page 204) with Gravy
(page 103)
Roasted Potatoes (page 110)
Sweet Potato Mash (page 109)
Roasted Brussels Sprouts (page 121)
Roasted Butternut Squash Halves (page 123)
filled with Couscous Salad with
Apricots (page 88)
Cranberry-Apple Sauce (page 206)

*

Chocolate Roulade (page 185)
Mincemeat Turnovers (page 207)

Alternative Quirky Christmas Menu

This is for those who can't face the thought of a whole roasted bird, and want something a bit more fun and informal, yet Christmassy. If you dislike turkey in any form, make the Moroccan-inspired Sausage Patties (page 172) into burgers and substitute for the Turkey Burgers.

Red Pepper Soup (page 75) scattered
with herbs

*

Grilled Turkey Burgers (page 162)
on baps or ciabatta bread with
Cranberry-Apple Sauce (page 206)
and Rémoulade (page 57)
Extra Crunchy, Spicy Oven-fried Potato Wedges
(page 107)
Roasted Beetroot Salad with Balsamic-Citrus
Dressing (page 119)
Roasted Fennel (page 121)

*

Spiced Angel Cake (page 183) with Maple
Vanilla Cream (page 202)

Vegetarian Christmas Menu

Plenty of flavour and colour despite the lack of meat; tempting enough for non-vegetarians to have a go!

Vegetarian Christmas Cracker Rolls or Turnovers (page 204) filled with the Sicilian Spinach mixture (page 41) and a dab of half-fat feta cheese

*

Sweet Potato and Smoked Corn Soup with Mushroom Stock (page 71)

*

Roasted Butternut Squash Halves (page 123) filled with Sicilian Vegetable Stew (page 129)
Garlic and Lemon Roasted Potatoes (pages 110–11)
Cranberry-Apple Sauce (page 206)

*

Mocha Roulade (page 188)

Elegant Dinner Party I

Onion Soup (page 73)

*

Salmon Fillets with Red Wine Sauce (page 142)
Roasted Asparagus (page 120)
Lemon-glazed Pan-braised New Potatoes (page 113)

*

Chocolate Chestnut Layer Cake (page 189)

Elegant Dinner Party II

Spinach Clafoutis (page 41)

*

Smoked Duck Breasts with Two Orange Salsas (page 160)
Spicy Oven-fried New Potatoes (page 106)
Italian-style Stir-fried Courgettes (page 128)

*

Spicy Plum Crumble (page 195)
with Orange Cream (page 201)

Elegant Vegetarian Dinner Party I

Sweet Potato and Smoked Corn Soup (page 71) with garnishes

*

Open Ravioli (page 86) with Spinach (page 41) and Piccadillo Sauce (page 92)
Green salad (make with a variety of interesting greens) with Grilled Peppers (page 32) and Grilled Red Pepper Vinaigrette (page 58)
Roasted Fennel (page 121)

*

Banana Ice-Cream (page 200) with fresh berries and puréed, strained, sweetened raspberries

Elegant Vegetarian Dinner Party II

Purée of Borlotti Bean Soup with Sherry (page 74)

*

Aubergine Gratin (page 116)
Caramelized Carrots (page 127)
Roasted Beetroot Salad with Balsamic-Citrus Dressing (page 119)

*

Layer Cake with Marmalade Glaze (page 186)

New York Style Sunday Brunch

This is one of those marvellously lavish, informal New York mid-morning spreads. The feast is meant to go on for hours with much reading of the Sunday papers, and lots of noshing and kibitzing.

Smoked Fish Clafoutis (page 42)

*

Bagels with a selection of spreads e.g. very low-fat fromage frais with horseradish;
Quark with chives; Goat's Cheese Spread (page 54); and Herbed Raita, drained to be spreadable (page 55).
Smoked salmon slices
Roasted Beetroot slices (page 119) with Beetroot Vinaigrette (page 60)
Flavourful cherry tomatoes, radishes, pickled cucumbers and black olives

*

Chocolate and Banana Cheesecake (page 197)
Poppy Seed and Sherry Banana Loaf (page 190)

Italian-inspired Feast

A bit multicultural (the chicken is smoked Chinese-style after all), but the dominant accent is Italian.

Very Quick Pizza (page 46) with grilled vegetables (pages 126–7)

*

Smoked Chicken Thighs in Tomato Gravy (page 158) served over pasta with Creamy Pesto (page 52) for garnish.
Italian-style Stir-fried Courgettes (page 128)

*

Berry Cream (page 193) topped with Amaretti crumbs

Summer Grill Party

Grill on the outdoor barbecue or on a grill pan indoors. This will satisfy a gang of mixed guests – vegetarians and meat-eaters.

A selection of dips, salsas and dippers (pages 52–69)

*

Smoked Chicken Thighs (page 157)
Moroccan-inspired Sausage Patties (page 172)
Unfried Beans (page 82) – don't purée these; serve as elegant baked beans
Couscous Vegetable Salad (page 87)
A selection of grilled vegetables (pages 126–7) with a selection of vinaigrettes (pages 58–60)

*

Fruit Salad (page 192)
Watermelon wedges (large ones!)

Indian-inspired Feast

Again, multicultural but with a definite hint of India

Red Pepper Soup (page 75)

*

Kofta Curry (page 176)
Mushrooms with Curry Spices, Port and Lime (page 115)
Aloo Chat (page 111)
Diced Carrot Salad (page 65)
Cucumber Raita (page 55)
Spring Onion Coriander Relish (page 66)
Cherry Tomato and Mango Salsa (page 62)
Basmati Rice

*

Banana Ice-Cream (page 200) flavoured with ground cinnamon and ground cardamom

Mail Order Guide

Terence Fisher,
Chocolate Wholesaler,
Earl Soham Business Centre,
Earl Soham,
Woodbridge,
Suffolk IP13 7SA.
Tel: 01728 685955
Fax: 01728 685956

Low-fat unsweetened cocoa powder. Excellent quality high cocoa solids dark chocolate

Lakeland Plastics,
Alexandra Buildings,
Windermere,
Cumbria LA23 1BQ.
Tel: 015394 88100
Fax: 015394 88300

Bakeware including: perforated baking trays, microwave rack for making fat free chips, air popper for popcorn, pure natural vanilla extract, pure natural almond extract and chocolate extract.

Made in America,
Hathaway Retail Park,
Chippenham SN15 1JG.
Tel: 01249 447558
Fax: 01249 446142

Oil sprays, pure natural vanilla extract

Divertimenti,
45-47 Wigmore Street,
London W1 H9LE
Tel: 020 7935 0689
Fax: 020 7224 0058

Bakeware including angel cake tins, cheescake tins

Index

almonds 4, 6
angel cakes 182–9
apples: Cranberry-Apple Sauce 206
apricots: Couscous Salad with Apricots, Fennel and Tomato and Red Onion Salsa 88
asparagus:
    Pasta with Asparagus, Yellow Peppers and Peas 85
    peeling 134
    Roasted Asparagus 120–1
aubergines:
    Aubergine Gratin 116–17
    Aubergine Tomato Sandwich 50
    Grilled Aubergines and Courgettes 126
    Grilled Vegetable Ratatouille 126–7
    Grilled Vegetable Sandwich with Grilled Pepper Chilli Spread 49
    infusion 31
    Moroccan-inspired Sausage Patties 172–3
    roasted purée 30–1
    Sausages 171
    Sicilian Vegetable Stew 129
    Tomato Aubergine Sauce 93
avocados 2, 4, 9

baked goods: store-bought 12
bananas:
    Banana Cream 202
    Banana Ice-Cream 200
    Banana Sandwich 44
    Chocolate and Banana Cheesecake 197
    Poppy Seed and Sherry Banana Loaf 190–1
    ripening 9
beans 76–7
    Bean Cakes 80–1
    dried: soaking 77
    Mexican Sausage Patties and Beans 174–5
    Purée of Borlotti Bean Soup with Sherry 74
    Tuna Bean and Rocket Sandwich 48–9
    Tuna Bean Salad 81
    Unfried Bean Tostados 82
    Unfried Beans 82
beef:
    Beef Steak in Red Wine Mustard Sauce 165
    Paprika Meatballs 173
    Thai-inspired Beef Salad 164
beetroot 11
    Beetroot Vinaigrette 60
    Herbed Beetroot Baguette 48
    Roasted Beetroot 119
    Roasted Beetroot Salad with Balsamic Citrus Dressing 119
Berry Cream 193
Blueberry Ice-Cream or Sorbet 200–1
bottled goods 23
brazils 4, 6
bread 29, 43
    bought: ingredients 5
breakfast 35–42
Brussels Sprouts, Roasted 121

burgers 162, 171
butter 4
Buttermilk Glaze 191

cabbage: raw 11
cakes 182–9
cancer 2
canned goods 23–4
carbohydrates: basic foods 25–6
carrots 11
    Caramelized Carrots 127
    Diced Carrot Salad 65
cauliflower:
    Cauliflower Cheese 117
    Roasted Cauliflower 120
celebration menus 210–12
celery: raw 11
cereal: as snack 13
cheese:
    Aubergine Gratin 116–17
    Blue Cheese Sauce 97
    Cauliflower Cheese 117
    Cheese Sauce 97
    Cheese on Toast 45
    cream toppings and fillings 201–2
    Creamy Spinach Dip 53
    Goat's Cheese Sauce 97
    Goat's Cheese Spread 54
    Herbed Goat's Cheese Raita 56
    low-fat 22, 29
    Quark as snack 12
    Sweet Potato Mash 109
cheesecakes 196–9
Cherry and Cranberry Chutney 161
chestnuts 4
    Chocolate Chestnut Spread 190
chicken:
    Chicken with Masses of Garlic 159
    Chicken Paprikash 150–1
    Chicken, Potatoes and Mushrooms in Smoky-Yogurt Sauce 154–5
    Creamy Chicken Curry 152
    Cuban Chicken 156
    Grilled Chicken Breasts Peperonata 148–9
    removing fat 32
    Roasted Orange Chicken Breasts 153
    Smoked Chicken Thighs 157
    Smoked Chicken Thighs in Tomato Gravy 158
chilli:
    Lentil Chilli 78
    Lentil Chilli Tacos 79
Chinese-glazed Mushrooms 114
Chinese-inspired Roasted Pork Tenderloin 169
Chips 105
chocolate 181
    Chocolate and Banana Cheesecake 197
    Chocolate Chestnut Layer Cake 189
    Chocolate Chestnut Spread 190
    Chocolate Crumb Crust 196
    chocolate extract 180

Chocolate Layer Cake with Mocha Cream Filling and Chocolate Glaze 187
Chocolate Roulade 185
cholesterol 3
Chorizo: de-fatting 178
Christmas 203–11
citrus fruits 180
clafoutis 40–2, 194
coconut cream 6
coconut milk 6
coconut oil 2
coconuts 2, 4, 6
coffee: Mocha Roulade 188
coffee bars 16
courgettes 11
    Grilled Aubergines and Courgettes 126
    Grilled Pepper and Courgette Clafoutis 40–1
    Grilled Vegetable Ratatouille 126–7
    Grilled Vegetable Sandwich with Grilled Pepper Chilli Spread 49
    Italian-style Stir-fried Courgettes 128
    Sicilian Vegetable Stew 129
couscous 86, 166–7
    Couscous Salad with Apricots, Fennel and Tomato and Red Onion Salsa 88
    Couscous Vegetable Salad 87
cranberries:
    Cherry and Cranberry Chutney 161
    Cranberry Port Cheesecake Mousse 199
    Cranberry-Apple Sauce 206
cream 29
cream toppings and fillings 201–2
crisps 13, 67, 68
crostini 46
    Open-faced Mushroom Crostini 51
crudités 10–12
crumble toppings 180
Cuban Chicken 156
cucumber 11
    Cucumber and Cherry Tomato Salsa 63
    Cucumber Raita 55
    Cucumber Relish 164
    preparing 134
    Tomato Salsa with a Hint of the Orient 62
    Tzatziki 55

dairy products 2, 22, 29, 181
desserts: ingredients for 180–1
dinner parties 20, 211
dippers 67–9
dips 12, 53–7
dried goods 23
duck:
    Grilled Duck Breast with Cherry and Cranberry Chutney 161
    Smoked Duck Breast with Two Orange Salsas 160

eggs 4, 6, 7, 22, 181
    for breakfast 36